$3
Meals in Minutes

$3
Meals in Minutes

Delicious, Low-Cost Dishes for Your Family
That Can Be Prepared in No Time!

Ellen Brown

The Lyons Press
Guilford, Connecticut
An imprint of The Globe Pequot Press

This book is dedicated to Constance Brown and Kenn Speiser, the best of neighbors and friends.

The Lyons Press is an imprint of The Globe Pequot Press.

Text design: Sheryl P. Kober

Library of Congress Cataloging-in-Publication Data is available on file.

ISBN 978-1-59921-822-9

Printed in the United States of America

10 9 8 7 6 5 4 3 2 1

Contents

With some advance planning at home, your trips to the supermarket can be less often and less expensive. You'll learn how to maximize the money saved by using coupons and other tricks to avoid sticker shock in the checkout lane.

Your cooking will go faster by learning how to work more efficiently in the kitchen, and in this chapter you'll also find some basic recipes for roasted meats and other foods that should become part of your low-cost pantry.

Entrée salads—either made with cold cooked protein or topping cold vegetables with hot meats—are easy to make and healthful to serve. These recipes include homemade dressings to save money in the condiment aisle.

Sandwiches have been getting really sexy in the past few years, with all sorts of international forms and options joining the category. Those are the recipes you'll find in this chapter.

It may never be decided if pasta was invented in Italy or China, but there's no cuisine today that doesn't have some recipes for quickly cooked sauces to top this ubiquitous carbohydrate. These sauces are ready in the same time it takes the pasta to cook, too.

Chapter 6: Stir-Fries and Sautés — 130

These quick-cooking dishes encompass all types of food and are ready to go onto the table in a matter of minutes. They range from Asian vegetarian dishes to European classics.

Chapter 7: Simmer and Skillet Suppers — 160

There is a whole repertoire of "one-dish meals" that are made from start to finish in one skillet or saucepan, and draw from a veritable United Nations of cuisines. Toss a salad and your meal is complete with the recipes in this chapter.

Chapter 8: Quick Casseroles and Oven-Baked Dishes — 194

After just a few minutes of your time to assemble these recipes, you can soak in the tub or read a book while they finish cooking in the oven. And none take longer than forty minutes from start to finish!

Chapter 9: Fast $1 Finales — 224

After saving money on your entrée, there's room remaining in your $3 per person budget for treats to tempt your sweet tooth. These are all recipes that can be prepared in the amount of time it takes to eat the courses that come before it.

Preface

It makes little difference——especially when you're holding your breath in the supermarket checkout line watching the total rise—that people in other industrialized countries envy the relatively small percentage of income that Americans spend on food. All you know is that a gallon of milk is now significantly more expensive than a gallon of gas, and a pound of *chopped* sirloin now costs what a *real* steak did a few years ago, even discounting the influence of inflation.

And you're not only spending more money at the supermarket now, you're spending more time, too. All those warnings! Does this contain trans fat? If this pudding is sugar-free, what's making it sweet? The alternative to cooking—stopping for the bucket of chicken or box of pizza on the way home—is now a luxury rather than a viable alternative to feed your family for mid-week meals.

Convenience foods may be a little faster, but they cost far more than ingredients, and I can show you how to beat the game. You're smart enough to know that there's no more than a few cents of ingredients in that $1 "value menu" burger, and the raw food that went into the $9 portion of Kung Po Chicken costs less than $1.

Perhaps you've weaned yourself away from restaurant food by purchasing convenience foods from the supermarket. The supermarket is certainly hoping to tempt you; that's why the rotisserie chickens—for which you're paying five times what the supermarket paid for the raw bird—are now found at every entrance, and the case space devoted to frozen pizza has grown as big as a Kansas cornfield.

But you've now realized that those purchases are a major factor in your supermarket "sticker shock." And, because you've glanced at the labels from time to time, you also know that these expensive convenience foods are loaded with chemicals and preservatives—as well as unwanted calories.

That's where this book, and other books in the *$3 Meals* series, comes in. You'll learn that in the same time it takes to use an expensive box of "Protein Helper," you can make a delicious pasta dish *from scratch.* And in less time than it takes to make a casserole with a can of "cream of something soup," you can be serving a nutritious custard made with fresh eggs and enlivened with cheese, meats, and vegetables.

I'll teach you not only how to save money, but also how to become a speed machine when you enter the kitchen. You'll learn how to slice 'n' dice like a pro, and how to pick whole, fresh food at the supermarket. It's not as if you're getting produce of lesser quality for less money! You'll learn how to save money by processing your own food. For example, you can bone your own chicken breasts to save money on the meat per pound, and then you have the bones to use to make your own chicken stock.

If you think that those sorts of tasks sound like what your grandmother would have done, you're right. But she had the right idea! We've gone from being a country of scratch cooks to being a country of convenience cooks. At first this was out of design, but now it's out of necessity because of the stressful lives we lead.

How did we get there?

The decades following World War II placed a premium on convenience as a domestic offshoot of science; the first frozen pot pie was introduced in 1951 and three years later it was joined by that truly American phenomenon, the TV dinner. The 20 million Victory Gardens that grew more than 40 percent of Americans' vegetables in 1943 gave way to a reliance on canned and frozen produce.

Yet this year First Lady Michelle Obama is growing vegetables (tomatoes and arugula, but no beets because the President is not a fan!) on the lawn at the White House, and the National Restaurant Association's study of members ranked "use of local produce" as the leading trend for upscale eateries for 2009.

So the adage that "everything old is new again" remains true. But with a significant difference: today's American cooks don't have that sort of time. Back in the 1960s, when only one in three American women worked outside the home, the prevalence of such labor-saving devices as blenders to prepare food and automatic dishwashers to speed cleanup led to a decrease in the time spent preparing meals—and cleaning up from them—to 15 hours per week! That was certainly a reduction from the 70-plus hours a week it took to perform the same tasks in the 1920s, but still more than twice the figure for American cooks today.

Now, however, time is at a premium. Two out of three American women work outside the home, and the percentage of America's single-parent households has grown from less than one in ten in 1960 to now more than one in three today—the highest for any industrialized country.

It's little wonder that almost every kitchen has a microwave oven! Any help to get dinner on the table fast is appreciated, and purchased.

But *$3 Meals in Minutes* will show you that you can prepare delicious meals that hide the fact that you made them on a strict budget. The reason why there's no mention of a precise number of minutes in the title of this book is that *$3 Meals in Less than 40 Minutes* seemed too cumbersome, and very few recipes take more than 30 minutes. But there are some that are on the table in 15 minutes—and that's if you're moving slowly. The good news is that the majority of the recipes in this book are on your table in less time than it takes to watch the evening news.

Frequently on that newscast are indications that the skyrocketing cost of food is global, and not just national. So there's a very good chance that we're not going to see a reduction soon—if ever.

The broadening middle classes in India and China are eating more meat, which is why that precious commodity will continue to escalate in price. And the downside of the quest to replace fossil fuels is that more of the world's corn crop—a staple for both animal feed and human consumption—is being diverted to ethanol production. If anything, this trend will accelerate in the years to come.

But have no fear. Stick with me and the recipes in the *$3 Meals* series, and you'll fulfill the wonderful proverb that "living well is the best revenge."

Happy Cooking!

—Ellen Brown
Providence, Rhode Island

Acknowledgments

While writing a book is a solitary endeavor, its publication is always a team effort. My thanks go to:

Ed Claflin, my agent, who had faith in the various iterations of this project, as well as for his constant support and great sense of humor.

Eugene Brissie, of The Lyons Press, for his faith in me and my ideas.

Ellen Urban, of The Lyons Press, editor extraordinaire, for her guidance and help all through the production process, and Jessie Shiers for her eagle-eyed copy editing.

My many friends who shared their culinary wisdom and tips for saving money.

Tigger and Patches, my furry companions, who personally endorse all fish and seafood recipes.

Introduction

If you're feeling stressed about the dilemma of how to feed your family healthy food in a jiffy each night for very little money, you're not alone. Your quandary is shared by millions of Americans, and the number continues to grow.

That's where *$3 Meals in Minutes,* and the other books in the *$3 Meals* series, enters your life and your kitchen. You'll learn that you can produce delicious meals that are on the table in less time than it takes to watch the evening news, *and* are more healthful because they contain real ingredients and not processed foods.

The goal of the *$3 Meals* series is an ambitious one; this small amount of money—less than the cost of a large fast food burger or a slice of gourmet pizza—is for your *whole meal!* That includes the greens for your tossed salad and the dressing with which it's tossed. It includes the pasta or rice you cook to enjoy all the gravy from a stew. And it includes a sweet treat for dessert. So unlike many books that promise cost-conscious cooking, this book shows you how to achieve savings beyond the entree.

You're cooking to combat what I call the "3 Cs" of modern living—cost, convenience, and chemicals. You pay more money for convenience foods that are loaded with chemicals. It's as simple as that. The "3 Cs" are an evil trio, and cooking these recipes, you'll learn how to avoid bumping into them.

These dishes are made with real ingredients that once grew from the land, walked upon it, or swam in its waters. These recipes do utilize canned beans and tomatoes, plus some inexpensive frozen vegetables that do not diminish the quality of a dish and speed its preparation. But those are foods that are minimally processed and represent a good value, too. Canned tomatoes, for example, have better flavor than fresh ones bought for a lot more money out of season, and frozen spinach delivers the same nutritional value as fresh and can be prepared in a fraction of the amount of time.

There are a few ingredient compromises taken to trim costs; however, these shortcuts trim preparation time, too. This is the first book I've written for which I used bottled lemon and lime juice in recipe development rather than freshly squeezed juices from the fruits themselves; I discovered it took a bit more juice to achieve the flavor I was after, but with the escalated cost of citrus fruits, this was a sacrifice I chose to make. I've also limited the range of herbs and spices specified to a core group of fewer than a dozen. There's no need to purchase an expensive dried herb that you may never use again.

On the other hand, there are standards I will never bend. I truly believe that unsalted butter has a flavor that is far superior to margarine, therefore, any minimal cost savings from using margarine was not worth the trade-down in flavor. Good quality Parmesan cheese, freshly grated when you need it, is another ingredient well worth the splurge. You use very little of it because once grated it takes up far more volume than in a block, and its innate flavor is far superior.

The same is true for using fresh parsley, cilantro, and dill. While most herbs deliver flavor in their dried form, these leafy herbs do not. Luckily, they are used so often that they are inexpensive to buy and don't go to waste—especially with the tricks I'll teach you on how to preserve their freshness.

You'll find cooking the recipes in this book that *budget* is hardly synonymous with *boring.* The recipes are for great American foods and foods from cuisines that are increasingly popular options in this country. These dishes have vibrant flavors, but they're not made with exotic ingredients that cost a lot of money and that you might not use again.

The recipes are arranged by category of food and cooking method rather than by the dominant ingredient. Within each chapter, the recipes follow the same sequence; they start with vegetarian options, and then progress through fish, poultry, and meats. The reason for this approach is to think of foods in terms of how they are prepared, and some methods—such as stir-frying and sautéing—are far faster than others. Also, many nights you know you want a salad for dinner, so all the entrée salads are grouped together rather than having to use the index to locate them. And at the beginning of each chapter is a discussion about each cooking method, if appropriate.

While specific cooking methods are important to learn, general tips for speeding up your time in the kitchen are detailed in Chapter 2. Like any activity, the more you do it, the more accomplished—and in this case, faster—you should become. But there are some skills, such as how to hold knives to achieve the best results, that are important to know for all cooking.

Many of the skill-building tips, as well as tips for saving money, come from my years running a professional kitchen. Waste—either of ingredients or staff time—eat away at profits, so they had to be avoided.

A good number of the recipes in *$3 Meals in Minutes* began as staff meals in the professional kitchen. These are the foods cooked in a short time to feed the hungry folk who work there. They could be dishwashers who were happy with anything I'd make because it was free, to chefs and sous chefs with discerning palates. They were always happy with the food, and I hope you will be, too.

Chapter 1:
Saving Money at the Supermarket

If your boss lists a task in your job description, you do it. So here's your task: You're going to save money on your grocery bill. But rather than *saving* money, you're going to think of it as *earning* money. And in the hour it takes you to follow some of the suggestions in this chapter, you'll earn anywhere from $25 to $60 a week. That might not seem like a lot. But how about if you earned $3,000 a year for something you're doing anyway? That would be a nice bonus, and I bet it would make a difference in your attitude. And with the money you're "earning" you can do anything from feeling unstressed about the heating bill that needs paying to taking the kids to that expensive theme park for a weekend.

Next to housing and auto expenses, food is our major annual expense, as it is around the world. The fact that Americans spend about a 12 percent chunk of disposable income on food still remains the envy of most people living in the industrialized world. Just across the border in Canada the figure is 14 percent, while in Mexico it is more than 25 percent.

Most of the tips are specific to food shopping; this *is* a cookbook. But there are also hints for saving money in other segments of your budget. It's all coming out of the same wallet.

I wish I could promise you a clear and uncluttered path. But every rule has an exception, as you'll see below. However, once you've accepted earning money on groceries as part of your job, the nuances are easy to grasp.

PLAN *BEFORE* YOU SHOP

The most important step to cost-effective cooking is to decide logically and intelligently what you're going to cook for the week. That many sound simple, but if you're in the habit of deciding when you're leaving work at the end of the day, chances are you've ended up with a lot of high-calorie frozen pizza or greasy Chinese carry-out. While this section on how to plan is very detailed, it really takes but minutes to compile your master plan once you've gotten in the habit.

First, look at the week, and what activities are listed. How many nights will you actually be home? Are there guests invited for any meals? How about the kids? Do they have activities that mean that the family won't be eating dinner together? Is there a sporting event on television that everyone will want to see, so eating may be on laps instead of a table? These are all questions to ponder before putting pen to paper.

The next step is to shop in your own house first. Look and see what's still in the refrigerator, and how that food—which you've already purchased and perhaps also cooked—can be utilized.

Now look and see what foods you have in the freezer. Part of savvy shopping is stocking up on foods when they're on sale; in fact, sales of free-standing freezers have grown by more than 10 percent during the past few years, while sales of all other major appliances have gone down. And with good reason—a free-standing freezer allows you to take advantage of sales. Especially foods like boneless, skinless chicken breasts—the time-crunched cook's best friend—which go on sale frequently and are almost prohibitive in price when they're not on sale. You should always have a cache of them ready to cook, for the recipes in this book as well as recipes that are more indulgent.

But preparing food for the freezer to ensure quality is important. Never freeze meats, poultry, or seafood in the supermarket wrapping alone. To guard against freezer burn, double wrap food in freezer paper or place it in heavy resealable plastic bags. Mark the purchase date on raw food, and the date when frozen on cooked items, and use them within three months. The recipes in this book use less meat, fish, and poultry than many other cookbooks. Therefore, it's important to repackage meats into smaller packages than those you buy, too. Scan recipes and look at the amount of the particular meat specified; that's what size your packages destined for the freezer should be.

Keep a list taped to the front of your freezer. It should list contents and date when they were frozen. Mark off foods as you take them out and add foods as you put them in.

Also, part of your strategy as a cook is to do it only a few nights a week; that means when you're making recipes that can be doubled—like a pasta sauce or stew—you make larger batches and freeze a portion. Those meals are "dinner insurance" for nights you don't want to cook. Those are the nights that you previously would have brought in the bucket of chicken or the box of pizza, and spent more money for food that is not as high in nutritional value.

The other factor that enters in to the initial planning is looking at your depletion list and seeing what foods and other products need to be purchased. A jar of peanut butter or a bottle of dishwashing liquid doesn't contribute to your meal plans, but they do cost money—so they have to be factored into your budget. Some weeks you might not need many supplies, but it always seems to me that all of the cleaning supplies seem to deplete the same week.

Now you've got the "raw data" to look at the weekly sales circulars from your newspaper or delivered with your mail. Those sales should form the core for your menu planning.

MAKING A LIST, AND CHECKING IT TWICE

So it's a new you entering the supermarket. First of all, you have a list, and it's for more than a few days. And you're going to buy what's on your list. Here's the first rule: stick to that list. Never go shopping when you're hungry; that's when non-essential treats wind up in your basket. Always go shopping alone; unwanted items end up in the cart to keep peace in the family. And—here's an idea that might seem counterintuitive—go shopping when you're in a hurry. It's those occasions when you have the time to dawdle that the shortcakes end up coming home when all you really wanted was the strawberries.

But as promised, here are some exceptions to the rule of keeping to your list. You've got to be flexible enough to take advantage of some unexpected great sales. It's easy if the sale is a markdown on meat; you see the $2 off coupon and put it in the cart, with the intention of either cooking it that night or freezing it. All supermarkets mark down meat on the day before the expiration sticker. The meat is still perfectly fine, and should it turn out not to be, you can take it back for a refund. So go ahead and take advantage of the markdown.

Then you notice a small oval sticker with the word "Save." Is turkey breast at $1.09 a real bargain? You'll know it is if you keep track of prices, and know that a few weeks ago it was $3.99 per pound.

You now have two options. Buy the off-list bargains and freeze them, or use them this week.

That's why I suggest freezing bargains, assuming you can absorb the extra cost on this week's grocery bill. If not, then look at what produce, shelf-stable, and dairy items on the list were tied to a protein you're now crossing off, and delete them too.

SHOPPING STRATEGY

It always helps when you know where you're going—including where to find what in the supermarkets you frequent. The next time you are at the market, have a pad and pen with you. Take notes of what is located where, such as "baking supplies (flour, sugar, chocolate chips) in aisle 2," and create a master form for your shopping list according to the layout of your market. Divide a sheet of paper into four columns, starting with the meats, fish, and other protein, and then make listings for produce, dairy products, and shelf-stable pantry items by aisle number. After a few times, this system becomes so familiar that you will probably not be referring to your master guide.

Supermarkets are almost all designed to funnel traffic first into the produce section; that is the last place you want to shop. Begin with the proteins, since many items in other sections of your list relate to the entrees of the dinners you have planned. Once they are gathered, go through and get the shelf-stable items, then the dairy products (so they will not be in the cart for too long), and end with the produce. Using this method, the fragile produce is on the top of the basket, not crushed by the gallons of milk.

The last step is packing the groceries. If you live in an area where you have the option of packing them yourself, place items stored together in the same bag. That way all of your produce can go directly into the refrigerator, and canned goods destined for the basement will be stored in one trip.

COUPON CLIPPING 101

It's part art, it's part science, and it all leads to more money in your wallet. Consider this portion of the chapter your Guerilla Guide to Coupons. There's more to it than just clipping them. Of course, unless you clip them or glean them from other channels (see some ideas below) then you can't save money. So that's where you're going to start—but, trust me, it's just the beginning.

Forget that image you have of the lady wearing the hairnet and the "sensible shoes" in line at the supermarket digging through what seems to be a bottomless pit of tiny pieces of paper looking for the right coupon for this or that. Clipping coupons—in case you haven't heard—is *cool*. And it should be. At any given moment there are *billions of dollars* of coupons floating around out there, according to the folks at www

.grocerycouponguide.com, one of the growing list of similar sites dedicated to helping you save money.

And not only is it becoming easier to access these savings, you're a Neanderthal if you don't. The fact that you're reading this book—and will be cooking from it—shows that you care about trimming the size of your grocery bill. So it's time to get with the program.

Every Sunday the newspaper (as long as they still exist) is a treasure-trove of coupons. I found a $5 off coupon for a premium cat food my finicky cats liked in a local paper, which cost 50 cents. It was worth it to buy four copies of the paper; I spent $2 but I then netted an $18 savings on the cat food.

The first decision you have to make is how you're going to organize your coupons. There are myriad ways and each has its fans. It's up to you to decide which is right for you, your family, and the way you shop:

- Arrange the coupons by aisle in the supermarket if you only shop in one store consistently.

- Arrange them by category of product (like cereals, cleaning supplies, dairy products, etc.) if you shop in many stores.

- Arrange them alphabetically if you have coupons that you use in various types of stores beyond the grocery store.

- Arrange them by expiration date. Coupons are only valid for a certain time period; it can be a few weeks or a few months. And part of the strategy of coupon clipping is to maximize the value, which frequently comes close to the expiration date. Some of the best coupons are those for "buy one, get one free." However, when the coupon first appears the item is at full price. But what about two weeks later when the item is on sale at your store? Then the "buy one, get one free" can mean you're actually getting four cans for the price of one at the original retail price.

Storage systems for arranging coupons are as varied as methods of organizing them. I personally use envelopes, and keep the stack held together with a low-tech paper clip. I've also seen people with whole wallets and tiny accordion binders dedicated to coupons. If you don't have a small child riding on the top of the cart, another alternative is to get a loose-leaf notebook with clear envelopes instead of pages.

BARGAIN SHOPPING 2.0

Every grocery store has weekly sales, and those foods are the place to start your planning for new purchases; that's how you're saving money beyond using coupons. And almost every town has competing super-market chains that offer different products on sale. It's worth your time to shop in a few venues, because it will generate the most savings. That way you can also determine which chain offers the best store brands, and purchase them while you're there for the weekly bargains. Here are other ways to save:

- **"Junk mail" may contain more than junk.** Don't toss those Val-pack and other coupon envelopes that arrive in the mail. Look through them carefully, and you'll find not only coupons for food products, but for many services, too.

- **Spend a stamp to get a rebate.** Many large manufacturers are now sending out coupon books or cash vouchers usable in many stores to customers who mail in receipts demonstrating that they have purchased about $50 of products. For example, Procter & Gamble, the country's largest advertiser and the company for which the term "soap opera" was invented, is switching millions of dollars from the airwaves to these sorts of promotions.

- **Find bargains online.** It's difficult for me to list specific Web sites because they may be defunct by the time you're reading this book, but there are hundreds of dollars worth of savings to be culled by printing coupons from Web sites, and for high end organic prod-ucts, it's the only way to access coupons. Ones I use frequently are www.couponmom.com and www.coupons.com; I also look for the coupon offers on such culinary sites as www.epicurious.com and www.foodnetwork.com. You will find coupons there, some tied to actual recipes. Also visit manufacturers' Web sites, which offer both coupons and redemption savings.

- **Find coupons in the store.** Look for those little machines projecting out from the shelves; they usually contain coupons that can be used instantly when you check out. Also, don't throw out your receipt until you've looked at it carefully. There are frequently coupons printed on the back. The cashier may also hand you other small slips of paper with your cash register receipt; most of them are coupons for future purchases of items you just bought. They may be from the same brand or they may be from a competing brand. Either way, they offer savings.

- **Stock up on cans.** Even if you live in a small apartment without a basement storage unit, it makes sense to stock up on canned goods when they're on sale. The answer is to use every spare inch of space. The same plastic containers that fit under your bed to hold out of season clothing can also become a pantry for canned goods.

- **Shuffle those cards.** Even if I can't convince you to clip coupons, the least you can do for yourself to save money is take the five minutes required to sign up for store loyalty cards; many national brands as well as store brands are on sale only when using the card. While the current system has you hand the card to the cashier at the checkout, that will be changing in the near future. Shopping carts will be equipped with card readers that will generate instant coupons according to your purchasing habits. I keep my stack of loyalty cards in the glove box of my car; that way they don't clutter my purse but I always have them when shopping.

- **Get a bargain buddy.** There's no question that supermarkets try to lure customers with "buy one, get one free" promotions, and sometimes one is all you really want. And what about those massive cases of paper towels at the warehouse clubs that are also a good deal—if you have unlimited storage space. The answer? Find a bargain buddy with whom you can split large purchases. My friends and I also swap coupons we won't use but the other person will. Going back to my example of the cat food savings, there were dog food coupons on the same page, so I turned them over to a canine-owning friend.

LEARNING THE ROPES

The well-informed shopper is the shopper who is saving money, and the information you need to make the best purchasing decision is right there on the supermarket shelves. It's the shelf tag that gives you the cost per unit of measurement. The units can be quarts for salad dressing, ounces for dry cereal, or pounds for canned goods. All you have to do is look carefully.

But you do have to make sure you're comparing apples to apples and oranges to oranges—or in this example, stocks to stocks. Some can be priced by the quart, while others are by the pound.

- **Check out store brands.** Store brands and generics have been improving in quality during the past few years, and according to *Consumer Reports,* buying them can save anywhere from 15 percent to 50 percent. Moving from a national brand to a store brand is a personal decision, and sometimes money is not the only factor. For example, I have used many store brands of chlorine bleach, and have returned to Clorox time and again. But I find no difference between generic corn flakes and those from the market leaders. Store brands can also be less expensive than national brands on sale—and with coupons.

- **Compare prices within the store.** Many foods—such as cold cuts and cheeses—are sold in multiple areas of the store, so check out those alternate locations. Sliced ham may be less expensive in cellophane package shelved with the refrigerated foods than at the deli counter.

- **Look high and low.** Manufacturers pay a premium price to shelve products at eye level, and you're paying for that placement when you're paying their prices. Look at the top and bottom shelves in aisles like cereal and canned goods. That's where you'll find the lower prices.

- **Buy the basics.** When is a bargain not a bargain? When you're paying for water or you're paying for a little labor. That's why even though a 15-ounce can of beans is less expensive than the same quantity of dried beans (approximately a pound), you're still better off buying the dried beans. One pound of dried beans makes the equivalent of four or five cans of beans. In the same way, a bar of Monterey Jack cheese is much less expensive per pound than a bag of grated Monterey Jack cheese. In addition to saving money, the freshly grated cheese will have more flavor because cheese loses flavor rapidly when grated. And pre-cut and pre-washed vegetables are truly exorbitant.

- **Watch the scanner.** I know it's tempting to catch up on pop culture by leafing through the tabloids at the checkout, but that's the last thing you should be doing. Watching the clerk scan your order usually saves you money. For example, make sure all the instant savings coupons are peeled off; this includes marked-down meats and coupons on boxes and bags. Then, make sure sale items are ringing up at the right price.

WASTE NOT, WANT NOT

We're now going to start listing exceptions to all the rules you just read, because a bargain isn't a bargain if you end up throwing some of it away. Remember that the goal is to waste nothing. Start by annotating your shopping list with quantities for the recipes you'll be cooking. That way you can begin to gauge when a bargain is a bargain. Here are other ways to buy only what you need:

- **Don't overbuy.** Sure, the large can of diced tomatoes is less per pound than the smaller can. But what will you do with the remainder of the can if all you need is a small amount? The same is true for dairy products. A half-pint of heavy cream always costs much more per ounce than a quart, but if the remaining three cups of cream will end up in the sink in a few weeks, go with the smaller size.

- **Sometimes bigger isn't better.** If you're shopping for snacks for a young child, look for the *small* apples rather than the giant ones. Most kids take a few bites and then toss the rest, so evaluate any purchases you're making by the pound.

- **Ring that bell!** You know the one; it's always in the meat department of the supermarket. It might take you a few extra minutes, but ask the real live human who will appear for *exactly* what you want; many of the recipes in *$3 Meals in Minutes* specify less than the weight of packages you find in the meat case. Many supermarkets do not have personnel readily available in departments like the cheese counter, but if there are wedges of cheeses labeled and priced then someone is in charge. It might be the deli department or the produce department, but find out who it is and ask for a small wedge of cheese if you can't find one the correct size.

- **Check out the bulk bins.** Begin buying from the bulk bins for shelf-stable items, like various types of rice, beans, dried fruits, and nuts. Each of these departments has scales so you can weigh ingredients like dried mushrooms or pasta. If a recipe calls for a quantity rather than a weight you can usually "eyeball" the quantity. If you're unsure of amounts start by bringing a 1-cup measure with you to the market. Empty the contents of the bin into the measuring cup rather than directly into the bag. One problem with bulk food bags is that they are difficult to store in the pantry; shelves were made for sturdier materials. Wash out plastic deli containers or even plastic containers that you bought containing yogurt or salsa. Use those for storage once the bulk bags arrive in the kitchen. Make sure you label your containers of bulk foods both at the supermarket and if you're transferring the foods to other containers at home so you know what they are, especially if you're buying similar foods. Arborio and basmati rice look very similar in a plastic bag, but they are totally different grains and shouldn't be substituted for each other.

- **Shop from the salad bar for tiny quantities.** There's no question that supermarkets charge a premium price for items in those chilled bins in the salad bar, but you get exactly what you need. When to shop there depends on the cost of the item in a larger quantity. At $4 per pound, you're still better off buying a 50-cent can of garbanzo beans, even if it means throwing some of them away. However, if you don't see how you're going to finish the $4 pint of cherry tomatoes, then spend $1 at the salad bar for the handful you need to garnish a salad.

SUPERMARKET ALTERNATIVES

All of the hints thus far in this chapter have been geared to pushing a cart around a supermarket. Here are some other ways to save money:

- **Shop at farmers' markets.** I admit it; I need a 12-step program to help me cure my addiction to local farmers' markets. Shopping *al fresco* on warm summer days turns picking out fruits and vegetables into a truly sensual experience. Also, you buy only what you want. There are no bunches of carrots; there are individual carrots sold by the pound. The U.S. Department of Agriculture began publishing the *National Directory of Farmers' Markets* in 1994, and at that time the number was fewer than 2,000. That figure has now doubled. To find a farmers' market near you go to www.ams.usda.gov/farmersmarkets. The first cousins of farmers' markets for small quantities of fruits are the sidewalk vendors in many cities. One great advantage to buying from them is that their fruit is always ripe and ready to eat or cook.

- **Shop at ethnic markets.** If you live in a rural area this may not be possible, but even moderately small cities have a range of ethnic markets, and that's where you should buy ingredients to cook those cuisines. All the Asian condiments used in *$3 Meals in Minutes* are far less expensive at Asian markets than in the Asian aisle of your supermarket, and you can frequently find imported authentic brands instead of U.S. versions. Even small cities and many towns have ethnic enclaves, such as a "Little Italy"; each neighborhood has some grocery stores with great prices for those ingredients and the fresh produce used to make the dishes, too.

- **Shop alternative stores.** Groceries aren't only at grocery stores; many "dollar stores" and other discount venues stock shelf-stable items. Also, every national brand of drugstore—including CVS and Walgreen's—carries grocery products, and usually has great bargains each week. In the same way that food markets now carry much more than foods, drug stores stock thousands of items that have no connection to medicine. Those chains also have circulars in Sunday newspapers, so check them out—even if you're feeling very healthy.

- **Shop online.** In recent years it's become possible to do all your grocery shopping online through such services as Peapod and Fresh Express. While there is frequently a delivery charge involved, for housebound people this is a true boon. If you really hate the thought of pushing the cart, you should explore it; it's impossible to make impulse buys. There are also a large number of online retailers for ethnic foods, dried herbs and spices, premium baking chocolate, and other shelf-stable items. Letting your cursor do the shopping for these items saves you time, and many of them offer free shipping at certain times of the year.

THAT FRUGAL FRAME OF MIND

In addition to all the tips listed above, you've got to get into a frugal frame of mind. You're out to save money on your food budget, but not feel deprived. You're going to be eating the delicious dishes in this book.

Think about where your food budget goes other than the grocery store. The cost of a few "designer coffee" treats at the local coffee shop is equal to a few dinners at home. Couldn't you brew coffee and take it to work rather than spend $10 a week at the coffee cart? And those cans of soft drinks in the vending machine are four times the cost of bringing a can from home. But do you really need soft drinks at all? For mere pennies you can brew a few quarts of iced tea, which has delicious flavor without chemicals.

Bringing your lunch to work does increase your weekly supermarket tab, but it accomplishes a few good goals. It adds funds to the bottom line of your total budget, and it allows you to control what you're eating—and when. While you may think that your choices for lunch are low-calorie, chances are you're kidding yourself, but you won't be kidding your body. That lean little salad comes with a packet of traditional dressing that may contain upwards of a few hundred calories! That's more than many of the entrees in this book.

If you have a pressured job, chances are there are days that you end up eating from snack food vending machines or eating fast food at your desk. If you bring your lunch you know what it will be—even if you don't know when. Almost every office has a microwave oven, so lunch can frequently be a leftover from a dinner the night or two before, so the extra cost and cooking time are minimal.

So now that you're becoming a grocery guru, you can move on to find myriad ways to save money on your grocery bill while eating wonderfully. That's what *$3 Meals in Minutes* is all about.

Chapter 2:

How to Save Time as Well as Money

This chapter is your reward for passing by all those convenience foods in the supermarket, and buying foods that are only minimally processed. Those are the foods we term *ingredients,* and they are the ones listed in these recipes.

The pointers and hints you learn here will give you both the physical and mental skills that will make you a better cook. Efficiency is as important in cooking as it is in any other aspect of your life. In this chapter you're getting some pointers on saving time.

A phrase we use a lot these days is "multitasking"; it began as a computer term for what the machine could do, but now it's become part of our daily parlance for what *we* can do. Merriam-Webster defines it as "the performance of multiple tasks at one time," and that's what you'll learn to do while cooking.

At the end of this chapter are some recipes I call your "homework." These are ways to roast a big chicken, a small turkey, or any size ham so that you'll have the building blocks with which to cook myriad fast meals during the week. Unlike our grandmothers, who spent *hours* in the kitchen on a daily basis, the premise of this book is that you can make a healthful, nutritious meal in less time than it takes to get a takeout pizza that tastes almost identical to the cardboard box in which it is delivered.

I promise you that you can have dinner on the table within 30 minutes of walking in the front door on Tuesday night. What you'll use for these "instant meals" some of the time are the anticipated leftovers from the lazy Saturday and Sunday afternoons during which you baked a ham while watching a football game or roasted some big chickens while gardening outside. Pre-cooked meats—found in very expensive small packages or in the deli department—fall under that evil definition of "convenience foods." It's so easy to get into the habit of cooking these foods yourself, and packaging them in convenient forms in your freezer.

A whole category of convenient, costly, and chemical-laden foods you can replace for virtually no money are stocks. Those carrot peels and parsley stems that you now throw into the garbage or add to the compost bin, along with the bones from boning your own chicken breasts and cutting up your own chuck roasts to make stews, are discarded no more!

A number of tricks in this chapter are ones that are commonly practiced in the professional kitchen—where waste means less profit and time is as important to chefs as it is to you. Once you get into the habit of wasting nothing, you'll be amazed how much further your limited food budget can go.

ESSENTIAL EQUIPMENT

I am not a big fan of kitchen gadgets; in fact, I've gathered a whole box of them in the garage for my next tag sale. But I'm so devoted to my food processor that it travels with me if I'm driving to see friends for a weekend who don't have one, and it has a dedicated corner in my dishwasher because it's used daily.

The food processor is an unpaid *sous chef* in your kitchen, and if you have no other piece of kitchen equipment, it's worth the money to buy one now that you're doing more slicing and dicing because you're cooking *real food*. For such tasks as grating Parmesan cheese or mincing garlic or parsley, it will shave literally hours a month off your cooking time.

Get one that has the ability to chop by pulsing it on and off, and then buy a slicing disc and a shredding disc. Those are really the only two that are used enough to merit a place in your kitchen.

In addition to a food processor, an immersion blender is an excellent investment if you have to replace your standard blender. These handheld machines can make smoothies as well as a larger model, but they are also more versatile. You can plunk one right into the middle of a pot of bean soup and puree it in the pot.

Other than these two electrical appliances, a good set of knives is the only other thing you need, plus a way to keep them sharp. A small paring knife and a chef's knife become like an extension of your hand.

READING RECIPES RIGHT

All of the recipes in this book have three annotations. Both "Yield" and "Start to finish" are self-explanatory. But then there's the one in the middle: "Active time." That's my shorthand for time you need to tend to the food, either before it's cooked or while it's cooking. It doesn't include time during which the food cooks on its own, while you can be doing something else.

For many of the salads in Chapter 3, "Active time" and "Start to finish" are identical. You finish the slicing and dicing, and then you're ready to eat. But in most recipes there is a discrepancy, and that's where your savvy reading comes into play.

I try to make it easier for you. In Step 1 you're bringing a pot of water to a boil to cook pasta; then in Step 2 I'll say, "While the water heats . . ." That's the time to multitask! Begin by reading each recipe to determine what has to be ready to be cooked when. Read the recipe from top to bottom, and until it becomes second nature, write down what should be done when. The ingredients are all listed in order of use, but when you get them into the necessary form can vary.

If you sauté onions and then add stock that must heat to a boil, you can be prepping all the vegetables that will be added to the simmering sauce while the liquid heats; there's no reason to have completed that task in advance.

The key to time-efficient cooking is this rule: "Make every minute count." There are few recipes—and none of them are in this book!—that require split-second timing. So if you don't have all the vegetables chopped by the time the liquid comes to a boil, either add them later or turn off the heat until you've finished your prepping.

KNIFE SKILLS

Do you watch cooking shows and marvel at the speed with which chefs slice and dice? I certainly hope they can; it's a skill that's vital to their profession. Time is money in the professional kitchen, and there's no reason why it shouldn't be in your kitchen, too.

Maybe you'll never be able to swing a golf club like Tiger Woods, but you can hold—and use—a paring knife with the best of them. That's what you'll learn to do in this section.

Knife skills are the backbone of cooking. In the same way that you started by crawling, and then walked before you ran, now it's time to truly learn how to use those sharp implements needed to cut up food to be cooked. Once you've mastered it, you're good for life.

Take it slow at first, and don't try to imitate a TV chef with great speed or bravado. Your speed will increase naturally as you become more confident about your knife skills. One maxim of cooking woven into this book is that small pieces cook faster than big pieces, so you'll be faster in the kitchen once you've learned how to efficiently make small pieces.

The goals for holding a knife are comfort, control, and safety—and using the knife with minimum stress on your hand. Grip the knife by its bolster; that's the official term for the handle. The bolster is both your knife's balance point and a finger guard. Only your last three fingers should rest on the handle. Your thumb and index finger should be on opposite sides of the blade. When you hold a knife at its balance point it becomes an extension of your hand.

Now that you're holding your knife properly, the best way to cut food is with a forward cutting motion. If you cut back to front the knife is doing the work. If you cut up and down your arm is doing the work.

For slicing, begin by initiating the cut with the tip of the knife and pushing the knife forward across the food until you reach the knife's heel. If you find you have to push down with the knife, chances are your knife needs sharpening. If you reach the heel and you haven't finished your cut, bring the knife back to the tip and repeat the motion.

For large items that sit high on the cutting board like potatoes or carrots, start with the tip of the blade on the food. For smaller foods like celery or herbs start with the tip on the cutting board.

Regardless of what you're cutting, the hand *not* holding the knife serves a vital role. It stabilizes the food you're cutting and guides the knife to determine the size of your cuts. Make sure your fingers are curled inward with your thumb tucked underneath the palm of your hand. The side of the knife—and *never* the blade—should rest against your knuckles.

For fine mincing and chopping you'll use your knife in a different way. Once food is cut into small pieces, and you want to make the pieces yet smaller, your guiding hand should be placed on top of the blade. This hand will help the one holding the knife pivot repeatedly along its curved edge in a rocking motion. You never lift your knife off of the cutting board except to scrape into a pile the food you're cutting.

DEFINING YOUR TERMS

While we understand the meaning of slicing, and only look for guidance as to the thickness of the slices, many recipes include such words as *julienne,* which may need some clarification. There are many traditional ways of cutting food, many of which can be done quickly in the food processor, using the steel blade for chopping and using special discs for shredding and cutting.

The reason to use one cut rather than another is determined by how the ingredient functions in a recipe. If the food must cook quickly in a sauté or stir-fry, the pieces will have to be smaller than if they are going into a stew that will simmer for hours. And if a food is intended as a garnish, chances are it will be cut in a manner that makes it as attractive as possible.

One constant for all cutting methods is to make the pieces uniform; this is important for both cooking and appearance. Here is a list of cutting methods used frequently in recipes:

- **Coarse chopping.** Coarse chopping is usually used for foods such as the vegetables that are added to stews or foods such as cooked potatoes or chicken that form the basis for cold salads.

- **Mincing.** This is an even, very fine cut that is especially appropriate for herbs, garlic, and shallots. Gather herbs or roughly chopped garlic or shallots in a pile on a cutting board and position the knife above the pile. Keeping the tip of the blade against the cutting board, lower the knife firmly and rapidly, repeatedly chopping through the herbs or vegetables. Continue chopping until desired fineness is attained.

- **Julienne and batonnets.** These are long, rectangular cuts that are used for vegetables and for any ingredient that is to be finely cut, like the julienne of prosciutto used to top a pizza. For hard vegetables like carrots or potatoes, trim them so that the sides are straight, which will make it easier to make even cuts. Slice the vegetable lengthwise, using parallel cuts of the proper thickness. Stack the slices, aligning the edges, and make parallel cuts of the same thickness through the stack. To make batonnets, the cuts should be thick. To make a fine julienne, the cuts should be very thin. For soft foods like cooked meats, it's easier to slice it thinly, trim the slices into a neat shape, and then make the thin cuts. Meats should be cut into a julienne with the grain because they'll fall apart if cut against the grain.

- **Dice.** The results of dicing are cube-shaped pieces, and a recipe usually specifies the size of the dice (¼ inch, for example) Everything from vegetables to meats, cheeses, and chocolate may be diced. Trim and cut the food as for julienne or batonnet. Gather the julienne or batonnets and cut through them cross-wise at evenly spaced intervals.

PRODUCE POINTERS

Cooking is at best an inexact science because every piece of food has a unique composition. Perhaps "a rose is a rose is a rose," but each individual apple—even if it comes from the same branch of the same tree—may have gotten a different amount of sunlight. In winemaking, the term the French use is *terroir;* it all depends on the soil. Even different brands of all-purpose flour contain differing amounts of protein so they perform differently when used in baking.

As a general rule, try to select your produce individually rather than putting a bag in your cart. Even though this takes a bit more time, you control the quality of each item, and you can also draw a range of sizes. For example, countless recipes in this book use onions. And there is always a size given—small, medium, or large. So there's no waste if you keep inventory on all three onion sizes.

This section will help you select, handle, and store produce, and give you tips for how to pare away time with your paring knife:

- **Apples.** Look for large apples that have good color, are free of bruises, and are firm to the touch. The bruised cells of apples release an enzyme, polyenoloxidase, which hastens the oxidation or decay of the flesh. Overripe apples feel soft, and the flesh will feel mushy. While traditional slicing methods call for quartering and coring apples to slice them, these steps are unnecessary. Once an apple is peeled, start shaving off slices from the outside with a paring knife, turning the apple in quarter turns. Continue slicing until you reach the core, and then discard the core.

- **Bell peppers.** The best peppers are plump, and have a vibrant color and a long, fresh-looking green stem. Peppers should look crisp and be firm when they are purchased. Flimsy stems, bruises or soft spots, and cracks are signs of an old pepper. Most recipes for bell peppers specify "seeds and ribs removed." To accomplish this faster, sculpt the pepper in relief: Cut a slice off the bottom of the pepper, so that it will stand firmly on the cutting board. You will see the ribs indenting the contour of the pepper. Holding the cap with your free hand, slice down the natural curvature of the pepper in sections. You will be left with all the pepper and none of the seeds and ribs. You can then chop the flesh, or cut as indicated in the recipe.

- **Cabbage.** A head of cabbage should be heavy for its size, free of brown spots or streaks, and have crisp leaves. In green cabbage, look for cabbage with dark green leaves still attached; many markets will pull these off since they are the first to turn yellow. Black edge in red cabbage is a sign of age. For best appearance, cut or shred cabbage just before cooking or serving. Discard outer leaves or any leaves that are discolored or wilted. Halve the head and cut out the tough core with a knife. For shredded cabbage or leaves, remove the entire core; for wedges to be boiled leave some of the core in place to keep the wedges from falling apart. To shred cabbage, put it cut side down on a board and cut crosswise in very fine slices.

- **Carrots.** It's best to buy carrots that still have the green tops attached, not in plastic bags with the greens removed. Look for firm, bright orange carrots with fresh, crisp green tops. Trim off the green tops before you store carrots, however, because the leafy tops will wilt and rot long before the sturdy roots. If you need to peel just a few carrots, the old fashioned way remains the best. But for a large number, cover the carrots with boiling water for 5 minutes, and then place them into ice water. The skins will then slip right off. While cross slices are always appropriate, they look more decorative with no additional work if cut on the bias. Hold the knife at a 20-degree angle to the carrot, and slice it beginning with the small end.

- **Celery.** Select a medium-size stalk that has a solid, rigid feel and a glossy surface of light to medium green. The leaves should be green and fresh, and the ribs should be crisp. Rinse the ribs, and trim off the bottom; save these pieces for making stock. Cut the ribs lengthwise into the size pieces you want. Then pile the thin strips and slice across them. If using ribs whole, slice them with the curved side up so they'll sit firmly on the cutting board.

- **Cucumber.** Select smaller cucumbers because they tend to have fewer seeds. Look for cucumbers that have a clean break at the stem end. An uneven stem means the cucumber was harvested from the vine before it was ready. All waxed cucumbers should be peeled. To seed a cucumber, halve it lengthwise and spoon out the seedy center with a melon baller, or use the tip of a teaspoon or a measuring spoon.

- **Eggplant.** The freshest eggplants are plump and have shiny skins and a bright green cap, and should not weigh more than 1 pound or they may be old and bitter. They should be firm and heavy for their size. Avoid damaged, bruised, or soft eggplant, since even slightly soft eggplants are bitter. Eggplants brown easily, so slice them just prior to cooking.

- **Garlic.** Look for whole heads with no cloves broken off, with tightly packed large cloves and no sign of green sprouts at the tips. The skin on cloves should be tight and snug because loose cloves indicate deterioration. When the cloves are pressed, they should feel firm and solid. If the papery skin is pulling away from the cloves, it is a sign of old garlic. Keep garlic in a cool, dark, dry space with fresh, circulating air. Fresh garlic should keep from three to six months if properly stored. Separate cloves from the head as needed. For a few cloves, you can easily pry the outer cloves with your thumb. To quickly separate the entire head, hit the base firmly onto a counter or cutting board, and the cloves will easily pull apart. **To peel a clove:** Place the side of a heavy knife over the clove and bring your fist down hard on the side of the blade. The skin can then easily be pulled off with your fingers. This is the easiest method, and it should be used if the clove is to be pounded or minced. **To mince garlic:** Cut the peeled clove lengthwise with a very sharp knife. Keeping the garlic together, make a quarter turn and slice again. Continue to chop the garlic, using a rocking motion with your knife. Hold the tip end with your other hand and use quick, small strokes. As garlic spreads out, use the knife to push it back to the center. Keep chopping until garlic is very fine.

- **Ginger.** The freshest ginger is plump and very firm, and the skin should be tan and shiny. Try to buy the largest knobs possible without many small bumps, which will be removed and are virtually useless for cooking. Store ginger refrigerated for up to 2 weeks, wrapped in paper towels to absorb moisture and placed inside a plastic bag. Ginger should be peeled not only for aesthetic reasons, but because the peel never softens. Use a sharp paring knife, and trim the small stubs off the knobs. Then peel with the curve of the knobs, along the grain rather than across it. Then cut the ginger into slices, and crush them with the flat side of a large knife; the crushing separates the fibers, which makes it easier to chop or slice further. To grate ginger, use the tiny-hole side of a box grater, or drop cubes through the feed tube of a food processor with the motor running and they will grate finely.

- **Mushrooms.** Fresh mushrooms are firm, smooth, plump, and have a consistent cream color. The caps should be spongy and tightly closed, hiding the gills. In small, delicate mushrooms, look for mushrooms with the veil—the membrane between the cap and the stem—still attached to the mushroom cap. Mushrooms should be slightly moist, but with no damp patches. Slimy mushrooms, or those with some yellow underneath, should be avoided. White mushrooms all taste the same regardless of size. So if you're chopping them it makes sense to buy the largest ones possible. It will take less time to clean them. If you purchased mushrooms loose, refrigerate them where they can get good air circulation and store them in a paper bag poked with a few holes, or cover them with wax paper or a damp cloth or paper towel to aid in retaining the moisture. Mushrooms should be handled gently, since they bruise easily. If mushrooms are pristine, simply rub them gently with a damp paper towel and trim the stem. Never soak mushrooms because they absorb water, and do not scrub them because this causes a loss of nutrients and a change in texture. Slice mushrooms just before cooking, since oxidation will cause the mushrooms to turn an unattractive purplish brown. **To slice:** Slice a mushroom in half, and place the cut side on the cutting board. Slice with a sharp paring knife, using a front to back motion. Do not press straight down or the knife can bruise the mushroom. **To dice:** Slice the stem so that it is level with the mushroom cap. Cut mushroom horizontally into medium to thick slices. Arrange slices, or stack them on top of each other. Cut mushroom into medium-size sticks. Now gather the mushroom slices together and cut across.

- **Onions.** Choose onions that are firm and nicely shaped. The skins should appear tight and healthy. Sprouting is a sign of age, and these onions should be avoided. Also avoid onions with soft spots, a dried appearance, or black or powdery spots, all of which are signs of internal decay. Store onions in a cool, dry area with good air circulation, and they should keep for three to four weeks. At cooler temperatures, 55 to 60°F, they may keep for several months. Refrigerate onions only after they have been cut. Wrap onions tightly in plastic wrap to avoid odors from affecting other foods. If only part of an onion is needed for a recipe, slice off only that much, leaving the remainder of the onion in its skin. **To peel:** Take a small slice off the top and root ends, using a stainless steel paring knife; iron can cause the onion to discolor. Pull away the papery skin using your hand as a guide. **To slice and dice:** Place the onion on a chopping board, and slice it in half lengthwise. To slice it, cut down at regular intervals holding the onion by its root end in the hand not holding the knife. To dice it, place the onion cut side down, and slice lengthwise at intervals from 1/4 to 1/2 inch, depending on the size pieces needed. Next, hold the knife horizontally, and slice at the same intervals from the bottom to the top. The third step is to slice down vertically, and the onion will be diced. To chop more finely, use a chef's knife in a rolling pattern on the diced onion.

- **Potatoes.** Whatever type of potato you buy, always choose firm, well-shaped ones free of blemishes, bruises, discolorations, or sprouting eyes. Especially avoid those with green spots, which indicate the presence of a toxic alkaloid called solanine that results from exposure to light. To reduce waste, choose ones with regular shapes that do not have deep eyes and are heavy for their size. To make sure that small raw potatoes truly are "new" potatoes, gently rub their skins; being immature, the skins should come off easily.

- **Tomatoes.** The best way to obtain a perfectly ripe tomato is to grow your own or buy them from a farmers' market. Tomatoes should be smooth and heavy for their size with firm flesh. Avoid any that appear watery. Avoid bruised tomatoes, many times damaged tomatoes are rotten inside. Mold growing around the stem is a bad sign, and the mold may be toxic. Vine-ripened varieties often have the green stems attached. Press them gently between your palms; they should give slightly. Never refrigerate unripe tomatoes. They will not ripen in the refrigerator. Store unripe tomatoes in a cool spot, out of direct sunlight that could encourage tomatoes to turn to mush and may also destroy the vitamins A and C. Store between 60 and 75°F. For quicker ripening, place unripe tomatoes in a closed paper bag or fruit-ripening bowl. Refrigerate only fully ripe tomatoes, and use them within three to five days after they are ripe. **To seed:** Slice the tomato in half through the middle. Squeeze gently over a bowl, and seeds should loosen and drop. Any clinging seeds can be removed with the tip of a paring knife or your finger. **To dice:** Cut the tomato in half. Slice it into strips and then cut the strips crosswise into dice.

FISHY BUSINESS

Fish cooks faster than any other type of protein; that's why there are so many ways to cook it in this book. While fish is usually higher in price than most meats, there is no waste to a fish fillet, and with its low fat content it doesn't shrink the way that meats do. So the price per edible ounce of fish is really about the same as for other forms of protein like a chuck roast or pork loin, if still more expensive than a chicken.

It's more important to use the freshest fish—and one that is reasonably priced—than any specific fish species; that's why these recipes are not written for cod, halibut, or pompano. They're written for two generic types of fish: thin white-fleshed fillets and thick white-fleshed fish fillets. These encompass the most types of fish. They are all low in fat, mild to delicate in flavor, and flake easily when cooked. The only species of fish that should *not* be used in these recipes are tuna, blue-fish, and mackerel; they will all be too strong. Salmon, if you find it at a good price, can be substituted for either classification of fish, depending on the thickness of the fillet.

There are thousands of species that fit these rather large definitions. Here are some of the most common:

- Thin fillets: Flounder, sole, perch, red snapper, trout, tilapia, ocean perch, catfish, striped bass, turbot, and whitefish.

- Thick fillets: Halibut, scrod, cod, grouper, sea bass, mahi-mahi, pompano, yellowtail, and swordfish.

Most supermarkets still display fish on chipped ice in a case rather than pre-packaging it, and they should. Fish should be kept at even a lower temperature than meats. Fish fillets or steaks should look bright, lustrous, and moist, with no signs of discoloration or drying.

When making your fish selection, keep a few simple guidelines in mind: above all, do not buy any fish that actually smells fishy, indicating that it is no longer fresh or hasn't been cut or stored properly. Fresh fish has the mild, clean scent of the sea—nothing more. Look for bright, shiny colors in the fish scales, because as a fish sits, its skin becomes more pale and dull looking. Then peer into the eyes; they should be black and beady. If they're milky or sunken, the fish has been dead too long. And if the fish isn't behind glass, gently poke its flesh. If the indentation remains, the fish is old.

Rinse all fish under cold running water before cutting or cooking. With fillets, run your fingers in every direction along the top of the fillet before cooking, and feel for any pesky little bones.

You can remove bones easily in two ways. Larger bones will come out if they're stroked with a vegetable peeler, and you can pull out smaller bones with tweezers. This is not a long process, but it's a gesture that will be greatly appreciated by all who eat the fish.

TALKING TUNA

There are a dizzying array of cans, and now pouches, on supermarket shelves, but they essentially fall into four categories. The options are solid white tuna packed in water, solid white tuna packed in oil, light tuna packed in water, and light tuna packed in oil. Water-packed tuna is a relative newcomer to the market, following decades of oil-packed tuna. While it does trim the fat from the fish, it also trims much of the flavor since it tends to be less moist.

There are health concerns as well as cost reasons for specifying light tuna rather than white tuna, sometimes called albacore tuna, in these recipes. White tuna has been found to be much higher in mercury than light tuna, so light tuna is better on both scores. Feel free in any of the recipes containing canned tuna to substitute canned salmon. Almost all canned salmon is packaged complete with bones and skin, however, so some preparatory work is needed before using it in recipes.

PROCEDURES FOR POULTRY

Just look at the range of prices for chicken in the supermarket! They can range from less than $1 per pound for whole birds and leg/thigh quarters to $5 or $6 per pound for coveted boneless, skinless breasts. Always keep in mind that you're paying for someone else's labor.

It is far more economical to purchase a whole chicken, and cut it up yourself, rather than buying one already cut. There are also times that your choice of chicken pieces aren't available, and you can always cut up a few chickens to glean the parts for that meal, and freeze what's left; another benefit is that you can save the scraps and freeze them to keep you "stocked up" for soups and sauces. Here are some methods of chicken cutting you should know:

- **Cutting up a whole chicken:** Start by breaking back the wings until the joints snap, then use the boning knife to cut through the ball joints and detach the wings. When holding the chicken on its side, you will see a natural curve outlining the boundary between the breast and the leg/thigh quarters. Use sharp kitchen shears to cut along this line. Cut the breast in half by scraping away the meat from the breastbone, and using a small paring knife to remove the wish bone. Cut away the breastbone using the shears, and save it for stock. Divide the thigh/leg quarters by turning the pieces over and finding the joint joining them. Cut through the joint and sever the leg from the thigh.

- **Boning chicken breasts:** If possible, buy the chicken breasts whole rather than split. Pull the skin off with your fingers, and then make an incision on either side of the breastbone, cutting down until you feel the bone resisting the knife. Treating one side at a time, place the blade of your boning knife against the carcass, and scrape away the meat. You will then have two pieces— the large fillet, and the small tenderloin. To trim the fillet, cut away any fat. Some recipes will tell you to pound the breast to an even thickness, so it will cook evenly and quickly. Place the breast between two sheets of plastic wrap or waxed paper, and pound with the smooth side of a meat mallet or the bottom of a small, heavy skillet or saucepan. If you have a favorite veal scallop recipe, and want to substitute chicken or turkey, pound it very thin—to a thickness of $1/4$ inch. Otherwise, what you are after is to pound the thicker portion so that it lies and cooks evenly. To trim the tenderloin, secure the tip of the tendon that will be visible with your free hand. Using a paring knife, scrape down the tendon, and the meat will push away.

Handling Poultry

Poultry should always be rinsed under cold running water after being taken out of the package. If it's going to be pre-browned in the oven or in a skillet on the stove, pat the pieces dry with paper towels and then wash your hands. Chicken often contains salmonella, a naturally occurring bacteria that is killed by cooking, but you don't want to transfer this bacteria to other foods.

Rules for both pork and poultry have changed during the past few years, and now poultry must be cooked to just 165°F, rather than the 180°F for dark meat in the past, to ensure that there's no chance for microorganisms to survive. The best way to test the temperature is to use an instant-read meat thermometer.

When the thickest part of the chicken is probed, the reading should be 165°F. But if you don't want to take the temperature of every piece of chicken, here are the visual signals: The chicken is tender when poked with the tip of a paring knife, there is not a hint of pink even near the bones, and the juices run clear. Always test the dark meat before the white meat. Dark meat takes slightly longer to cook, so if the thighs are the proper temperature, you know the breasts will be fine.

Basic Roast Chicken

While we credit President Herbert Hoover with the expression "a chicken in every pot," the phrase praising this luxury actually dates back to the kings of seventeenth-century France. There are few foods as wonderful, and there's so much you can do with the leftovers.

Yield: 6–8 servings | **Active time:** 15 minutes | **Start to finish:** 2 hours

1 (5–7-pound) roasting chicken
4 sprigs fresh parsley, divided
4 sprigs fresh rosemary, divided
6 garlic cloves, peeled and minced, divided
2 sprigs fresh thyme
Salt and freshly ground black pepper to taste
4 tablespoons ($\frac{1}{2}$ stick) unsalted butter, softened
1 large onion, peeled and roughly chopped
1 carrot, peeled and thickly sliced
1 celery rib, rinsed, trimmed, and sliced
1 cup Chicken Stock (recipe on page 35) or purchased stock

1. Preheat the oven to 425°F. Rinse chicken, and pat dry with paper towels. Place 2 sprigs parsley, 2 sprigs rosemary, 4 garlic cloves, and thyme in cavity of chicken. Sprinkle salt and pepper inside cavity, and close it with skewers and string.

2. Chop remaining parsley, rosemary, and garlic. Mix with butter, and season to taste with salt and pepper. Gently stuff butter mixture under the skin of breast meat. Rub skin with salt and pepper. Place chicken on a rack in a roasting pan, breast side up.

3. Bake for 30 minutes, reduce the oven temperature to 350°F, and add onion, carrot, and celery to the roasting pan. Cook an additional 1–1½ hours, or until chicken is cooked through and no longer pink, and dark meat registers 165°F on an instant-read thermometer. Remove chicken from the oven, and allow it to rest on a heated platter for 10 minutes.

4. Spoon grease out of the pan, and discard, or save for another use. Add chicken stock to the pan. Stir over medium-high heat until the liquid is reduced to a syrupy consistency. Strain sauce into a sauce boat, and add to it any liquid that accumulates on the platter when the chicken is carved. Serve immediately.

Note: The chicken can be roasted up to 3 hours in advance and kept at room temperature, covered with aluminum foil.

Variations: While the method remains the same, here are some other seasoning blends to flavor the chicken:
- Use 3 tablespoons smoked Spanish paprika, 1 tablespoon ground cumin, 1 tablespoon dried thyme, and 3 minced garlic cloves.
- Use 3 tablespoons Italian seasoning, 3 tablespoons chopped fresh parsley, and 3 garlic cloves.
- Use 3 tablespoons dried oregano and 5 garlic cloves, and add 1 sliced lemon to the cavity.
- Rather than chicken stock, deglaze the pan with white wine.

Here's how to carve a roast chicken or turkey: To add a flourish to carving that also assures crisp skin for all, first "unwrap" the breast. Use a well-sharpened knife and fork. Carve and serve one side at a time. From neck, cut just through skin down middle of breast and around side. Hook fork on skin at tail and roll skin back to neck. Holding bird with fork, remove leg by severing hip joint. Separate drumstick from thigh and serve. Cut thin slices of breast at slight angle and add a small piece of rolled skin to each serving. Repeat all steps for other side. Remove wings last.

Basic Roast Turkey

There are two schools of thought to roasting a turkey—either relatively low heat or high heat—and I prefer the latter. Using this roasting method, the turkey basically steams; the meat remains juicy since it is being cooked by a moist rather than dry heat method.

Yield: 8–10 servings, plus enough for leftovers | **Active time:** 15 minutes | **Start to finish:** at least 2¼ hours, but varies by the weight of the turkey

    1 (12–16-pound) turkey
    6 tablespoons (¾ stick) unsalted butter, softened and divided
    3 garlic cloves, peeled and minced
    3 tablespoons smoked Spanish paprika
    1 tablespoon dried thyme
    Salt and freshly ground black pepper to taste
    1 large onion, peeled and diced
    1½ cups Chicken Stock (recipe on page 35) or purchased stock
    1 tablespoon cornstarch
    2 tablespoons cold water

1. Preheat the oven to 450°F. Rinse turkey inside and out under cold running water, and place it in a large roasting pan.
2. Combine 3 tablespoons butter, garlic, paprika, thyme, salt, and pepper in a small bowl, and mix well. Rub mixture over skin of turkey and inside cavity. Place onion and stock in the roasting pan, and place turkey on top. Create a tent with two sheets of heavy-duty aluminum foil, crimping foil around the edges of the roasting pan, and joining the two sheets in the center by crimping.
3. Place turkey in the oven, and roast for 12–15 minutes per pound. After 2 hours, remove the foil, and remove liquid from the roasting pan with a bulb baster and reserve for gravy. Return turkey to the oven, covered as before.
4. Reduce the oven temperature to 350°F, and uncover turkey for the last 1 hour of roasting so skin browns. Rub skin with remaining butter after removing the foil. Turkey is done when it is cooked through and no longer pink, and dark meat registers 165°F on an instant-read thermometer. Remove turkey from the oven, and allow it to rest on a heated platter for 10–15 minutes, lightly covered with foil.

5. While turkey rests, prepare gravy. Pour all juices and flavoring ingredients from the roasting pan into a saucepan. If there are any brown bits clinging to the bottom of the pan, add 1 cup of turkey or chicken stock. Stir over medium heat, scraping brown bits from bottom of pan. In a small bowl, mix cornstarch and water, and set aside. Remove as much fat as possible from the surface of juices with a soup ladle, and then reduce liquid by at least ¼ to concentrate flavor. Stir cornstarch mixture into the pan, and cook for 3–5 minutes, or until liquid boils and slightly thickens. Season gravy to taste with salt and pepper.

6. To serve, carve turkey, and pass gravy separately.

Note: The turkey can be left at room temperature for up to 1 hour after removing it from the oven; keep it lightly tented with aluminum foil.

Variations: While the method remains the same, here are some other seasoning blends to flavor the turkey:

- Use 2 tablespoons herbes de Provence or Italian seasoning along with 3 garlic cloves.
- Use ¼ cup chopped fresh rosemary, 1 tablespoon grated lemon zest, and 3 garlic cloves.

Basic Baked Ham

Not only does this recipe render the ham succulent and moist, it also creates some wonderful stock to use for your next batch of soup or a stew! This is a master recipe, and creates enough meat for a lavish Sunday dinner plus leftovers for myriad recipes located in other chapters of this book. Plus, always save the ham bone for making soups.

Yield: 10–12 servings | **Active time:** 10 minutes | **Start to finish:** 3–3¼ hours

HAM

1 (8–10-pound) fully cooked ham (*not* spiral-sliced)
1½ cups Chicken Stock (recipe on page 35) or purchased stock
1 small onion, peeled and diced
1 small carrot, peeled and sliced
3 parsley sprigs

GLAZE (OPTIONAL)

½ cup apricot preserves
3 tablespoons grainy mustard
2 tablespoons grated fresh ginger

1. Preheat the oven to 325°F, and grease a large roasting pan.
2. Remove ham from plastic, if necessary, and rinse well under cold water. Cut away and discard any thick skin with a sharp knife, and trim all fat to an even ¼-inch layer.
3. Place ham, cut side down, in the prepared pan, and add stock, onion, carrot, and parsley. Cover the pan with heavy-duty aluminum foil, and bake ham for 1¾ hours. Remove ham from the oven, discard foil, and remove pan juices; save juices and freeze for soups and stews. Turn ham over, and bake for an additional 1–1½ hours, or until an instant-read thermometer registers 145°F.
4. While ham bakes, make glaze, if using. Combine apricot preserves, mustard, and ginger in a small mixing bowl, and stir well. Increase oven temperature to 400°F, if serving glazed ham. Remove ham from the oven. Cut off all ham to be used for future dishes, and apply glaze to remaining ham.

5. Return ham to the oven and bake for an additional 15 minutes, basting with glaze every 5 minutes.

Note: The ham can be prepared up to 3 days in advance and refrigerated, tightly covered. Serve it cold, or slice and reheat it in a 350°F oven for 10–20 minutes, or until warm.

Variations:
- Substitute ¾ cup dry sherry or white wine for ¾ cup of stock.
- Substitute ½ cup orange marmalade or red currant jelly for the apricot preserves.
- Glaze alternative: Reduce 3 cups of pineapple juice to ¾ cup, and add ¼ cup Dijon mustard, ¼ cup firmly packed dark brown sugar, and ¼ teaspoon ground cloves.
- Glaze alternative: Substitute prepared horseradish for the grainy mustard.

I have no idea why spiral-sliced hams have become the norm rather than the exception; they are always more expensive than ham that is not sliced and it's nearly impossible to cook one without having dried-out slices. Also, because the slices are so thin, you are severely limited as to the recipes you can make with the leftovers.

STOCKING UP

Stocks are no more difficult to make than boiling water; all they are is lots of water in which other ingredients simmer for many hours to create water with an enriched flavor.

You may be thinking, "Why should I make stock when there are so many bargain brands on the supermarket shelves?" There are two compelling reasons to make your own—money and flavor. Homemade stock costs virtually pennies to make, and its flavor is far superior to that found in even the highest-priced containers, which are more expensive than a quart of milk or jug of juice—foods you can't make yourself. Plus commercial stocks are frequently very high in sodium.

In the same way that you can utilize bits of leftover vegetables in soups, many of the vegetables that go into stocks would otherwise end up in the garbage or compost bin. Save those carrot and onion peelings, parsley stems, the base off a celery stalk, and the dark green scallion tops. All of those foods might not wend their way into cooking a dish, but they're fine for stock!

I keep different bags in my freezer in anticipation of making stock on a regular basis. There are individual ones for chicken trimmings, beef (but not pork) trimmings, fish skin and bones, and vegetables past their prime and their trimmings. When one bag is full, it's time to make stock.

Once your stock is cooked—and the fat removed from chicken and beef stock—you should freeze it in containers of different sizes. I do about half a batch in heavy, resealable quart bags; they are the basis for soups. Bags take up less room in the freezer than containers. Freeze them flat on a baking sheet and then they can be stacked on a freezer shelf or in the cubbyholes on the freezer door.

I then freeze stock in 1-cup measures and some in ice cube trays. Measure the capacity of your ice cube tray with a measuring tablespoon; it will be somewhere between 1 and 3 tablespoons. Keep a bag of stock cubes for those recipes that require just a small amount.

Chicken Stock

You'll be amazed at the difference in flavor homemade chicken stock makes to all your dishes. And you'll notice a change in your grocery bill when you can stop buying it!

Yield: 4 quarts | **Active time:** 10 minutes | **Start to finish:** 4 hours

6 quarts water

5 pounds chicken bones, skin, and trimmings

4 celery ribs, rinsed and cut into thick slices

2 onions, trimmed and quartered

2 carrots, trimmed, scrubbed, and cut into thick slices

2 tablespoons whole black peppercorns

6 garlic cloves, peeled

4 sprigs parsley

1 teaspoon dried thyme

2 bay leaves

1. Place water and chicken in a large stockpot, and bring to a boil over high heat. Reduce the heat to low, and skim off foam that rises during the first 10–15 minutes of simmering. Simmer stock, uncovered, for 1 hour, then add celery, onions, carrots, peppercorns, garlic, parsley, thyme, and bay leaves. Simmer for 2$\frac{1}{2}$ hours.

2. Strain stock through a fine-meshed sieve, pushing with the back of a spoon to extract as much liquid as possible. Discard solids, spoon stock into smaller containers, and refrigerate. Remove and discard fat from surface of stock, then transfer stock to a variety of container sizes.

Note: The stock can be refrigerated and used within 3 days, or it can be frozen for up to 6 months.

Variation:

• For turkey stock, use the same amount of turkey giblets and necks as chicken pieces.

Beef Stock

While beef stock is not specified as often as chicken stock in recipes, it is the backbone to certain soups and the gravy for stews and roasts.

Yield: 2 quarts | **Active time:** 15 minutes | **Start to finish:** 3½ hours

   2 pounds beef trimmings (bones, fat) or inexpensive beef shank
   3 quarts water
   1 carrot, trimmed, scrubbed, and cut into thick slices
   1 medium onion, peeled and sliced
   1 celery rib, trimmed and sliced
   1 tablespoon whole black peppercorns
   3 sprigs fresh parsley
   1 teaspoon dried thyme
   2 garlic cloves, peeled
   2 bay leaves

1. Preheat the oven broiler, and line a broiler pan with heavy-duty aluminum foil. Broil beef for 3 minutes per side, or until browned. Transfer beef to a large stockpot, and add water. Bring to a boil over high heat. Reduce the heat to low, and skim off foam that rises during the first 10–15 minutes of simmering. Simmer for 1 hour, uncovered, then add carrot, onion, celery, peppercorns, parsley, thyme, garlic, and bay leaves. Simmer for 3 hours.
2. Strain stock through a fine-meshed sieve, pushing with the back of a spoon to extract as much liquid as possible. Discard solids, and spoon stock into smaller containers. Refrigerate; remove and discard fat from surface of stock.

Note: The stock can be refrigerated and used within 3 days, or it can be frozen for up to 6 months.

Vegetable Stock

You may think it not necessary to use vegetable stock if making a vegetarian dish that includes the same vegetables, but that's not the case. Using stock creates a much more richly flavored dish that can't be replicated by increasing the quantity of vegetables cooked in it.

Yield: 2 quarts | **Active time:** 10 minutes | **Start to finish:** 1 hour

> 2 quarts water
> 2 carrots, scrubbed, trimmed, and thinly sliced
> 2 celery ribs, trimmed and sliced
> 2 leeks, white part only, trimmed, rinsed, and thinly sliced
> 1 small onion, peeled and thinly sliced
> 1 tablespoon whole black peppercorns
> 3 sprigs fresh parsley
> 1 teaspoon dried thyme
> 2 garlic cloves, peeled
> 1 bay leaf

1. Pour water into a stockpot, and add carrots, celery, leeks, onion, peppercorns, parsley, thyme, garlic, and bay leaf. Bring to a boil over high heat, then reduce the heat to low and simmer stock, uncovered, for 1 hour.
2. Strain stock through a fine-meshed sieve, pushing with the back of a spoon to extract as much liquid as possible. Discard solids, and allow stock to cool to room temperature. Spoon stock into smaller containers, and refrigerate.

Note: The stock can be refrigerated and used within 3 days, or it can be frozen for up to 6 months.

Seafood Stock

Seafood stock is a great reason to make friends with head of the fish department of your supermarket. You can arrange in advance to have them save bodies for you if the store cooks lobster meat, or purchase them at minimal cost. The same is true with fish bones, if the store fillets the fish on site.

Yield: 2 quarts | **Active time:** 15 minutes | **Start to finish:** $1^3/_4$ hours

3 lobster bodies (whole lobsters from which the tail and claw meat has been removed), shells from 3 pounds raw shrimp, or 2 pounds bones and skin from firm-fleshed white fish such as halibut, cod, or sole

3 quarts water

1 cup dry white wine

1 carrot, scrubbed, trimmed, and cut into 1-inch chunks

1 medium onion, peeled and sliced

1 celery rib, rinsed, trimmed and sliced

1 tablespoon whole black peppercorns

3 sprigs fresh parsley

1 teaspoon dried thyme

2 garlic cloves, peeled

1 bay leaf

1. If using lobster shells, pull top shell off 1 lobster body. Scrape off and discard feathery gills, then break body into small pieces. Place pieces into the stockpot, and repeat with remaining lobster bodies. If using shrimp shells or fish bones, rinse and place in the stockpot.

2. Add water, wine, carrot, onion, celery, peppercorns, parsley, thyme, garlic, and bay leaf. Bring to a boil over high heat, then reduce the heat to low and simmer stock, uncovered, for $1^1/_2$ hours.

3. Strain stock through a fine-meshed sieve, pushing with the back of a spoon to extract as much liquid as possible. Discard solids, and allow stock to cool to room temperature. Spoon stock into smaller containers, and refrigerate.

Note: The stock can be refrigerated and used within 3 days, or it can be frozen for up to 6 months.

Chapter 3:
Salad Savvy

Rising right alongside our concerns about eating more frugally is interest in eating more healthfully, and entrée salads—your complete meal on one plate—are one way to accomplish both goals. Entrée salads are a delicious way to ensure you're getting all nine daily servings of fruits and vegetables into your diet. And they can be on the table in a matter of minutes.

It used to be that salads were relegated to the warm summer months, but that's no longer the case. While chef salads and the now ubiquitous grilled chicken Caesar salad have been around for decades, a trend gaining favor is the warm salad. Not a misnomer, warm, freshly cooked protein—be it a chicken breast or fillet of fish—tops cold vegetables (with the occasional fruit thrown in) and then all components are napped with a light dressing.

Entrée salads are also a great way to stretch some leftover protein, like the chicken or ham that's not enough to serve on its own. If using a pre-cooked protein, it's possible to prep the ingredients and make the salad dressing earlier in the day and refrigerate the various elements in plastic bags or bowls; you'll need one for the "wet" ingredients like onions or beans, and another for the "dry" salad greens.

A LESSON ON LETTUCE

Decades ago there was no problem choosing a lettuce for a salad because iceberg was all you'd find in the supermarket, and it remains the country's leading lettuce. Today, however, the produce section is a cornucopia of salad greens (plus some whites and reds), some of which are much more expensive than others. But there's no reason to spend $4 a pound on lettuce when your protein is half that cost.

All the types of greens specified in these recipes are drawn from the less expensive options. So this chart is intended to help you save money on recipes you may already have, or will glean in the future. While making substitutions for some ingredients is difficult if wanting to retain the character of the finished dish, this is hardly a problem with lettuces, as long as they're in the same flavor and texture family.

NAME	TEXTURE	FLAVOR
Arugula	Tender	Pungent
Belgian endive	Crisp	Slightly bitter
Curly endive	Crisp	Bitter
Escarole	Crisp	Bitter
Frisee	Crisp	Bitter
Lettuce, butter	Very tender	Mild
Lettuce, iceberg	Crisp	Very mild
Lettuce, leaf	Crisp tender	Mild
Lettuce, romaine	Mainly crisp with tender outer leaves	Fairly mild
Radicchio	Tender leaves with crisp veins	Slightly bitter
Watercress	Tender leaves on crisp stalks	Peppery, pungent

REDRESSING YOUR DRESSING

The reason why traditional recipes for salad dressing contain so much oil is that the oil is needed to balance the acidity of the other ingredients. Imagine drinking a glass of pure lemon juice; it's not very appealing.

But the fat can be trimmed with the inclusion of mild ingredients other than oil. You'll find recipes in this chapter that list orange juice and grapefruit juice, which are not as acidic and tart as lemon juice or vinegar. This principle of diluting acids with other liquid can be applied to all your vinaigrette dressings to cut back on the fat.

Spanish White Bean and Orange Salad

Oranges are an ingredient commonly found in Spanish cuisine, and their sweet flavor is amplified by the heady aroma of smoked paprika in the dressing.

Yield: 4–6 servings | **Active time:** 15 minutes | **Start to finish:** 30 minutes

2 (15-ounce) cans white cannellini beans, drained and rinsed

3 navel oranges, peeled and cut into $\frac{1}{2}$-inch dice

2 Red Delicious or McIntosh apples, peeled, cored, and cut into $\frac{1}{2}$-inch dice

$\frac{1}{2}$ green bell pepper, seeds and ribs removed, cut into $\frac{1}{2}$-inch dice

$\frac{1}{4}$ cup chopped fresh cilantro

3 garlic cloves, peeled and minced

1 small onion, peeled and finely chopped

2 tablespoons smoked Spanish paprika

1 teaspoon ground cumin

$\frac{1}{4}$ teaspoon ground cinnamon

$\frac{1}{3}$ cup orange juice

3 tablespoons lime juice

3 tablespoons cider vinegar

Salt and cayenne to taste

$\frac{1}{3}$ cup olive oil

1. Combine beans, oranges, apples, green bell pepper, and cilantro in a mixing bowl.
2. Combine garlic, onion, paprika, cumin, cinnamon, orange juice, lime juice, vinegar, salt, and cayenne in a jar with a tight-fitting lid. Shake well, add olive oil and shake well again.
3. Toss salad with dressing, and refrigerate salad for at least 15 minutes before serving.

Note: The salad can be made 1 day in advance and refrigerated, tightly covered.

Variation:
- Substitute mango or papaya for the oranges, and substitute jicama for the apples.

Warm Asian Eggplant Salad

Eggplant has an earthy, hearty flavor and texture, and it's used extensively in Asian as well as Western cuisines. The dressing for this salad is spicy, with tiny white sesame seeds adding visual appeal.

Yield: 4–6 servings | **Active time:** 10 minutes | **Start to finish:** 25 minutes

- 2 (1-pound) eggplants
- 6 tablespoons vegetable oil, divided
- Salt and freshly ground black pepper to taste
- 1/4 cup sesame seeds *
- 3 tablespoons soy sauce
- 3 garlic cloves, peeled and minced
- 2 teaspoons granulated sugar
- 1 teaspoon Chinese chile paste with garlic *
- 3 tablespoons Asian sesame oil *
- 6–9 cups salad greens, rinsed and dried

1. Preheat the oven to 400°F, and cover 2 baking sheets with aluminum foil. Cut eggplant into 1/4-inch slices. Spread 3 tablespoons vegetable oil on the baking sheets, and arrange eggplant slices. Sprinkle with salt and pepper. Bake eggplant for 15–20 minutes, or until soft.
2. While eggplant bakes, place sesame seeds in a small, dry skillet over medium heat. Toast seeds for 2 minutes, or until browned, shaking the pan frequently. Set aside. Combine soy sauce, garlic, sugar, and chile paste in a jar with a tight-fitting lid. Shake well, add sesame oil and remaining vegetable oil, and shake well again. Set aside.
3. To serve, toss greens with 1/2 of dressing, and arrange greens on individual plates or on a large platter. Top with warm eggplant slices. Drizzle with remaining dressing, sprinkle with sesame seeds, and serve immediately.

Note: The eggplant can be baked up to 1 day in advance and refrigerated, tightly covered. Reheat it in a 350°F oven for 5–10 minutes, or until hot. The dressing can also be made in advance and refrigerated; allow it to sit at room temperature for 30 minutes prior to serving.

Variation:
- Substitute 4 large green bell peppers, seeds and ribs removed, and cut into 2-inch wedges, for the eggplant.

* Available in the Asian aisle of most supermarkets and in specialty markets.

Tabbouleh with Fish and Feta

Tabbouleh, pronounced *ta-BOOL-a,* is the potato salad of the Middle East; it's served as an accompaniment to almost everything and as an entrée if augmented with protein. The characteristic ingredients are bulgur, parsley, and lemon juice. From that base it's open to interpretation.

Yield: 4–6 servings | **Active time:** 15 minutes | **Start to finish:** 45 minutes, including 15 minutes for chilling

> ¾ pound bulgur wheat
> ½ cup lemon juice
> 2⅓ cups very hot water
> ¾ pound thin white-fleshed fish fillets
> ½ cup olive oil, divided
> Salt and freshly ground black pepper to taste
> 1 cucumber, rinsed, seeded, and chopped
> 4 ripe plum tomatoes, rinsed, cored, seeded, and chopped
> 1 small red onion, peeled and minced
> 2 garlic cloves, peeled and minced
> 1 cup chopped fresh parsley
> ½ cup crumbled feta cheese

1. Preheat the oven to 400°F, and line a baking sheet with aluminum foil. Place bulgur in a large mixing bowl and add lemon juice and hot water. Let stand, covered, for 30 minutes, or until bulgur is tender. Drain off any excess liquid.
2. While bulgur soaks, rinse fish and pat dry with paper towels. Rub fish with 2 tablespoons olive oil, and sprinkle with salt and pepper. Bake fish for 6–8 minutes, or until it is cooked through and flakes easily. Remove fish from the oven, and break into 1-inch pieces.
3. Add fish, cucumber, tomatoes, onion, garlic, parsley, and feta to bulgur and toss to combine. Add remaining olive oil, a few tablespoons at a time, to make salad moist but not runny. Season to taste with salt and pepper.
4. Refrigerate tabbouleh for at least 15 minutes. Serve cold or at room temperature.

Note: The tabbouleh can be made up to 1 day in advance and refrigerated, tightly covered.

Variation:
- Omit the fish, and increase the feta to 1¼ cups.

Warm Fish, Avocado, and Grapefruit Salad

The pairing of two tropical ingredients—buttery avocado and tart grapefruit—has been popular for decades with good reason; it's delicious. In this salad it's joined with delicate fish fillets that absorb flavor from the mild and lean dressing.

Yield: 4–6 servings | **Active time:** 15 minutes | **Start to finish:** 25 minutes

1¼ pounds thin white-fleshed fish fillets
Salt and freshly ground black pepper to taste
1 tablespoon paprika
1 tablespoon chili powder
1 teaspoon ground cumin
1 teaspoon dried oregano
¼ cup grapefruit juice
2 tablespoons rice vinegar
2 garlic cloves, peeled and minced
⅔ cup olive oil, divided
2 pink grapefruits
4–6 cups bite-sized pieces romaine lettuce, rinsed and dried
4 scallions, white parts and 3 inches of green tops, rinsed, trimmed, and sliced
1 small cucumber, peeled, halved lengthwise, seeded, and sliced
1 ripe avocado, peeled and thinly sliced

1. Rinse fish and pat dry with paper towels. Cut fish into 2-inch squares. Sprinkle fish with salt and pepper. Combine paprika, chili powder, cumin, and oregano in a small bowl. Rub spice mixture on both sides of fillets.
2. Combine grapefruit juice, vinegar, garlic, salt, and pepper in a jar with a tight-fitting lid, and shake well. Add ⅓ cup olive oil, and shake well again. Set aside.
3. Peel grapefruit, and cut off white pith. Cut grapefruit into thin slices, discarding seeds if necessary. Arrange grapefruit on individual plates or on a serving platter. Top grapefruit with lettuce, and divide scallions, cucumber, and avocado on top.

4. Heat remaining oil in a large skillet over medium-high heat. Cook fish for 2 minutes per side, turning it gently with a slotted spatula. Remove fish from the skillet, and drain on paper towels. Arrange fish on top of salad, and drizzle all with dressing. Serve immediately.

Note: The fish can also be cooked up to 1 day in advance and refrigerated, tightly covered, and the dressing can be prepared at the same time. Serve the fish cold; do not reheat.

Variation:

- Substitute boneless, skinless chicken breast halves, pounded between 2 sheets of plastic wrap to an even thickness of 1/4 inch. Cook chicken for 2–3 minutes per side, or until chicken is cooked through and no longer pink.

Avocados are expensive, so you don't want to waste one. If you think an avocado is ripe and it turns out to be hard, coat the cut surfaces with mayonnaise, and push the halves back together. It will continue to ripen at room temperature.

Pasta Salad Niçoise

Traditional French *salade Niçoise* is a composed salad that takes longer to arrange than to eat. But all its traditional ingredients—from tuna and green beans to olives and hard-cooked eggs—are in this easy and fast pasta version.

Yield: 4–6 servings | **Active time:** 15 minutes | **Start to finish:** 25 minutes

> ½ pound green beans, rinsed, trimmed, and cut into 1-inch lengths
> ⅔ pound small pasta shells or gemelli
> 3 (6-ounce) cans light tuna packed in oil
> ¼ cup lemon juice
> 1 tablespoon anchovy paste
> 1 tablespoon Dijon mustard
> 1 tablespoon chopped fresh parsley
> 1 teaspoon herbes de Provence
> 2 garlic cloves, peeled and minced
> Salt and freshly ground black pepper to taste
> 2 tablespoons olive oil
> ½ green bell pepper, seeds and ribs removed, and chopped
> ½ small red onion, peeled and chopped
> 3 ripe plum tomatoes, rinsed, cored, seeded, and chopped
> ⅓ cup oil-cured black olives
> 2–3 cups bite-sized pieces salad greens, rinsed and dried
> 2 hard-cooked eggs, cut into wedges (optional)

1. Bring a pot of salted water to a boil, and have a bowl of ice water handy. Boil green beans for 2–3 minutes, or until crisp-tender. Remove beans from the water with a slotted spoon, and plunge them into the ice water to stop the cooking action. Drain when chilled, and place beans in a large mixing bowl.
2. Add pasta to the boiling water and cook according to package directions until al dente. Drain and run under cold water until cold. Add pasta to the mixing bowl, along with tuna and oil from tuna.
3. Combine lemon juice, anchovy paste, mustard, parsley, herbes de Provence, garlic, salt, and pepper in a jar with a tight-fitting lid, and shake well. Add olive oil, and shake well again.

4. Add dressing to the mixing bowl, and allow to sit for 5 minutes so pasta absorbs flavor. Add green bell pepper, onion, tomatoes, and olives, and toss. To serve, arrange lettuce on individual plates or on a serving platter, and top with salad. Serve immediately, garnished with egg wedges, if using.

Note: The salad can be prepared up to 1 day in advance and refrigerated, tightly covered. Allow it to sit at room temperature for 30 minutes prior to serving.

Variation:
- Substitute 1½ cups diced cooked chicken for the tuna, and increase the amount of olive oil in the dressing to ½ cup.

Running pasta under cold water after draining speeds up the completion of all pasta salads. It's not as effective to soak it in cold water because the water heats up rapidly and the pasta can become soggy.

Italian Garbanzo Bean and Tuna Salad

This hearty salad is delicious for a summer supper, and can also be used as part of an Italian *antipasto* table. The dressing is merely the oil from the tuna with some lemon juice.

Yield: 4–6 servings | **Active time:** 15 minutes | **Start to finish:** 15 minutes

> 2 (15-ounce) cans garbanzo beans, drained and rinsed
> 3 (6-ounce) cans light tuna packed in oil, not drained
> 1/3 cup chopped fresh parsley
> 4 scallions, white parts and 3 inches of green tops, rinsed, trimmed, and chopped
> 1/2 green bell pepper, seeds and ribs removed, and chopped
> 1/2 cup chopped pimiento-stuffed green olives
> 1/4 cup lemon juice
> 2 garlic cloves, peeled and minced
> Salt and freshly ground black pepper to taste
> 4–6 cups shredded iceberg lettuce
> 2–3 ripe plum tomatoes, rinsed, cored, and thinly sliced

1. Combine beans, tuna, parsley, scallions, green bell pepper, and olives in a mixing bowl.
2. Mix lemon juice, garlic, salt, and pepper in a small cup, and stir well. Pour dressing over mixture in the mixing bowl, and toss gently. To serve, arrange lettuce on individual plates or on a serving platter, and mound salad in the center. Place tomato slices around salad, and serve immediately.

Note: The salad can be prepared up to 2 days in advance and refrigerated, tightly covered with plastic wrap. Allow it to reach room temperature before serving.

Variation:
- Substitute white beans for the garbanzo beans.

Asian Chicken Salad

This salad delivers vibrant flavor from the combination of assertive Asian seasonings in the dressing. The crunchy Napa cabbage is delicious and adds visual appeal as well as texture.

Yield: 4–6 servings | **Active time:** 15 minutes | **Start to finish:** 15 minutes

¼ cup soy sauce
¼ cup rice vinegar
¼ cup vegetable oil
2 tablespoons Asian sesame oil *
2 tablespoons Dijon mustard
2 tablespoons grated fresh ginger
1–2 teaspoons Chinese chile paste with garlic *
2–3 garlic cloves, peeled and minced
2 cups shredded cooked chicken
4–6 cups shredded Napa cabbage, rinsed and dried
2 cucumbers, peeled, halved lengthwise, seeded, and thinly sliced
6 scallions, white parts and 4 inches of green tops, rinsed, trimmed, and finely chopped
⅓ cup chopped fresh cilantro

1. Combine soy sauce, vinegar, vegetable oil, sesame oil, mustard, ginger, chile paste, and garlic in a jar with a tight-fitting lid. Shake well.
2. Combine chicken, Napa cabbage, cucumbers, scallions, and cilantro in a large mixing bowl. Toss salad with dressing, and serve immediately.

Note: Both the salad and dressing can be prepared up to 6 hours in advance and refrigerated, tightly covered. Do not dress the salad until just prior to serving.

Variation:
- Substitute roast pork or cooked fish for the chicken.

* Available in the Asian aisle of most supermarkets and in specialty markets.

> Many a cook has suffered a scraped knuckle when grating fresh ginger. A solution to this problem is to peel only a small portion of the rhizome, and then hold on to the unpeeled portion as a handle.

Southern Fried Chicken Salad with Honey-Mustard Dressing

Nuggets of crispy pan-fried chicken on a salad napped with an old-fashioned honey and mustard dressing is one that appeals to all generations, and is a great way to induce children to eat more vegetables. Serve it with cornbread or biscuits.

Yield: 4–6 servings | **Active time:** 30 minutes | **Start to finish:** 30 minutes

SALAD

1 pound boneless, skinless chicken breast halves
Salt and freshly ground black pepper to taste
1/2 cup all-purpose flour
3 large eggs
1/4 cup whole milk
1/2 cup plain breadcrumbs
6–9 cups bite-sized pieces salad greens of your choice, rinsed and dried
2 carrots, peeled and cut into thin strips
1 green bell pepper, seeds and ribs removed, and cut into thin slices
1 small red onion, peeled, halved lengthwise, and cut into thin rings
2 cups vegetable oil for frying

DRESSING

3 tablespoons honey
3 tablespoons Dijon mustard
1/3 cup cider vinegar
Salt and freshly ground black pepper to taste
1/2 cup olive oil

1. Rinse chicken and pat dry with paper towels. Trim chicken of all visible fat, and cut chicken into 1-inch nuggets. Sprinkle nuggets with salt and pepper. Place flour on a sheet of plastic wrap, beat eggs with milk in a shallow bowl, and place breadcrumbs on another sheet of plastic wrap. Dip chicken pieces in flour, shaking to remove any excess, then dip in egg mixture, and then in breadcrumbs.

2. Arrange lettuce, carrots, green pepper, and onion on individual plates or on a serving platter. Combine honey, mustard, vinegar, salt, and pepper in a jar with a tight-fitting lid. Shake well, add olive oil, and shake well again. Set aside.

3. Heat vegetable oil in a deep-sided saucepan over medium-high heat to a temperature of 375°F. Add chicken pieces, being careful not to crowd the pan, and fry for 5 minutes, or until golden brown and chicken is cooked through and no longer pink; this may have to be done in batches. Remove chicken from the pan with a slotted spoon and drain well on paper towels.

4. To serve, arrange chicken pieces on top of the salad, and drizzle dressing over all.

Note: Chicken and dressing can be prepared 1 day in advance and refrigerated, tightly covered. Reheat chicken, uncovered, in a 375°F oven for 8–10 minutes, or until hot and crisp. Allow dressing to sit at room temperature for at least 30 minutes if chilled.

Variation:
- Substitute cubes of thick white-fleshed fish fillet for the chicken.

The best way to judge oil temperature is with a thermometer, but here's a trick if you don't have one. Drop a cube of bread into the hot oil. If a ring of white bubbles surrounds the bread and the bread turns golden brown in about 15 seconds, the oil is hot enough.

Warm Mediterranean Chicken Salad

The grilled chicken topping this salad—dotted with olives, tomatoes, and garbanzo beans—is moistened with an herbed dressing flavored with aromatic smoked Spanish paprika.

Yield: 4–6 servings | **Active time:** 20 minutes | **Start to finish:** 20 minutes

> 1 pound boneless, skinless chicken breast halves
> ½ cup olive oil, divided
> Salt and freshly ground black pepper to taste
> 2 tablespoons smoked Spanish paprika
> 1 tablespoon ground cumin
> 1 tablespoon dried oregano
> 3 tablespoons lemon juice
> 3 tablespoons orange juice
> 2 tablespoons chopped fresh parsley
> 2 garlic cloves, peeled and minced
> 1 (15-ounce) can garbanzo beans, drained and rinsed
> 4 ripe plum tomatoes, rinsed, cored, seeded, and diced
> ¼ cup pitted kalamata olives
> 4–6 cups bite-sized pieces iceberg or romaine lettuce, rinsed and dried

1. Light a charcoal or gas grill, or preheat the oven broiler or an electric double-sided grill pan.

2. Rinse chicken and pat dry with paper towels. Trim chicken of all visible fat and pound to an even thickness of ½ inch between 2 sheets of plastic wrap. Rub chicken with 2 tablespoons olive oil, and sprinkle with salt and pepper. Combine paprika, cumin, and oregano in a small cup. Rub mixture on both sides of chicken. Cook chicken for 3–4 minutes per side, if not using a double-sided grill pan, or until chicken is cooked through and no longer pink. Set chicken aside.

3. While chicken cooks, combine lemon juice, orange juice, parsley, garlic, salt, and pepper in a jar with a tight-fitting lid, and shake well. Add remaining oil, and shake well again.

4. Place beans, tomatoes, and olives in a mixing bowl, and add ½ of dressing. Stir well.

5. To serve, arrange lettuce on individual plates or onto a large serving platter, and top with bean mixture. Slice chicken into 2-inch strips, and place on top of vegetables. Drizzle salad greens with remaining dressing, and serve immediately.

Note: The chicken can also be cooked up to 1 day in advance and refrigerated, tightly covered, and the dressing can be prepared at the same time. Serve the chicken cold; do not reheat.

Variation:

- Substitute boneless pork loin, cut into ¼-inch slices, for the chicken. Cook the pork for 2–3 minutes per side.

You should always add granular seasonings like salt or sugar to a salad dressing before adding the oil. These ingredients dissolve in liquids like vinegar or fruit juice, but not in oil.

Warm Tropical Chicken Salad

In this easy recipe the chicken is quickly stir-fried, and then the dressing is also warmed before being plated with succulent fresh pineapple and vegetables. I like to serve it with flour tortillas.

Yield: 4–6 servings | **Active time:** 20 minutes | **Start to finish:** 20 minutes

    1 pound boneless, skinless chicken breast halves
    ½ cup orange juice
    ½ small onion, peeled and diced
    3 garlic cloves, peeled
    ⅓ cup cider vinegar
    2 tablespoons fresh ginger, peeled and sliced
    Salt and freshly ground black pepper to taste
    ⅔ cup vegetable oil, divided
    4–6 cups bite-sized pieces salad greens, rinsed and dried
    1 ripe avocado, peeled and sliced
    2 cups diced fresh pineapple
    1 large green bell pepper, seeds and ribs removed, and thinly sliced
    2 tablespoons soy sauce

1. Rinse chicken and pat dry with paper towels. Trim chicken of all visible fat and slice it into ¼-inch slices against the grain.
2. Place orange juice, onion, garlic, vinegar, ginger, salt, and pepper in a food processor fitted with the steel blade or in a blender. Puree until smooth. Add ½ cup vegetable oil, and blend again. Set aside. Arrange lettuce, avocado, and pineapple on individual plates or a large platter.
3. Heat remaining oil in a large skillet over medium-high heat. Add chicken and green bell pepper, and cook, stirring constantly, for 3 minutes, or until chicken is cooked through and no longer pink. Add soy sauce, and stir well. Turn off heat, and add dressing to the skillet. Stir to warm dressing, but do not let mixture boil.
4. To serve, mound chicken mixture on top of greens and fruits, and serve immediately.

Note: The dressing can be prepared up to 2 days in advance and refrigerated, tightly covered.

Variation:
- Substitute pork loin for the chicken.

Gazpacho Chicken and Garbanzo Bean Salad

No, this isn't a mistake; I know that gazpacho is a Spanish vegetable soup. But all the ingredients are in this refreshing salad, which is napped with a dressing similar to the other flavors in the soup.

Yield: 4–6 servings | **Active time:** 20 minutes | **Start to finish:** 30 minutes, including 10 minutes for chilling

- 1½ cups cooked chicken, cut into ½-inch dice
- 2 green bell peppers, seeds and ribs removed, and cut into ½-inch dice
- 2 cucumbers, peeled, halved lengthwise, seeded, and cut into ½-inch dice
- 1 small red onion, peeled and cut into ½-inch dice
- 2 large ripe tomatoes, rinsed, cored, seeded, and cut into ½-inch dice
- 1 (15-ounce) can garbanzo beans, drained and rinsed
- ⅓ cup chopped fresh cilantro
- 1 jalapeño or serrano chile, seeds and ribs removed, and finely chopped
- 3 garlic cloves, peeled and minced
- ⅓ cup balsamic vinegar
- Salt and freshly ground black pepper to taste
- ½ cup olive oil
- 4–6 cups salad greens, rinsed and dried

1. Combine chicken, green bell peppers, cucumbers, red onion, tomatoes, and garbanzo beans in a large mixing bowl.
2. Combine cilantro, chile, garlic, vinegar, salt, and pepper in a jar with a tight-fitting lid. Shake well, add olive oil, and shake well again. Pour ⅔ of dressing over salad, and refrigerate 10 minutes.
3. Place salad greens in a mixing bowl, and toss with remaining dressing. Arrange lettuce on individual plates or on a large serving platter, and mound salad in the center. Serve immediately.

Note: The salad can be prepared 1 day in advance and refrigerated, tightly covered. Do not add dressing until 10 minutes prior to serving.

Variation:
- Omit the chicken, and add an additional can of garbanzo beans.

Peanut Chicken and Pasta Salad

This is another child-pleasing dish because it contains most kids' favorite food—peanut butter—in the somewhat spicy dressing. It's a whole meal because it contains pasta as well as vegetables and chicken.

Yield: 4–6 servings | **Active time:** 15 minutes | **Start to finish:** 30 minutes

³/₄ pound linguine, broken into 2-inch lengths
¼ cup peanut butter, preferably chunky
¼ cup very hot tap water
¼ cup Asian sesame oil *
2 tablespoons soy sauce
2 tablespoons rice vinegar *
2 tablespoons firmly packed dark brown sugar
3 garlic cloves, peeled and minced
2 tablespoons grated fresh ginger
2 tablespoons chopped fresh cilantro
1–2 tablespoons Chinese chile paste with garlic *
2 cups shredded cooked chicken
6 scallions, white parts and 4 inches of green tops, rinsed, trimmed, and thinly sliced
1 cucumber, peeled, halved lengthwise, seeded, and thinly sliced
1 carrot, peeled and coarsely grated
1 cup bean sprouts, rinsed
½ cup finely chopped roasted peanuts

1. Bring a large pot of salted water to a boil. Add pasta, and cook according to package directions until al dente. Drain pasta, and rinse under cold running water until pasta is cool. Drain, and refrigerate.

2. While water heats, combine peanut butter and hot tap water in a mixing bowl, and whisk until smooth. Add sesame oil, soy sauce, vinegar, brown sugar, garlic, ginger, cilantro, and chile paste. Whisk well again.

* Available in the Asian aisle of most supermarkets and in specialty markets.

3. Add sauce, chicken, scallions, cucumber, carrot, and bean sprouts to pasta. Mix well, and serve immediately, sprinkled with peanuts.

Note: The salad can be prepared up to 1 day in advance and refrigerated, tightly covered.

Variations:
- Substitute shredded pork or beef for the chicken.
- Omit the chicken, and add 2 cups shredded Napa cabbage.

When you need a small quantity of a food, look at the smallest size possible; in this case it's the peanut garnish. While those little packets at the convenience store are more expensive per ounce than a large can, if you're not going to finish the large can, then think small.

Greek Chicken Salad

Sharp feta cheese in a tart lemon juice and oregano dressing are the hallmarks of a Greek salad, and that Mediterranean favorite is transformed into a more filling meal with the addition of cooked chicken.

Yield: 4–6 servings | **Active time:** 15 minutes | **Start to finish:** 15 minutes

⅓ cup lemon juice

2 tablespoons chopped fresh parsley

3 garlic cloves, peeled and minced

2 teaspoons dried oregano

Salt and freshly ground black pepper to taste

½ cup olive oil

6–9 cups bite-sized pieces iceberg lettuce, rinsed and dried

2 small cucumbers, peeled, seeded, and cut into ½-inch dice

4 ripe plum tomatoes, rinsed, cored, seeded, and cut into ½-inch dice

2 cups cooked chicken, cut into ½-inch dice

½ red onion, peeled and cut into ½-inch dice

½ cup sliced kalamata olives

½ cup crumbled feta cheese

1. Combine lemon juice, parsley, garlic, oregano, salt, and pepper in a jar with a tight-fitting lid, and shake well. Add olive oil, and shake well again.
2. Combine lettuce, cucumber, tomato, chicken, onion, and olives in a large mixing bowl, and toss with enough dressing to moisten ingredients well. Serve immediately, sprinkling feta over each serving and passing extra dressing separately.

Note: The salad ingredients and dressing can be prepared up to 6 hours in advance and refrigerated, tightly covered. Do not dress the salad until just prior to serving.

Variation:
- Substitute cubes of cooked fish for the chicken.

Southwestern Turkey Salad

There are very few mayonnaise-bound salads in this chapter because I find them generally heavy, but the barbecue sauce mixed with it in this dressing adds a lively flavor. The corn and beans add color and texture as well as flavor to the dish.

Yield: 4–6 servings | **Active time:** 15 minutes | **Start to finish:** 15 minutes

> 2 cups shredded roast turkey
> 3 hard-cooked eggs, peeled and diced
> 1 cup cooked corn kernels
> 1 (15-ounce) can red kidney beans, drained and rinsed
> 1 small red onion, peeled and chopped
> 2 celery ribs, rinsed, trimmed, and thinly sliced
> ½ cup barbecue sauce
> ⅓ cup mayonnaise
> 2 garlic cloves, peeled and minced
> 2 tablespoons chopped fresh cilantro
> 4–6 cups bite-sized pieces salad greens, rinsed and dried
> 3 ripe plum tomatoes, rinsed, cored, seeded, and sliced

1. Combine turkey, eggs, corn, beans, onion, and celery in a mixing bowl.
2. Whisk together barbecue sauce, mayonnaise, garlic, and cilantro. Toss dressing with salad, and refrigerate.
3. Arrange lettuce and tomatoes on individual plates or on a serving platter and mound salad in the center. Serve immediately.

Note: The salad can be prepared 1 day in advance and refrigerated, tightly covered.

Variation:
- Substitute baked ham for the turkey.

The large celery ribs around the outside of a bunch can be tough and fibrous. Starting at the tip, break off the top inch and it will be attached to the strings, which can then be easily pulled off.

Thai Beef Salad

Thai is one of the Asian cuisines that has a hallowed spot for entrée salads, and this salad—made with spicy radishes and crispy romaine—is based on one I remember enjoying on the beaches of Phuket many years ago.

Yield: 4–6 servings | **Active time:** 20 minutes | **Start to finish:** 20 minutes

> 1 pound thinly sliced cooked roast beef
> 4–6 cups bite-sized pieces romaine lettuce, rinsed and dried
> 8 scallions, white parts and 4 inches of green tops, rinsed, trimmed, and thinly sliced
> 1 cup fresh bean sprouts, rinsed
> 2–4 radishes, rinsed, trimmed, and thinly sliced
> 1/4 cup lime juice
> 3 tablespoons fish sauce (*nam pla*) *
> Salt and freshly ground black pepper to taste
> 1/4 cup Asian sesame oil *
> 2 tablespoons vegetable oil

1. Trim roast beef of all visible fat, and cut it into 1/2-inch strips. Place beef in a large mixing bowl, and add romaine, scallions, bean sprouts, and radishes.
2. Combine lime juice, fish sauce, salt, and pepper in a jar with a tight-fitting lid. Shake well, add sesame oil and vegetable oil, and shake well again.
3. Toss salad with dressing, and serve immediately.

Note: The dressing can be made up to 1 day in advance and refrigerated, tightly covered. Allow it to sit at room temperature for at least 30 minutes prior to serving.

Variation:
  • Substitute shredded chicken or turkey for the roast beef.

* Available in the Asian aisle of most supermarkets and in specialty markets.

Chef's Salad with Warm Bacon Dressing

When I was growing up, a chef's salad was about the only entrée salad that found its way onto restaurant menus as well as kitchen tables. This is an updated version because the chicken is stir-fried and the dressing is warm.

Yield: 4–6 servings | **Active time:** 15 minutes | **Start to finish:** 30 minutes

> ½ pound boneless, skinless chicken breast halves
> ¼ pound bacon, cut into 1-inch pieces
> 2 garlic cloves, peeled and minced
> ¼ cup cider vinegar
> 1 tablespoon Dijon mustard
> Salt and freshly ground black pepper to taste
> 6–9 cups bite-sized pieces iceberg lettuce, rinsed and dried
> 2 hard-cooked eggs, diced
> 2 ripe plum tomatoes, rinsed, cored, seeded, and diced
> ½ ripe avocado, peeled and diced
> ½ cup crumbled blue cheese

1. Rinse chicken and pat dry with paper towels. Cut chicken into ½-inch cubes, and set aside.
2. Cook bacon in a large skillet over medium-high heat for 5–7 minutes, or until crisp. Remove bacon from the skillet with a slotted spatula, drain on paper towels, and place bacon in a large mixing bowl.
3. Add chicken and garlic to the skillet, and cook, stirring frequently, for 5–7 minutes, or until chicken is cooked through and no longer pink. Remove chicken from the pan with a slotted spoon, and place in the mixing bowl with bacon.
4. Add vinegar and mustard to the skillet, stir well to dislodge any brown bits, and season to taste with salt and pepper. Add lettuce, eggs, tomatoes, avocado, and blue cheese to the mixing bowl. Pour dressing over salad, and toss well. Serve immediately.

Note: The bacon, chicken, and dressing can be prepared up to 1 day in advance and refrigerated, tightly covered. Reheat bacon and chicken in a microwave oven, and reheat dressing as well.

Variation:
- Substitute ½ pound boneless pork loin, cut into ½-inch cubes, for the chicken.

Bacon and Egg Salad

This is a fantastic salad to serve for brunch. It contains soft-scrambled eggs as well as bacon, dressed lightly and tossed with bitter escarole. It's based on an Italian prototype that uses pancetta.

Yield: 4–6 servings | **Active time:** 15 minutes | **Start to finish:** 15 minutes

SALAD

3/4 pound bacon
2 tablespoons unsalted butter
8 large eggs
1/4 cup sour cream
Salt and freshly ground black pepper to taste
6 cups bite-sized pieces escarole, rinsed and dried

DRESSING

3 tablespoons balsamic vinegar
1 tablespoon lemon juice
2 garlic cloves, peeled and minced
1 teaspoon dried oregano
Salt and freshly ground black pepper to taste
1/3 cup olive oil

1. Place bacon in a heavy, large skillet, and cook over medium-high heat, turning it as necessary with tongs, for 5–7 minutes, or until bacon is crisp. Remove bacon from the skillet, drain well on paper towels, and crumble bacon. Set aside. Discard bacon grease from the skillet.
2. While bacon cooks, prepare dressing. Combine vinegar, lemon juice, garlic, oregano, salt, and pepper in a jar with a tight-fitting lid, and shake well. Add oil, and shake well again. Set aside.
3. Melt butter in the same skillet over low heat. Whisk eggs with sour cream, salt, and pepper. When butter melts, pour eggs into the pan, then cover the pan. After 3 minutes, scrape cooked egg mixture to the sides of the pan with a spatula, and cover the pan again. Cook for another 2–3 minutes, or until eggs are 3/4 set.

4. While eggs cook, place escarole in a salad bowl. Toss with ⅓ cup dressing. Add reserved bacon and hot eggs to the salad bowl, and toss gently. Serve immediately, passing extra dressing separately.

Note: The bacon can be cooked and the dressing can be made up to 2 days in advance and refrigerated, tightly covered. Reheat the bacon, and allow dressing to sit at room temperature for at least 30 minutes before serving.

Variation:

- Substitute bulk Italian sausage for the bacon. Cook it for 5-7 minutes, breaking up lumps with a fork, or until cooked through and no pink remains.

An alternative to frying bacon is to bake it on baking pans in a 350°F oven for 20–30 minutes, or until crisp. The length of time will depend on the thickness of the bacon. This is a good way to cook bacon for a crowd in a hurry!

Sesame Stir-Fried Pork and Vegetable Salad

All of the vegetables in this salad are cooked, and then it's served at room temperature. The sesame flavor in the dressing is reinforced by the tiny toasted sesame seeds sprinkled over the top.

Yield: 4–6 servings | **Active time:** 20 minutes | **Start to finish:** 35 minutes, including 15 minutes for chilling

- ¼ cup sesame seeds *
- ¾ pound boneless pork loin
- 2 tablespoons vegetable oil
- 2 tablespoons Asian sesame oil *
- 3 garlic cloves, peeled and minced
- 2 tablespoons finely minced fresh ginger
- 4 scallions, white parts and 4 inches of green tops, rinsed, trimmed, and thinly sliced
- ½ pound mushrooms, wiped with a damp paper towel, trimmed, and sliced
- 1 (1-pound) bunch Napa cabbage or bok choy, rinsed and cut into ½-inch slices on the diagonal
- ½ pound green beans, rinsed, trimmed, and cut on the diagonal into ½-inch slices
- ½ cup oyster sauce *
- ¼ cup Chicken Stock (recipe on page 35) or purchased stock
- 2 tablespoons soy sauce
- 2 tablespoons dry sherry

1. Place sesame seeds in a small, dry skillet over medium heat. Toast seeds for 2 minutes, or until browned, shaking the pan frequently. Set aside. Trim pork of all visible fat. Cut into thin slices, then stack slices and cut into thin slices in the opposite direction.
2. Heat vegetable oil and sesame oil in a wok or large skillet over medium-high heat. Add garlic, ginger, and scallions. Stir-fry for 30 seconds, or until fragrant. Add mushroom and pork, and stir-fry for 2 minutes. Add cabbage and green beans, and stir-fry for 2 additional minutes. Add oyster sauce, stock, soy sauce, and sherry. Stir well and bring to a boil. Boil for 1 minute, then remove pan from heat.

* Available in the Asian aisle of most supermarkets and in specialty markets.

3. Transfer mixture to a mixing bowl or serving dish with a slotted spoon. Chill for at least 15 minutes to reach room temperature, or refrigerate, tightly covered, and serve chilled. Sprinkle salad with toasted sesame seeds just before serving.

Note: The salad can be prepared up to 1 day in advance and refrigerated, tightly covered. Do not sprinkle with sesame seeds until just prior to serving.

Variation:
- Substitute boneless, skinless chicken breast for the pork.

Mushrooms are relatively expensive, so you don't want them to go to waste. Always store mushrooms in a paper bag rather than a plastic bag. Plastic causes mushrooms to become moist and soggy. An alternative method is to line a bowl with paper towels, add the mushrooms, then cover the bowl with more paper towels.

Warm Ham and Sweet Potato Salad

Ham and sweet potatoes hold a place of honor on many Southern dinner tables, and their flavor blends beautifully in this salad, too. Chopped pickles and Dijon mustard add flavor accents to the dish.

Yield: 4–6 servings | **Active time:** 20 minutes | **Start to finish:** 35 minutes, including 15 minutes for cooling

2 pounds sweet potatoes, scrubbed

¼ cup cider vinegar

2 tablespoons Dijon mustard

Salt and freshly ground black pepper to taste

2 garlic cloves, peeled and minced

½ cup olive oil

2 cups diced baked ham

¼ small red onion, peeled and finely chopped

1 small green bell pepper, seeds and ribs removed, and finely chopped

¼ cup finely chopped sweet pickles

4–6 cups bite-sized pieces iceberg lettuce, rinsed and dried

1. Bring a pot of salted water to a boil over high heat. Quarter sweet potatoes lengthwise, and cut quarters into 2-inch sections. Place sweet potatoes in the saucepan, and boil for 10 minutes, or until potatoes are tender. Drain and run under cold water. Peel potatoes when cool enough to handle. Cut potatoes into 1-inch cubes, and place in a mixing bowl.

2. Combine vinegar, mustard, salt, pepper, and garlic in a jar with a tight-fitting lid, and shake well. Add oil, and shake well again. Add dressing to potatoes along with ham, onion, green pepper, and pickles. Toss gently, and season to taste with salt and pepper.

3. To serve, arrange greens on individual plates or on a large platter, and top with salad. Salad can be served at room temperature or chilled.

Note: The salad can be made 1 day in advance and refrigerated, tightly covered with plastic wrap.

Variation:
- Substitute turkey or chicken for the ham.

It's much faster to peel potatoes once they're cooked rather than when they're raw. That's why these sweet potatoes are cooked and then peeled. And that's why red-skinned potatoes are such a time-saver; they don't need peeling at all!

Chapter 4:

Between the Bread, on Top of the Bread, and under Wraps

Everyone loves sandwiches, and like all the salads in Chapter 3, these hand-holdable meals are on the table in a matter of minutes. Most of these are hot sandwiches, because I think there's a special magic about a hot sandwich—be it a slice of white toast topped with leftover turkey and gravy on Thanksgiving weekend to any manner of gooey grilled cheese and crispy quesadillas.

The whole genre of sandwiches has come a long way quickly from the "stuff between two slices of bread is a sandwich" definition of my youth. It was just a decade ago that I wrote a book titled *All Wrapped Up;* it was in the vanguard of cookbooks that featured cold sandwiches wrapped in lavash, and crispy and hot quesadillas with non-Hispanic fillings. Since then we've seen panini, Italian pressed sandwiches, become a craze. Those are some of the forms you'll find explored in this chapter. In addition to hot sandwiches, there are many exotic combinations for cold wraps, too.

As a trick to speed up sandwich-making, think of your kitchen counter as an assembly line. Every time you put down one ingredient to pick up another it wastes time. So to use your time in the most efficient manner, do every step only once but multiple times. For example, if bread or tortillas are to be spread with mustard, do the bread for all the sandwiches at once. Then layer each meat or other ingredient in the sequence listed for the number of sandwiches you're making.

HAUTE HOT SANDWICHES

While the Earl of Sandwich was English, sandwiches of some type exist in every cuisine around the world. One of the most popular forms now is the quesadilla. It used to be that quesadillas—the word comes from the Spanish word *queso,* which means cheese—were only found on Mexican menus, and they had a traditional filling of cheese and perhaps some strips of peppers. But that's all changed today. Quesadilla, pronounced *case-ah-DEE-ya,* now means any hot sandwich made in a flour tortilla.

While some cookbooks call for frying quesadillas, I prefer to bake them to cut back on the amount of fat. Also, by baking them you can leave them unattended while you do something else.

If you don't want to wait for the oven to preheat, then heat 2 tablespoons of vegetable oil in a heavy 12-inch skillet over medium-high heat. Add the quesadillas, and cook for 2 minutes per side, or until browned and the cheese melts. Turn the quesadillas gently with a slotted spatula, and blot them with paper towels before serving.

Any of the hot sandwich recipes made with cheese in this chapter can be transformed into quesadillas. All you have to do is follow the procedure in a quesadilla recipe for layering the filling and baking them.

Even newer in popularity are panini (or the singular in Italian, *panino*). These grilled Italian sandwich snacks, which traditionally have stripe marks on both sides from being grilled, have only become familiar in this country during the past five years.

Panini, pronounced *pah-NEE-nee,* are traditionally grilled on small, square loaves of Italian ciabatta bread that has been sliced horizontally. There is no set filling for a panino, although cheese is frequently included but does not have to be.

One of the greatest small appliances to come on the market in the past decade is the sloping double-sided grill. Boxing great George Forman's moniker is famous in this field, although many companies now manufacture these grills. I love these grills for indoor cooking because they cook from both sides to cut down on cooking time.

What I've recently discovered is how great they are for making sandwiches. While there are expensive panini presses on the market, they're really superfluous unless you want every gadget in the aisle. But the double-sided grill is a great investment not only for the recipes in this chapter but for your general cooking.

An alternative for cooking panini is to grill them in a skillet and press them with a rather low-tech device—a brick wrapped in aluminum foil. Or should you not have a brick around, another option is to weigh down the sandwiches with another skillet or pan.

Pinto Bean and Vegetable Quesadillas

One convenience food that I applaud is the pre-blended grated cheese package; the mixed Italian version is perfect for many dishes, and the taco cheese contains all the necessary seasonings to give food Mexican flavor. Quick-cooking squash, along with beans, makes this a hearty vegetarian dish.

Yield: 4–6 servings | **Active time:** 15 minutes | **Start to finish:** 30 minutes

> 4–6 (10-inch) flour or whole-wheat tortillas
> 3 tablespoons olive oil
> ½ small red onion, peeled and diced
> 2 garlic cloves, peeled and minced
> 1 medium zucchini or yellow squash, rinsed, trimmed, and thinly sliced
> 1 (15-ounce) can pinto beans, drained and rinsed
> ¼ cup chopped fresh cilantro
> Salt and freshly ground black pepper to taste
> 2 ripe plum tomatoes, rinsed, cored, seeded, and thinly sliced
> 1 (8-ounce) bag grated taco cheeses
> Vegetable oil spray

1. Preheat the oven to 450°F, cover 2 baking sheets with heavy-duty aluminum foil, and grease the foil with vegetable oil spray. Soften tortillas, if necessary, by wrapping them in plastic wrap and heating them in a microwave oven on High (100 percent power) for 10–15 seconds, or until pliable. Place tortillas on a counter.

2. Heat olive oil in a large skillet over medium-high heat. Add onion, garlic, and zucchini, and cook, stirring frequently, for 3 minutes, or until onion is translucent. Add beans, and cook for an additional 2–3 minutes, or until vegetables soften. Stir in cilantro, and season to taste with salt and pepper. Divide mixture onto ½ of each tortilla, and spread evenly. Top with tomato slices and cheese.

3. Fold empty side of tortillas over filling, and press closed with the palm of your hand or a spatula. Arrange tortillas on prepared baking sheets, and spray tops with vegetable oil spray.

4. Bake quesadillas for 5 minutes. Turn them gently with a spatula, and press them down if the top has separated from the filling. Bake for an additional 5–7 minutes, or until crispy. Allow to sit for 2 minutes, then cut each in half, and serve immediately.

Note: The quesadillas can be formed up to 1 day in advance and refrigerated, tightly covered. Add 3 minutes to the baking time if chilled.

Variations:
- Substitute ¼ pound mushrooms, wiped with a damp paper towel, trimmed, and sliced, for the zucchini.
- Substitute ½ pound chorizo sausage for the zucchini. Cook sausage for 2 minutes before adding onion and garlic, breaking up lumps with a fork.

Quesadillas can easily be transformed into hors d'ouevres for a party, too. Bake them as directed, and then cut each into 5 or 6 wedges.

Fish Po' Boys

The Po' Boy sandwich is native to Louisiana, and this version is topped with a succulent tartar sauce variation. Serve it with a bowl of coleslaw, another Southern treat.

Yield: 4-6 servings | **Active time:** 25 minutes | **Start to finish:** 30 minutes

SAUCE

- ½ cup mayonnaise
- 2 tablespoons chili sauce
- 2 tablespoons chopped fresh parsley
- 2 tablespoons mustard
- 2 tablespoons pickle relish

SANDWICH

- 1¼ pounds thin white-fleshed fish fillets
- 2 large eggs, lightly beaten
- 2 tablespoons milk
- Salt and freshly ground black pepper to taste
- ¾ cup yellow cornmeal
- ⅔ cup vegetable oil
- 4-6 (6-inch) sub rolls, halved horizontally
- 4-6 leaves romaine, rinsed and dried
- 2-3 ripe plum tomatoes, rinsed, cored, seeded, and thinly sliced

1. Preheat the oven to 200°F, and line a baking sheet with paper towels. For sauce, combine mayonnaise, chili sauce, parsley, mustard, and pickle relish in a mixing bowl, and whisk well.
2. Rinse fish and pat dry with paper towels. Cut fish into 2-inch sections. Place eggs in a shallow bowl, and beat with milk. Season to taste with salt and pepper. Place cornmeal on a sheet of plastic wrap.
3. Heat oil in a large skillet over medium-high heat. Dip fish pieces in egg mixture, allowing excess to drip back into the bowl, and then into cornmeal. Fry fish for 2 minutes per side, turning it gently with a slotted spatula, or until fish is browned and crisp and flakes easily; this may have to be done in batches. Drain fish on paper towels, and keep warm in the oven while frying remaining fish.

4. To serve, spread sauce on both halves of rolls. Place fish on bottom half, and cover with lettuce and tomato slices. Serve immediately.

Note: The sauce can be prepared up to 2 days in advance and refrigerated, tightly covered.

Variation:

- Add 1–2 teaspoons hot red pepper sauce to the sauce for a spicier dish.

You don't have to worry that the paper towels you're placing in the oven will catch fire at a temperature as low as 200ºF. The reason you want them on the baking sheet is to absorb moisture from the cooked fish and keep it crisp as well as warm.

Pan Bagnat

This phrase means "bathed bread" in French, and this sandwich from the sun-drenched coast of Provence is basically a tuna salad pressed in a hollowed-out loaf of bread.

Yield: 4–6 servings | **Active time:** 10 minutes | **Start to finish:** 20 minutes

1 (1-pound) loaf French bread, unsliced
2 tablespoons olive oil
1 cup firmly packed shredded iceberg lettuce
3 (6-ounce) cans light tuna packed in oil, undrained
3 ripe plum tomatoes, rinsed, cored, seeded, and diced
1/2 small red onion, peeled and chopped
1/2 cup chopped pitted kalamata olives
2 hard-cooked eggs, peeled and diced
3 tablespoons lemon juice
Salt and freshly ground black pepper to taste

1. Slice bread in half lengthwise. Using your hands, remove interior of loaf, leaving 3/4-inch-thick shell. Brush interior of both halves with olive oil and line both halves with lettuce.
2. Combine tuna, tomatoes, onion, olives, eggs, and lemon juice in a mixing bowl. Stir gently, and season to taste with salt and pepper.
3. Spoon salad evenly into bottom bread shell. Cover with top bread shell, and wrap loaf tightly with plastic wrap. Place loaf in a shallow dish, top with a second dish, and weight top dish with cans. Allow loaf to sit for 10 minutes. To serve, cut into 2-inch slices.

Note: You can prepare the loaf up to 2 hours in advance and then refrigerate it.

Variation:
- Substitute 1 1/2 cups chopped cooked chicken for the tuna, and add 1/4 cup olive oil to the ingredients.

> Remember, we don't believe in wasting food! Make croutons from the bread pulled out of the loaf; cut the bread into 1/2-inch pieces, and sauté them in olive oil until browned and crispy.

Tomato, Cheese, and Basil Panini

Sometimes it's the small touches that make a dish special, such as adding some fresh basil leaves to this pressed grilled cheese and tomato sandwich.

Yield: 4–6 servings | **Active time:** 10 minutes | **Start to finish:** 15 minutes

> 8–12 slices Italian bread, $\frac{1}{4}$ inch thick and 8 inches wide
> $\frac{1}{4}$ cup olive oil
> 3 tablespoons mayonnaise
> $\frac{2}{3}$ pound sliced sharp cheddar cheese
> 3 ripe plum tomatoes, rinsed, cored, seeded, and sliced
> $\frac{1}{4}$ cup shredded fresh basil

1. Preheat a two-sided grill, if using one. Brush 1 side of bread slices with olive oil. Place slices, oiled sides down, on the counter or a plate, and spread mayonnaise on bread.
2. Divide half of cheese among half of bread slices. Top with tomato slices, basil, remaining cheese, and remaining bread slices, oiled sides up.
3. Grill sandwiches in a two-sided grill for 3–4 minutes, or until bread is brown and cheese melts. Alternatively, fry sandwiches in a ridged grill pan, turning once, weighed down by a foil-covered brick. Cut sandwiches in half, and serve immediately.

Note: The sandwiches can be prepared for cooking up to 6 hours in advance and refrigerated, tightly covered.

Variations:
- Add $\frac{1}{3}$ pound thinly sliced baked ham or smoked turkey to the sandwiches. Layer it on top of the tomatoes.
- Substitute fresh oregano for the basil.
- Substitute provolone cheese for the cheddar.

Smoked Turkey, Broccoli Rabe, and Cheese Panini

This sandwich is a great way to introduce children to a new vegetable, because the broccoli rabe is hidden beneath cheese! Serve this with a tossed salad, and the meal is complete.

Yield: 4-6 servings | **Active time:** 15 minutes | **Start to finish:** 20 minutes

> 1½ pounds broccoli rabe, rinsed with tough ends discarded
> ⅓ cup olive oil, divided
> 3 garlic cloves, peeled and minced
> 1 tablespoon anchovy paste
> 8-12 slices Italian bread, ¼ inch thick and 8 inches wide
> ⅔ pound sliced Swiss cheese
> ½ pound thinly sliced smoked turkey

1. Bring a large pot of salted water to a boil over high heat. Add broccoli rabe, and boil for 3 minutes, or until tender. Drain well, squeeze dry, and chop coarsely. Set aside.
2. Heat 3 tablespoons olive oil in a heavy over medium heat. Add garlic, and cook, stirring frequently, for 1 minute, or until garlic is golden. Add anchovy paste and broccoli rabe and cook, stirring frequently, for 1 minute.
3. Preheat a two-sided grill, if using one. Brush 1 side of bread slices with remaining olive oil. Place slices, oiled sides down, on the counter or a plate. Divide ½ of cheese among ½ of bread slices. Top with smoked turkey, broccoli rabe mixture, remaining cheese, and remaining bread slices, oiled sides up.
4. Grill sandwiches in a two-sided grill for 3-4 minutes, or until bread is brown and cheese melts. Alternatively, fry sandwiches in a ridged grill pan, turning once, weighted down by a foil-covered brick. Cut sandwiches in half, and serve immediately.

Note: The broccoli rabe can be cooked up to 2 days in advance and refrigerated, tightly covered. Reheat it in a microwave oven or over low heat before assembling and grilling sandwiches.

Variations:

- Cooked broccoli can be substituted for the broccoli rabe, and fontina cheese can be used in place of Swiss.
- Omit the turkey and increase the broccoli rabe by ½ pound for a vegetarian sandwich.

Broccoli rabe, called *rapini*—its Italian name—in some supermarkets, is a vegetable related to both classic broccoli and the turnip family. It has leafy green stalks about 9 inches long that have clusters of small florets attached. It has flavor that is both more pungent and more bitter than that of broccoli.

Greek Chicken Quesadillas

This sandwich is the portable version of a Greek salad; it contains the same feta, cucumber, and tomato with a lemon and oregano dressing. But there's chicken added for additional protein, and then the sandwich is baked to give it a crispy texture.

Yield: 4–6 servings | **Active time:** 15 minutes | **Start to finish:** 25 minutes

> Vegetable oil spray
> 4–6 (10-inch) flour or whole-wheat tortillas
> 1½ cups shredded cooked chicken
> ½ cup crumbled feta cheese
> ¼ cup grated mozzarella cheese
> ¼ cup chopped cucumber
> 2 tablespoons chopped fresh parsley
> 1 teaspoon dried oregano
> 3 tablespoons lemon juice
> 3 tablespoons olive oil
> Salt and freshly ground black pepper to taste
> ¼ small red onion, peeled and thinly sliced
> 2 ripe plum tomatoes, rinsed, cored, seeded, and thinly sliced

1. Preheat the oven to 450°F, cover 2 baking sheets with heavy-duty aluminum foil, and grease the foil with vegetable oil spray. Soften tortillas, if necessary, by wrapping them in plastic wrap and heating them in a microwave oven on High (100 percent power) for 10–15 seconds, or until pliable.

2. Place tortillas on a counter. Combine chicken, feta, mozzarella, cucumber, parsley, oregano, lemon juice, and olive oil in a mixing bowl. Season to taste with salt and pepper. Toss to combine. Divide filling on half of each tortilla, and top with onion and tomato. Fold empty side of each tortilla over filling, and press closed with the palm of your hand or a spatula. Arrange tortillas on prepared baking sheets, and spray tops with vegetable oil spray.

3. Bake quesadillas for 5 minutes. Turn them gently with a spatula, and press them down if the top has separated from the filling. Bake for an additional 5–7 minutes, or until crispy. Allow to sit for 2 minutes, then cut each in half, and serve immediately.

Note: The quesadillas can be formed up to 1 day in advance and refrigerated, tightly covered. Add 3 minutes to the baking time if chilled.

Variation:
- Substitute shredded roast beef or lamb for the chicken.

> Plum tomatoes are not only less expensive than most on the market, they are also "meatier" so they don't give off very much liquid, which might make a baked sandwich soggy.

Buffalo Chicken Wraps

First it was wings to chew, and now the same hot and spicy chicken can be placed in a wrap sandwich with its traditional accompaniments of blue cheese dressing to cool it and celery sticks to give it crunch. There's enough lettuce inside the wrap, too, that your meal is really complete.

Yield: 4–6 servings | **Active time:** 15 minutes | **Start to finish:** 15 minutes

> ³/₄ pound boneless, skinless chicken breast halves
> Salt and freshly ground black pepper to taste
> 3 tablespoons unsalted butter
> 2–3 tablespoons hot red pepper sauce, or to taste
> ½ cup mayonnaise
> ½ cup sour cream
> ³/₄ cup crumbled blue cheese
> 1 tablespoon lemon juice
> 3 celery ribs, rinsed and trimmed
> 4–6 (8-inch) flour or whole-wheat tortillas
> 8–12 leaves romaine, rinsed and dried

1. Rinse chicken and pat dry with paper towels. Pound chicken to an even thickness of ½ inch between 2 sheets of plastic wrap. Cut chicken into 2-inch strips, and sprinkle chicken with salt and pepper.
2. Melt butter in a large skillet over medium-high heat. Add chicken and cook for 2–3 minutes per side, turning strips with tongs. Chicken should be cooked through and no longer pink. Drizzle hot red pepper sauce over chicken, and shake the pan to distribute hot sauce.
3. While chicken cooks, combine mayonnaise, sour cream, blue cheese, and lemon juice in a mixing bowl. Whisk well. Cut each celery rib into 4 lengthwise strips, and cut pieces into 6-inch lengths. Set aside.
4. Soften tortillas, if necessary, by wrapping them in plastic wrap and heating them in a microwave oven on High (100 percent power) for 10–15 seconds, or until pliable. Place tortillas on a counter.
5. Arrange lettuce leaves on tortillas, and place celery sticks down the center of each tortilla. Place a portion of chicken on bottom half of tortillas, and top with dressing. Tuck sides of tortillas over filling, and roll gently but firmly beginning at the filled side. Cut in half on the diagonal, and serve immediately.

Note: The chicken can be cooked, and the dressing can be made, up to 1 day in advance and refrigerated, tightly covered. Reheat the chicken in a microwave oven until warm before assembling sandwiches.

Variation:
- This dish can also be served as an entrée salad if you omit the tortillas and double the amount of lettuce. Shred the lettuce, dice the celery, and mound the chicken and dressing on top.

Few dishes in American cuisine have an exact parentage, but Buffalo chicken wings are one of them. They started at the Anchor Bar in Buffalo, New York, and were a totally serendipitous snack served one night by the owner to regular patrons.

Cajun Wraps

It's only in the past decade that small producers have brought the pan-oply of great American regional sausages onto the national scene, and one of my favorites is spicy andouille (pronounced *ahn-DEW-ee*) from the bayous of Louisiana. This wrap is like holding red beans and rice in your hands, and should be served with a crisp green salad.

Yield: 4–6 servings | **Active time:** 15 minutes | **Start to finish:** 25 minutes

> 3 cups water
> Salt to taste
> ¾ cup white long-grain rice
> 2 tablespoons olive oil
> ¾ pound andouille sausage, sliced ¼ inch thick
> 1 medium onion, peeled and diced
> 3 garlic cloves, peeled and minced
> 1 green bell pepper, seeds and ribs removed, and chopped
> 1 (8-ounce) can tomato sauce
> 1–2 teaspoons hot red pepper sauce, or to taste
> 1 (15-ounce) can kidney beans, drained and rinsed
> Freshly ground black pepper to taste
> 4–6 (10-inch) flour or whole-wheat tortillas

1. Bring salted water to a boil over high heat, and add rice. Reduce the heat to low and cook rice, covered, for 15–18 minutes, or until tender. Drain rice, and keep warm.

2. While rice cooks, heat oil in a large skillet over medium-high heat. Add sausage to the pan, and cook, stirring occasionally, for 3–5 minutes, or until sausage is browned. Add onion, garlic, and green bell pepper to the skillet. Cook for 3 minutes, stirring frequently, or until onion is translucent.

3. Add tomato sauce, hot red pepper sauce, and beans to the skillet. Stir well, and bring to a boil over medium heat. Reduce the heat to low, and simmer mixture for 15 minutes, or until slightly reduced and the vegetables are soft. Season to taste with salt and pepper.

4. To serve, place a portion of rice in the center of each tortilla. Spoon sausage mixture on top. Tuck sides of tortillas over filling, and roll gently but firmly beginning at the filled side. Cut in half on the diagonal, and serve immediately.

Note: The sausage mixture and rice can be cooked up to 1 day in advance and refrigerated, tightly covered. Reheat in a microwave oven or over low heat until hot before wrapping.

Variation:
- Substitute bulk Italian sausage for the andouille, substitute white beans for the kidney beans, and omit the hot red pepper sauce and add 1 teaspoon Italian seasoning for a milder dish.

> To reduce in cooking is to make something thicker, not thinner. The term means to boil a liquid until the volume is decreased through evaporation, thereby intensifying the flavor. The resulting liquid is called a reduction.

Cobb Salad Wraps

Transforming salads from plate food to finger food is one of the trends of the late 1990s that continues to grow in popularity. This wrap contains bacon, turkey, avocado, eggs, and tomatoes—all the components of a Cobb salad—moistened with a blue cheese vinaigrette.

Yield: 4-6 servings | **Active time:** 20 minutes | **Start to finish:** 20 minutes

- ¼ pound bacon
- 4–6 (10-inch) flour or whole-wheat tortillas
- 8–12 leaves romaine, rinsed and dried
- ½ pound thinly sliced turkey
- 4 hard-cooked eggs, shelled and sliced
- 3 ripe plum tomatoes, rinsed, cored, seeded, and sliced
- ½ ripe avocado, peeled and thinly sliced
- ¾ cup crumbled blue cheese
- 3 tablespoons balsamic vinegar
- Salt and freshly ground black pepper to taste
- 3 tablespoons olive oil

1. Place bacon slices in a large skillet and cook over medium-high heat, turning slices with tongs, for 5–7 minutes, or until bacon is crisp. Drain bacon on paper towels, and set aside.
2. Soften tortillas, if necessary, by wrapping them in plastic wrap and heating them in a microwave oven on High (100 percent power) for 10–15 seconds, or until pliable. Place tortillas on a counter.
3. Arrange lettuce leaves on tortillas. Layer turkey, egg slices, tomato slices, and avocado slices on bottom ½ of each tortilla, and sprinkle with blue cheese. Combine vinegar, salt, and pepper in a small cup, and stir well. Add olive oil, and stir well again. Drizzle dressing over filling.
4. Tuck sides of tortillas over filling, and roll gently but firmly beginning at the filled side. Cut in half on the diagonal, and serve immediately.

Note: The bacon can be cooked, and the dressing can be made, up to 1 day in advance and refrigerated, tightly covered. Reheat the bacon briefly in a microwave oven before assembling wraps.

Variation:

• Substitute baked ham for the turkey.

Remember how nothing should go to waste in your kitchen? That includes bacon grease. Not only is it free, because you've already bought the bacon, but it has a very high smoke point, which makes it an excellent choice for sautéing hearty dishes.

Beef Fajitas

Fajitas (pronounced *fah-HEE-taz*) are authentically Mexican, but have also been absorbed into Southwestern cooking. These use economical sirloin tips, which are one of the best buys in the meat case, and blend them with the traditional sautéed onions and peppers.

Yield: 4–6 servings | **Active time:** 25 minutes | **Start to finish:** 25 minutes

> 1 pound sirloin tips
> ¼ cup olive oil, divided
> 1 large red onion, peeled and thinly sliced
> 1 large green bell pepper, seeds and ribs removed, and thinly sliced
> 2 jalapeño or serrano chiles, seeds and ribs removed, and finely chopped
> 3 garlic cloves, peeled and minced
> 2 medium ripe tomatoes, rinsed, cored, seeded, and diced
> ¼ cup lime juice
> 2 teaspoons ground cumin
> ¼ cup chopped fresh cilantro
> Salt and freshly ground black pepper to taste
> 8–12 (6-inch) flour tortillas
> Garnish (optional): Sour cream, salsa, and guacamole

1. Cut beef into ½-inch slices against the grain.
2. Heat 2 tablespoons oil in a large skillet over medium-high heat. Add beef and cook, stirring frequently, for 1½–2 minutes, or to desired doneness. Remove beef from the skillet with a slotted spoon, set aside, and keep warm. Discard fat from the skillet, and wipe out the skillet with paper towels.
3. Heat remaining oil in the skillet over medium-high heat. Add onion, green bell pepper, chiles, and garlic. Cook, stirring frequently, for 4–6 minutes, or until onion is soft. Add tomato, and cook for 1 minute. Add lime juice, cumin, cilantro, and beef, and heat through, stirring constantly. Season to taste with salt and pepper.

4. Wrap tortillas in plastic wrap, and microwave on High (100 percent power) for 20–30 seconds, or until warm and pliable. To serve, roll up filling in tortillas, and serve with small bowls of sour cream, salsa, and guacamole, if using. Serve immediately.

Note: The vegetable mixture can be made 6 hours in advance and kept at room temperature. Sauté the beef just prior to serving.

Variation:

- Substitute boneless, skinless chicken for the beef. Cook the chicken for 4–5 minutes, or until cooked through and no longer pink.

Cumin, pronounced *KOO-men*, is frequently found in markets under its Spanish name, *comino*. The seeds from which it's ground are the dried fruit from a plant in the parsley family, which is very aromatic. It's one of the major ingredients in commercial chili powder, so you can always substitute chili powder if necessary.

Sloppy Joes

While the exact origins of this American classic are not known, recipes for this indeed sloppy dish date back to the early 1940s, and by the 1960s, it was a fixture in every school cafeteria. While served on toasted hamburger buns, these are definitely "fork food."

Yield: 4–6 servings | **Active time:** 15 minutes | **Start to finish:** 30 minutes

3 tablespoons olive oil, divided
1 pound lean ground beef
1 medium onion, peeled and chopped
3 garlic cloves, peeled and minced
1 large green bell pepper, seeds and ribs removed, and chopped
2 tablespoons chili powder
1 cup ketchup
1 cup beer
2 tablespoons Worcestershire sauce
Salt and freshly ground black pepper to taste
4–6 hamburger buns, split and toasted
1 1/2–2 cups shredded iceberg lettuce, rinsed and dried

1. Heat 1 tablespoon oil in a saucepan over medium-high heat. Add beef, breaking up lumps with a fork, and cook for 3–5 minutes, or until no pink remains. Remove beef from the pan with a slotted spoon, and set aside. Discard fat from the pan.
2. Heat remaining oil in the pan over medium-high heat. Add onion, garlic, and green bell pepper, and cook, stirring frequently, for 3 minutes, or until onion is translucent. Add chili powder, and cook for 1 minute, stirring constantly.
3. Return beef to the pan, and add ketchup, beer, and Worcestershire sauce. Bring to a boil, reduce the heat to medium, and cook for 10–15 minutes, stirring occasionally, or until slightly thickened. Season to taste with salt and pepper.
4. To serve, mound beef mixture on bottom half of toasted buns, top with lettuce, and replace top of buns. Serve immediately.

Note: Make the beef mixture up to 2 days ahead and refrigerate, tightly covered. Reheat over low heat, covered, stirring occasionally.

Variation:
- Substitute ground turkey for the ground beef.

Croque Madame

The Croque Madame, and its egg-free brother, the Croque Monsieur, are traditional French sandwiches usually served in mid-morning. This recipe is basically just a grilled ham and Swiss sandwich, and goes well with a tossed salad.

Yield: 4–6 servings | **Active time:** 5 minutes | **Start to finish:** 8 minutes

> 8–12 slices firm white sandwich bread, crusts trimmed
> 6 tablespoons (¾ stick) unsalted butter, softened, divided
> ¾ pound Swiss cheese
> ½ pound thinly sliced smoked ham
> 4–6 large eggs
> Salt and freshly ground black pepper to taste

1. Preheat a two-sided grill, if using one. Spread both sides of bread slices with 4 tablespoons softened butter. Layer cheese on all bread slices. Layer ham on ½ of slices. Turn cheese side down on ham to enclose filling.

2. Grill sandwiches in a two-sided grill for 3–4 minutes, or until bread is brown and cheese melts. Alternatively, fry sandwiches in a ridged grill pan, turning once, weighted down by a foil-covered brick.

3. While sandwiches grill, heat remaining butter in a large skillet over medium heat. Break eggs into the skillet, and sprinkle with salt and pepper. Cook sunny-side up or flip over lightly. To serve, cut sandwiches in half, and top each with an egg.

Note: The sandwiches can be prepared for grilling up to 1 day in advance and refrigerated, tightly covered.

Variations:
- Substitute smoked turkey for the ham.
- Substitute cheddar cheese for the Swiss cheese.

Ham and Cheese French Toast Sandwich

This is another French sandwich, termed a Monte Cristo, and I've included it more for the method than for the simple ham and cheese filling. Dipping the sandwich in an egg bath creates a richer taste, and it's a great way to get additional protein into children.

Yield: 4–6 servings | **Active time:** 15 minutes | **Start to finish:** 15 minutes

> 8–12 slices egg bread
> 3 tablespoons Dijon mustard
> 1/3 pound thinly sliced baked ham
> 1/4 pound sliced cheddar cheese
> 3 ripe plum tomatoes, rinsed, cored, seeded, and diced
> 3 large eggs
> 1/4 cup milk
> Salt and freshly ground black pepper to taste
> 4 tablespoons (1/2 stick) unsalted butter

1. Arrange bread on the counter, and spread each slice with mustard. Divide ham, cheese, and tomatoes on 1/2 of slices, and top with remaining slices, mustard side down.

2. Whisk eggs and milk in a shallow bowl, and season to taste with salt and pepper. Melt butter in a heavy, large skillet over medium-low heat. Dip both sides of each sandwich into egg mixture and place sandwiches in the skillet; this may have to be done in batches. Cook, covered, for 4 minutes per side, or until cheese melts and sandwiches are golden. Blot sandwiches with paper towels, and serve immediately, cut on the diagonal.

Note: The sandwiches can be prepared up to 4 hours in advance and kept at room temperature. Reheat them in a 350°F oven for 5–7 minutes, or until warm, and do not cut in half until just prior to serving.

Variations:
- Add 1 teaspoon Italian seasoning or herbes de Provence to the egg mixture.
- Substitute Swiss cheese for the cheddar cheese.
- Substitute thinly sliced roast or smoked turkey for the ham.
- Omit the meat, and increase the number of tomatoes to 5.
- Substitute jalapeño Jack for the cheddar cheese, omit the mustard, and add 2 tablespoons chili powder to the egg mixture.

Cooking eggs covered over low heat is a way to keep them tender; it's the way I make scrambled eggs as well as French toast and its variations, like this sandwich. The proteins in eggs becomes tough when treated to high heat, which is why you need high heat for a fried egg if you want to turn it.

Gyros with Yogurt Sauce in Pita Pockets

The spiced meat mixture for the traditional gyro is roasted on a vertical skewer that slowly spins like a gyroscope, and is then carved off to form the basis for the sandwich. It's much easier and faster to cook the meat as a long, skinny meatloaf. Serve this with a Greek salad.

Yield: 4–6 servings | **Active time:** 15 minutes | **Start to finish:** 35 minutes

> 1½ cups plain yogurt
> 1 ripe plum tomato, rinsed, cored, seeded, and chopped
> ½ cup chopped peeled and seeded cucumber
> 4 garlic cloves, peeled and minced, divided
> Salt and freshly ground black pepper to taste
> 1 pound ground lamb
> ½ small onion, peeled and finely chopped
> 3 garlic cloves, peeled and chopped
> 2 teaspoons ground cumin
> 2 teaspoons chili powder
> 1 teaspoon dried basil
> ½ teaspoon dried thyme
> ¼ cup chopped fresh parsley
> ⅓ cup Italian breadcrumbs
> 4–6 (7–8-inch) pita breads, cut in half with pockets opened

1. Preheat the oven to 400°F, and line a rimmed baking sheet with heavy-duty aluminum foil. Place yogurt in a strainer set over a mixing bowl, and allow it to drain for 30 minutes. After draining, discard whey, and mix yogurt with tomato, cucumber, and 1 garlic clove. Season to taste with salt and pepper, and set aside.
2. While yogurt drains, combine lamb, onion, remaining garlic, cumin, chili powder, basil, thyme, parsley, and breadcrumbs in a mixing bowl. Mix well, and season to taste with salt and pepper. Form meat mixture into a log the length of the baking sheet, about 1½-inches high
3. Bake lamb for 15–20 minutes, or until browned. Remove lamb from the oven, and cut into 1-inch slices. To serve, fill each ½ of pita breads with lamb. Divide sauce on top of lamb, and serve immediately.

Note: The lamb and sauce can be prepared up to 1 day in advance and refrigerated, tightly covered. Reheat the lamb, covered in aluminum foil, in a 325°F oven for 10–15 minutes, or until warmed through.

Variation:

- Substitute ground beef or ground turkey for the lamb.

It's amazing how much liquid is in most yogurt. Draining it while the lamb is prepared gives it the consistency of sour cream so it delivers a better flavor and texture to the sauce.

Grilled Reuben Sandwich

While there are conflicting stories, most food historians agree that the Reuben sandwich dates to a deli in New York in the early twentieth century. The key ingredients are sauerkraut, corned beef, and Swiss cheese—all moistened with Russian (also called Thousand Islands) dressing.

Yield: 4 servings | **Active time:** 15 minutes | **Start to finish:** 20 minutes

SANDWICH

1 cup sauerkraut, drained
8 slices rye bread or pumpernickel
2 tablespoons unsalted butter, softened
$\frac{1}{2}$ pound thinly sliced Swiss cheese
$\frac{3}{4}$ pound thinly sliced corned beef

DRESSING

$\frac{1}{4}$ cup mayonnaise
2 tablespoons bottled chili sauce
1 scallion, white part and 3 inches of green tops, rinsed, trimmed, and chopped
1 tablespoon sweet pickle relish
1 tablespoon Dijon mustard
Salt and freshly ground black pepper to taste

1. Preheat a two-sided grill, if using one. Place sauerkraut in a large mixing bowl of cold water, and swirl it around well. Drain, and repeat three more times. Press dry after the last draining, and set aside.

2. For dressing, combine mayonnaise, chili sauce, scallion, pickle relish, mustard, salt, and pepper in a small mixing bowl. Whisk well, and set aside.

3. Butter one side of each slice of bread. Spread dressing on 4 of the non-buttered sides. Layer sauerkraut, Swiss cheese, and corned beef on top of dressing. Enclose filling by topping it with other slices of bread, buttered side up.

4. Grill sandwiches in a two-sided grill for 3–4 minutes, or until bread is brown and cheese melts. Alternatively, fry sandwiches in a ridged grill pan, turning once, weighted down by a foil-covered brick or pan. Cut sandwiches in half, and serve immediately.

Note: The sandwiches can be prepared for grilling up to 4 hours in advance and refrigerated, tightly covered.

Variation:
- Substitute sliced turkey for the corned beef.

> What most people find objectionable about sauerkraut is the salty brine in which it's pickled. By repeatedly rinsing it, you'll wash most of this brine away.

Mock Mu Shu Pork

While authentic Mandarin pancakes are still difficult to find in super-markets, or even Asian markets, and expensive if you do find them, flour tortillas are an excellent substitute with this stir-fried filling of pork and vegetables or any other Asian dish.

Yield: 4–6 servings | **Active time:** 25 minutes | **Start to finish:** 25 minutes

    8 large dried shiitake mushrooms *
    1 ounce dried wood ear mushrooms *
    1 cup boiling water
    ³/₄ pound boneless pork loin
    ¹/₄ cup soy sauce
    1 tablespoon dry sherry
    2 tablespoons cornstarch
    2 tablespoons vegetable oil
    6 scallions, white parts and 4 inches of green tops, rinsed,
       trimmed, and sliced
    3 garlic cloves, peeled and minced
    3 large eggs, lightly beaten
    Salt and freshly ground black pepper to taste
    8–12 (6-inch) flour tortillas
    ¹/₃ cup plum sauce *

1. Place dried shiitake mushrooms and wood ear mushrooms in a small mixing bowl. Pour boiling water over mushrooms, pressing them into water with the back of a spoon. Soak mushrooms for 10 minutes, then drain, squeezing out as much liquid as possible. Discard stems from shiitake mushrooms, and slice mushrooms thinly. Set aside.

2. Trim pork of all visible fat. Cut pork into thin slivers by cutting into thin slices and then cutting slices lengthwise. Combine soy sauce, sherry, and cornstarch in a mixing bowl. Stir well, and add pork to the mixing bowl. Toss to coat pork evenly.

* Available in the Asian aisle of most supermarkets and in specialty markets.

3. Heat oil in a heavy wok or large skillet over medium-high heat. Add scallions and garlic and stir-fry for 30 seconds, or until fragrant. Add pork and stir-fry for 2 minutes, or until pork is no longer pink. Add mushrooms and eggs to the pan, and stir. Cook for 1 minute, then scrape the bottom of the pan to dislodge cooked egg. Cook for an additional 1–2 minutes, or until eggs are just set. Season to taste with salt and pepper.

4. Wrap tortillas in plastic wrap, and microwave on High (100 percent power) for 20–30 seconds, or until warm and pliable. To serve, spread plum sauce on the surface of each tortilla. Place a portion of filling in the center. Tuck one edge over filling, and roll tortillas firmly to enclose filling. Serve immediately.

Note: The filling can be made up to 1 day in advance and refrigerated, tightly covered. Reheat it over low heat, covered, stirring occasionally, or in a microwave oven.

Variation:

- Substitute boneless, skinless chicken breasts for the pork.

Wood ear mushrooms, also called cloud ear, are a form of Asian dried mushroom with a slightly crunchy texture and very delicate flavor. They are almost brownish black and expand to five times their size when rehydrated.

Cuban Quesadillas

The Cuban sandwich, called a *medianoche* (or midnight) in some parts of South Florida because it is a late-night snack, combines ham and pork with pickles, mustard, and Swiss cheese.

Yield: 4–6 servings | **Active time:** 10 minutes | **Start to finish:** 25 minutes

    4–6 (10-inch) flour or whole wheat tortillas
    6 tablespoons Dijon mustard
    2/3 pound thinly sliced roast pork
    2/3 pound thinly sliced baked ham
    1 cup thinly sliced dill pickles
    3 cups grated Swiss cheese
    Vegetable oil spray

1. Preheat the oven to 450°F, cover 2 baking sheets with heavy-duty aluminum foil, and grease the foil with vegetable oil spray. Soften tortillas, if necessary, by wrapping them in plastic wrap and heating them in a microwave oven on High (100 percent power) for 10–15 seconds, or until pliable.
2. Place tortillas on a counter. Spread mustard on each tortilla. Layer roast pork, baked ham, and pickles on one half of each. Sprinkle Swiss cheese over filling. Fold empty side of tortillas over filling, and press closed with the palm of your hand or a spatula. Arrange tortillas on prepared baking sheets, and spray tops with vegetable oil spray.
3. Bake quesadillas for 5 minutes. Turn them gently with a spatula, and press them down if the top has separated from the filling. Bake for an additional 5–7 minutes, or until crispy. Allow to sit for 2 minutes, then cut each in half, and serve immediately.

Note: The quesadillas can be formed up to 1 day in advance and refrigerated, tightly covered. Add 3 minutes to the baking time if chilled.

Variation:
- Substitute thinly sliced turkey for the pork.

> Dijon mustard, known for its clean, sharp flavor, is made from a combination of brown and black mustard seeds, and the essential ingredients are white wine and unfermented grape juice.

Muffuletta Quesadillas

A great American regional sandwich is the muffuletta, invented at the Central Grocery in New Orleans' French Quarter. It is similar to many other Italian sandwiches that use up bits of cold cuts and cheese, but what is distinctive is the olive salad topping. I love it hot, with the cheese melted.

Yield: 4–6 servings | **Active time:** 10 minutes | **Start to finish:** 25 minutes

> Vegetable oil spray
> 4–6 (10-inch) flour or whole wheat tortillas
> $2/3$ cup chopped pimiento-stuffed green olives, drained well
> 2 garlic cloves, peeled and minced
> 2 tablespoons olive oil
> $1/4$ pound baked ham
> $1/4$ pound mortadella
> $1/4$ pound Genoa salami
> $1/3$ pound provolone cheese

1. Preheat the oven to 450°F, cover 2 baking sheets with heavy-duty aluminum foil, and grease the foil with vegetable oil spray. Soften tortillas, if necessary, by wrapping them in plastic wrap and heating them in a microwave oven on High (100 percent power) for 10–15 seconds, or until pliable. Combine olives, garlic, and olive oil in a small bowl, and stir well.

2. Place tortillas on a counter. Layer ham, mortadella, salami, and cheese on $1/2$ of each tortilla, and top with olive mixture. Fold empty side of each tortilla over filling, and press closed with the palm of your hand or a spatula. Arrange tortillas on prepared baking sheets, and spray tops with vegetable oil spray.

3. Bake quesadillas for 5 minutes. Turn them gently with a spatula, and press them down if the top has separated from the filling. Bake for an additional 5–7 minutes, or until crispy. Allow to sit for 2 minutes, then cut each in half, and serve immediately.

Note: The quesadillas can be formed up to 1 day in advance and refrigerated, tightly covered. Add 3 minutes to the baking time if chilled.

Variation:
- Use the same filling but make it into a panini sandwich. Consult a similar recipe in this chapter for the method.

Ham and Mushroom Quesadillas

These quesadillas have a subtle flavor, with aromatic smoked Spanish paprika giving them great appeal in terms of both taste and color. Serve them with a tossed salad.

Yield: 4–6 servings | **Active time:** 15 minutes | **Start to finish:** 30 minutes

Vegetable oil spray
4–6 (10-inch) flour or whole-wheat tortillas
½ pound thinly sliced baked ham
3 tablespoons unsalted butter
2 tablespoons olive oil
2 garlic cloves
2 tablespoons smoked Spanish paprika
1 teaspoon ground cumin
1 teaspoon dried oregano
½ pound mushrooms, wiped with a damp paper towel, trimmed, and thinly sliced
Salt and freshly ground black pepper to taste
2 cups grated Monterey Jack cheese

1. Preheat the oven to 450°F, cover 2 baking sheets with heavy-duty aluminum foil, and grease the foil with vegetable oil spray. Soften tortillas, if necessary, by wrapping them in plastic wrap and heating them in a microwave oven on High (100 percent power) for 10–15 seconds, or until pliable.
2. Place tortillas on a counter, and arrange ham on ½ of each tortilla. Heat butter and oil in a large skillet over medium-high heat. Add garlic, paprika, cumin, and oregano, and cook for 30 seconds, stirring constantly. Add mushrooms, and cook for 5–7 minutes, or until mushrooms soften. Season to taste with salt and pepper, and spread evenly on top of ham. Top mushrooms with cheese.
3. Fold empty side of each tortilla over filling, and press closed with the palm of your hand or a spatula. Arrange tortillas on prepared baking sheets, and spray tops with vegetable oil spray.

4. Bake quesadillas for 5 minutes. Turn them gently with a spatula, and press them down if the top has separated from the filling. Bake for an additional 5–7 minutes, or until crispy. Allow to sit for 2 minutes, then cut each in half, and serve immediately.

Note: The quesadillas can be formed up to 1 day in advance and refrigerated, tightly covered. Add 3 minutes to the baking time if chilled.

Variations:
- Substitute jalapeño Jack for the Monterey Jack for a spicier filling.
- Substitute sliced turkey or chicken for the ham.

> While I don't believe in many kitchen gadgets, if you have an egg slicer, use it for slicing mushrooms. The slices are the right width, and all the slices are the same size.

Open-Faced Welsh Rarebit with Bacon and Tomato

Welsh rarebit, also called Welsh rabbit, was a hearty dish served to laborers for high tea, because their main meal was at lunch. In this version, the cheddar cheese sauce made with beer tops slices of crisp bacon and succulent tomato.

Yield: 4–6 servings | **Active time:** 15 minutes | **Start to finish:** 15 minutes

⅔ pound bacon
3 ripe plum tomatoes, rinsed, cored, seeded, and thinly sliced
Salt and freshly ground black pepper to taste
4–6 slices white or whole-wheat bread
1 (12-ounce) can lager beer
1 tablespoon prepared mustard, preferably English
2 teaspoons paprika
½ teaspoon cayenne
1 pound (4 cups) grated sharp cheddar cheese
1 tablespoon cold water
1 tablespoon cornstarch

1. Place bacon in a large, heavy skillet. Cook over medium-high heat, turning as necessary with tongs, for 5–7 minutes, or until bacon is crisp. Remove bacon from the pan, and drain on paper towels. Sprinkle tomatoes with salt and pepper, and set aside. While bacon cooks, toast bread slices, and set aside.
2. Combine beer, mustard, paprika, and cayenne in a heavy 2-quart saucepan, and stir well. Bring to a simmer over medium heat, stirring occasionally.
3. Add cheddar to beer by ½ cup measures, stirring constantly with a whisk in a figure-eight pattern. Add additional cheese only after the previous addition melts.
4. Combine water and cornstarch in a small bowl, and stir to dissolve cornstarch. Add to beer mixture, and bring to a simmer, stirring constantly. Cook over low heat for 1–2 minutes, or until thickened. Season to taste with salt and pepper.
5. To serve, place toast slices on individual plates and top toast with sliced tomatoes and bacon. Spoon cheese mixture over all, and serve immediately.

Note: The components of the dish can be prepared up to 4 hours in advance and kept at room temperature. Reheat the cheese to a simmer before serving.

Variations:
- Substitute sliced turkey, roast beef, or ham for the bacon.
- Substitute Swiss cheese for the cheddar.
- Omit the bacon for a vegetarian dish.

Sprinkling tomatoes with salt and pepper in advance of eating them, even by a few minutes, increases the taste of the tomato. Also the fruit absorbs the salt so that it tastes succulent but not salty.

Chapter 5:
Pasta Power

Pasta is a more expensive meal than it was a few years ago; many wheat fields in the regions of Umbria and Tuscany have been converted to grow sunflowers rather than the species of hard durum wheat used for making dried pasta. While it creates an enchanting vista for summer tourists, the sunflowers are destined for ethanol production, which farmers are finding more lucrative at present than growing wheat.

While the increase in the price of pasta has caused me some sticker shock, it's still one of the most economical meals to make. And with a few boxes of dried pasta in the pantry, you know you'll always eat! Many of the recipes in this chapter use other pantry staples, too.

And because it's never been conclusively proven if pasta started in Italy and went to China with Marco Polo, or the Italian explorer imported it from China, you'll find a few Asian recipes interspersed amongst those drawn from Western cuisines.

It takes longer to bring the water to a boil to cook the pasta than it does to make many of these sauces. So here are a few ways to speed up that process:

- You don't have to use gallons of water. For 1 pound of pasta, 3 quarts of water is enough to cook it properly.

- Start with very hot tap water. It takes less energy to heat the water before it comes out of the tap than to heat cold water on the stove.

- Cover the pan while the water heats.

These three things may seem elementary, but after years of observing cooks at work, I can assure you they aren't second nature. And the difference between heating 6 quarts of cold water, uncovered, and 3 quarts of hot water, covered, is more than 15 minutes!

THE PASTA PARADE

Good-quality dried pasta is made with a high percentage of high-gluten semolina, the inner part of the grain of hard durum wheat. The gluten gives the pasta resilience, and allows it to cook while remaining somewhat firm—the elusive al dente. Many pasta recipes are written for a specific shape of pasta; however, there is wide latitude for substitution. What's important is to find a pasta of about the same dimensions that cooks in the same amount of time. Those are your guides for matching a shape with a sauce. The times given below should be used as guidance, but the best way to cook pasta is according to the times listed on the individual box; each manufacturer has a slightly different formula and tests its pasta for timing.

Here are the types of dried pasta found most often:

NAME (Meaning)	DESCRIPTION	COOKING TIME
Anelli (Rings)	Medium, ridged tubes cut into thin rings	6–8 minutes
Cannelloni (Large pipes)	Large cylinders	8–10 minutes with further baking
Capellini (Hair)	Thinnest strands	2–4 minutes
Cavatappi (Corkscrews)	Short, ridged pasta twisted into a spiral	8–10 minutes
Conchiglie (Shells)	Shells about 1 inch long	8–10 minutes
Ditalini (Little thimbles)	Very short round pieces	6–9 minutes
Farfalle (Butterflies)	Flat rectangles pinched in the center to form a bow	10–12 minutes
Fettuccine (Little ribbons)	Long, flat ribbon shapes, about ¼ inch wide	6–9 minutes
Fusilli (Twisted spaghetti)	Long, spring-shaped strands	10–12 minutes

NAME (Meaning)	DESCRIPTION	COOKING TIME
Gemilli (Twins)	Medium strands woven together and cut into 2-inch lengths	8–10 minutes
Linguine (Little tongues)	Thin, slightly flattened solid strands about $1/8$-inch wide	6–9 minutes
Maccheroni (Macaroni)	Thin, tubular pasta in various widths	8–10 minutes
Manicotti (Small muffs)	Thick, ridged tubes	10–12 minutes
Mostaccioli (Small mustaches)	Medium-sized tubes with angle-cut ends	8–10 minutes
Orecchiette (Ears)	Smooth, curved rounds about $1/2$ inch in diameter	6–9 minutes
Orzo (Barley)	Tiny, rice-shaped pasta	6–9 minutes
Penne (Quills)	Small tubes with angle-cut ends	8–10 minutes
Radiatore (Radiators)	Short, thick, and ruffled	8–10 minutes
Rigatoni (Larged grooved)	Thick, ridged tubes about $1^1/2$ inches long	10–12 minutes
Riso (Rice)	Tiny grains	4–6 minutes
Rotelli (Wheels)	Spiral-shaped with spokes	8–10 minutes
Rotini (Spirals)	Two thick strands twisted	8–10 minutes
Spaghetti (Length of cord)	Thin, long strands	8–10 minutes
Vermicelli (Little worms)	Thinner than spaghetti	6–8 minutes
Ziti (Bridegroom)	Medium-sized tubes about 2 inches long	10–12 minutes

Rigatoni with Roasted Vegetables and Olives

Roasting caramelizes the natural sugars in vegetables as well as evaporating their water. This is a simple sauce with an intense and hearty flavor; serve the dish with a tossed salad.

Yield: 4–6 servings | **Active time:** 15 minutes | **Start to finish:** 40 minutes

> ⅔ pound rigatoni
> 1 (1-pound) eggplant, cut into ¾-inch dice
> 1 large onion, peeled, and diced
> 8 ripe plum tomatoes, rinsed, cored, seeded, and diced
> ½ cup olive oil
> 4 garlic cloves, peeled and minced
> Salt and freshly ground black pepper to taste
> ½ cup chopped pitted kalamata olives
> ½ cup freshly grated Parmesan cheese

1. Preheat the oven to 450°F, and line a rimmed baking sheet with heavy-duty aluminum foil. Bring a large pot of salted water to a boil. Add pasta, and cook according to package directions until al dente. Drain, reserving ½ cup of pasta water, and return pasta to the pot.
2. While water heats, combine eggplant, onion, and tomatoes on the prepared pan. Add olive oil and garlic, and mix well to coat vegetables. Season to taste with salt and pepper, and roast vegetables for 20–25 minutes, or until tender. Stir vegetables after 10 minutes.
3. Add roasted eggplant mixture, olives, and Parmesan to the pot with pasta. Toss to coat, adding ¼–½ cup pasta water, if mixture seems dry. Serve immediately.

Note: The vegetable mixture can be made 1 day in advance and refrigerated, tightly covered. Reheat it, covered, in a 350°F oven for 10–12 minutes, or until hot.

Variation:
- Add 1½ cups shredded cooked chicken to the pot along with the vegetables and olives.

Pasta with Garlic and Oil (*Pasta Aglio e Olio*)

Getting a delicious dinner on the table doesn't get any easier than this recipe! As long as you cook with garlic, you've probably got everything you need right in the kitchen, so as soon as the pasta is cooked you're ready to eat.

Yield: 4-6 servings | **Active time:** 10 minutes | **Start to finish:** 25 minutes

⅔ pound spaghetti or linguine
½ cup olive oil
8 garlic cloves, peeled and minced
¾-1 teaspoon crushed red pepper flakes
Salt to taste
½ cup freshly grated Parmesan cheese

1. Bring a large pot of salted water to a boil. Add pasta, and cook according to package directions until al dente. Drain, reserving 1 cup of cooking liquid, and set aside.
2. While pasta cooks, heat olive oil in a large skillet over medium-high heat. Add garlic and red pepper flakes. Reduce heat to low, and cook, stirring constantly, for 1 minute, or until garlic is golden brown.
3. Remove the pan from the heat, and add the pasta. Toss the pasta well, adding some reserved cooking liquid if mixture seems dry. Season to taste with salt, and serve immediately, passing Parmesan cheese separately.

> Reserving some of the pasta cooking water is a traditional step in Italian cooking for pastas cooked in relatively dry sauces. It can moisten the sauce with the same innate flavor of the dish without making it taste watery.

Penne in Creamy Tomato Sauce

Here is an easy and creamy pasta dish that the whole family will adore. Serve it with a green salad.

Yield: 4–6 servings | **Active time:** 15 minutes | **Start to finish:** 35 minutes

- $^2/_3$ pound penne pasta
- 3 tablespoons olive oil
- 1 large onion, peeled and diced
- 2 celery ribs, rinsed, trimmed, and chopped
- 3 garlic cloves, peeled and minced
- 1 (8-ounce) can tomato sauce
- 1 (14.5-ounce) can diced tomatoes, undrained
- 1 cup heavy cream
- 2 tablespoons chopped fresh parsley
- $1^1/_2$ teaspoons dried oregano
- 1 teaspoon dried thyme
- Salt and freshly ground black pepper to taste
- $^1/_2$ cup freshly grated Parmesan cheese

1. Bring a large pot of salted water to a boil. Add pasta, and cook according to package directions until al dente. Drain, and set aside.
2. While water heats, heat olive oil in a saucepan over medium-high heat. Add onion, celery, and garlic, and cook, stirring frequently, for 3 minutes, or until onion is translucent. Stir in tomato sauce, tomatoes, cream, parsley, oregano, and thyme.
3. Bring to a boil, reduce the heat to low, and simmer sauce, uncovered, stirring occasionally, for 20 minutes. Add pasta to sauce, season to taste with salt and pepper, and serve immediately, passing Parmesan cheese separately.

Note: The sauce can be prepared up to 3 days in advance and refrigerated, tightly covered. Reheat over low heat, stirring occasionally, until simmering. Cook pasta just prior to serving.

Pasta Primavera

Spaghetti dotted with a cornucopia of colorful fresh vegetables in a creamy sauce laced with cheese is a nutritious as well as delicious dish. In addition to being served as an entrée, the recipe will also feed 8–10 people as a side dish to glamorize a simple baked or grilled dish.

Yield: 4–6 servings | **Active time:** 20 minutes | **Start to finish:** 25 minutes

½ pound thin spaghetti
⅓ cup olive oil, divided
1 small onion, peeled and finely chopped
3 garlic cloves, peeled and minced
2 small zucchini, rinsed, trimmed, and cut into ½-inch dice
½ pound mushrooms, wiped with a damp paper towel, trimmed, and thinly sliced
1 green bell pepper, seeds and ribs removed, and sliced
1 (14-ounce) can diced tomatoes, drained
1 cup Vegetable Stock (recipe on page 37) or purchased stock
1 cup heavy cream
¼ cup chopped fresh parsley
2 teaspoons Italian seasoning
1 cup broccoli florets
½ cup frozen peas, thawed
Salt and crushed red pepper flakes to taste
¾ cup freshly grated Parmesan cheese

1. Bring a large pot of salted water to a boil. Add pasta, and cook according to package directions until al dente. Drain, toss with 2 tablespoons olive oil, and keep warm.
2. While water heats, heat remaining oil in a large skillet over medium-high heat. Add onion and garlic and cook, stirring frequently, for 3 minutes, or until onion is translucent. Add zucchini, mushrooms, and green bell pepper. Cook for 3 minutes, stirring frequently.
3. Add tomatoes, stock, cream, parsley, Italian seasoning, broccoli, and peas to the skillet. Bring to a boil over medium-high heat, and simmer, uncovered, for 3 minutes. Season to taste with salt and red pepper flakes, and simmer for an additional 2 minutes.

4. To serve, add drained pasta to skillet, and toss with cheese. Serve immediately.

Note: The sauce can be prepared up to 4 hours in advance and kept at room temperature. Reheat it over low heat to a simmer before adding the pasta.

Variation:

- Add ½ pound boneless, skinless chicken breast halves, cut into ½-inch dice, to the skillet along with the zucchini, mushrooms, and green bell pepper.

Primavera is the Italian word for "springtime," and although this dish sounds quintessentially Italian, it was born and bred in New York. Restaurateur Sirio Maccioni created it in the mid-1970s for his famed Le Cirque restaurant, and food writers popularized the dish nationally.

Linguine with Garlicky Fish Sauce

The delicate flavor of fish is enlivened with lots of heady garlic, which is softened in an herbed white wine and cream sauce. While a tossed salad is always a good choice, grilled vegetables are also excellent with this dish.

Yield: 4–6 servings | **Active time:** 20 minutes | **Start to finish:** 25 minutes

$^2/_3$ pound linguine

1 pound thick white-fleshed fish fillets

$^1/_4$ cup olive oil

6 garlic cloves, peeled and minced

$^2/_3$ cup dry white wine

1 (14.5-ounce) can diced tomatoes, drained well

1 teaspoon dried basil

$^1/_2$ cup heavy cream

Salt and freshly ground black pepper to taste

$^1/_3$ cup freshly grated Parmesan cheese

1. Bring a large pot of salted water to a boil. Add pasta, and cook according to package directions until al dente. Drain, and set aside.
2. While water heats, rinse fish, and pat dry with paper towels. Cut fish into 1-inch cubes. Heat oil in a large skillet over medium-high heat. Add fish and garlic, and cook, stirring constantly, for 1 minute.
3. Add wine, tomatoes, basil, and cream, and bring to a boil. Cook over medium heat for 3 minutes, or until fish is cooked through and flakes easily. Remove fish from the pan with a slotted spoon, and reduce sauce for 3 minutes over medium-high heat, or until it coats the back of a spoon. Season to taste with salt and pepper.
4. Toss pasta and fish with sauce and cheese to heat through. Serve immediately.

Note: The fish and sauce can be prepared 1 day in advance and refrigerated, tightly covered. Reheat over low heat, covered, stirring occasionally, until hot before tossing with pasta and cheese.

Variation:

- Substitute $^1/_2$-inch cubes of boneless, skinless chicken breast for the fish.

Pasta with Tuna and Olive Sauce

Canned tuna makes a wonderful addition to a zesty tomato sauce to serve over pasta. A green salad is all you need to complete the meal.

Yield: 4–6 servings | **Active time:** 15 minutes | **Start to finish:** 30 minutes

⅔ pound linguine
2 tablespoons olive oil
1 small onion, peeled and diced
3 garlic cloves, peeled and minced
1 celery rib, rinsed, trimmed, and thinly sliced
1 (28-ounce) can crushed tomatoes in tomato puree
½ cup dry white wine
¾ cup chopped pimiento-stuffed green olives
¼ cup chopped fresh parsley
2 teaspoons Italian seasoning
1 bay leaf
Salt and freshly ground black pepper to taste
2 (6-ounce) cans light tuna, drained and broken into chunks
½ cup freshly grated Parmesan cheese

1. Bring a large pot of salted water to a boil. Add pasta and cook according to package directions until al dente. Drain, and return pasta to the pot.
2. While water heats, heat oil in a large skillet over medium-high heat. Add onion, garlic, and celery. Cook, stirring frequently, for 3 minutes, or until onion is translucent. Add tomatoes, wine, olives, parsley, Italian seasoning, and bay leaf. Bring to a boil, reduce the heat to medium, and simmer sauce, uncovered, for 15 minutes. Season to taste with salt and pepper, and stir in cooked pasta and tuna. Cover the pan, and cook for 2 minutes.
3. Remove and discard bay leaf. Serve immediately, sprinkling individual servings with Parmesan cheese.

Note: The sauce can be made up to 2 days in advance and refrigerated, tightly covered. Reheat it over low heat, covered.

Variation:

- Substitute red wine for the white wine, and substitute herbes de Provence for the Italian seasoning.

Creamy Tuna and Pasta

You could call this recipe "Nouvelle Tuna Noodle Casserole"; it has tuna in a creamy mushroom sauce with other vegetables, but instead of being joined to egg noodles and baked, the sauce tops pasta.

Yield: 4–6 servings | **Active time:** 20 minutes | **Start to finish:** 30 minutes

- ²/₃ pound spaghetti, broken into 2-inch sections
- 4 tablespoons (½ stick) unsalted butter
- 3 celery ribs, rinsed, trimmed, and diced
- 1 large onion, peeled and diced
- ¼ pound mushrooms, wiped with a damp paper towel, trimmed, and diced
- ¼ cup all-purpose flour
- 2 cups half-and-half
- 3 tablespoons chopped fresh parsley
- 2 (6-ounce) cans light tuna, drained
- ½ cup grated mozzarella cheese
- Salt and pepper to taste

1. Bring a large pot of salted water to a boil. Cook pasta according to package directions until al dente. Drain pasta, and return it to the pot.
2. While water heats, heat butter in a saucepan over medium-high heat. Add celery, onion, and mushrooms, and cook, stirring frequently, for 5–7 minutes, or until vegetables are soft. Reduce the heat to low, stir in flour, and cook, stirring constantly, for 2 minutes. Whisk in half-and-half, and bring to a boil over medium-high heat, stirring frequently. Reduce the heat to low, and simmer sauce, stirring occasionally, for 3 minutes.
3. Stir parsley and tuna into sauce, and simmer sauce, stirring occasionally, for an additional 3 minutes. Stir cheese into sauce, and stir for 30 seconds, or until cheese melts. Stir sauce into pasta, and reheat over low heat, if necessary. Season to taste with salt and pepper, and serve immediately.

Note: The sauce can be prepared up to 2 days in advance and refrigerated, tightly covered. Reheat it over low heat, covered, stirring frequently.

Variation:
- Substitute 1½ cups cooked shredded chicken for the tuna.

Spaghetti with Egg and Bacon (*Pasta Carbonara*)

It takes longer for the water to come to a boil to cook the pasta than it does to create this classic Italian dish that's spicy with black pepper, and rich from eggs and cheese. A tossed salad is all you need to complete the meal.

Yield: 4-6 servings | **Active time:** 15 minutes | **Start to finish:** 25 minutes

$^2/_3$ pound spaghetti
$^3/_4$ pound bacon, sliced into $^1/_2$-inch strips
6 garlic cloves, peeled and minced
Freshly ground black pepper to taste (at least 1$^1/_2$ teaspoons)
6 large eggs, well beaten
1$^1/_2$ cups freshly grated Parmesan cheese
Salt to taste

1. Bring a large pot of salted water to a boil. Add pasta, and cook according to package directions until al dente. Drain, and set aside.

2. While water heats, place bacon in a large, heavy skillet over medium-high heat. Cook, stirring occasionally, for 5–7 minutes, or until crisp. Remove bacon from the skillet with a slotted spoon, and set aside. Discard all but 2 tablespoons bacon grease from the pan. Add garlic and black pepper, and cook for 30 seconds. Return bacon to the pan, and turn off heat.

3. Add drained pasta to the skillet, and cook over medium heat for 1 minute. Remove the pan from the stove, and stir in the eggs. Allow eggs to thicken but do not put the pan back on the stove or they will scramble. Add cheese, and season to taste with salt and additional pepper. Serve immediately.

The last place you want your food dollars to go is to an expensive visit from the plumber, and bacon grease is notorious for clogging kitchen plumbing, even if it's put down the sink with hot water running. Rinse out empty half-pint cream containers and keep them under the sink. Pour unwanted bacon fat into a bowl, and after it cools dispose of it in the container.

Szechwan Pasta with Fish in Black Bean Sauce

One of the beauties of fish is how quickly it cooks, and that is demonstrated by this Asian pasta recipe. The spicy sauce gives the fish its flavor, and a large amount of Napa cabbage, which remains crisp-tender, makes this a meal in a bowl.

Yield: 4–6 servings | **Active time:** 15 minutes | **Start to finish:** 25 minutes

> ²/₃ pound thin spaghetti, broken into 2-inch lengths
> 1¼ pounds thick white-fleshed fish fillet
> 3 tablespoons Chinese fermented black beans, coarsely chopped but not rinsed *
> ⅓ cup dry sherry
> 6 scallions, white parts and 4 inches of green tops, rinsed, trimmed, and thinly sliced, divided
> 2 tablespoons Asian sesame oil *
> 4 garlic cloves, peeled and minced
> 3 tablespoons grated fresh ginger
> 3 cups shredded Napa cabbage
> 1 green bell pepper, seeds and ribs removed, and thinly sliced
> ¼ cup soy sauce
> 2 tablespoons oyster sauce *
> 1 tablespoon Chinese chile paste with garlic

1. Bring a large pot of salted water to a boil. Add spaghetti, and cook according to package directions until al dente. Drain, and set aside. Rinse fish and pat dry with paper towels. Cut fish into 1-inch cubes, and set aside. Stir black beans into sherry to plump for 10 minutes. Reserve 3 tablespoons of scallions, and set aside.

2. Heat sesame oil in a large skillet over medium-high heat. Add remaining scallions, garlic, and ginger, and cook, stirring constantly, for 30 seconds, or until fragrant. Add cabbage and green bell pepper to the pan, and cook, stirring constantly, for 2 minutes.

* Available in the Asian aisle of most supermarkets and in specialty markets.

3. Add fish, sherry mixture, soy sauce, oyster sauce, and chile paste to the pan. Cover the pan, and cook over medium heat for 3 minutes, or until fish is cooked through and flakes easily. Stir pasta into the pan to reheat. Sprinkle with remaining 3 tablespoons scallion rings, and serve immediately.

Note: The dish can be prepared up to 1 day in advance and refrigerated, tightly covered. Reheat it over low heat, covered, stirring occasionally.

Variation:

- Substitute 1 pound boneless, skinless chicken thighs or chicken breasts, cut into ½-inch dice, for the fish, and cook for 3 minutes before adding the vegetables. Cook the dish until the chicken is cooked through and no longer pink.

All of the recipes in the $3 Meals series specify green bell peppers rather than red, orange, or yellow. That's purely a matter of cost, because green bell peppers are immature red bell peppers that are less perishable and, therefore, less expensive. But if you find red bell peppers on sale, feel free to substitute them in any recipe.

Spaghetti with Fast Bolognese Sauce

A few ingredients that define a true Bolognese sauce are milk, which makes the meat tender, and white wine, along with vegetables. But once you make this sauce you'll learn that a great sauce does not need to simmer for hours! Serve the pasta with a green salad.

Yield: 4-6 servings | **Active time:** 20 minutes | **Start to finish:** 40 minutes

½–⅔ pound spaghetti
½ pound ground beef
½ pound mild or spicy bulk Italian sausage
2 tablespoons olive oil
1 medium onion, peeled and chopped
2 garlic cloves, peeled and minced
1 celery rib, rinsed, trimmed, and diced
1 carrot, peeled and chopped
1 (28-ounce) can crushed tomatoes in tomato puree
½ cup dry white wine
½ cup whole milk
3 tablespoons chopped fresh parsley
2 teaspoons Italian seasoning
1 teaspoon dried thyme
Salt and freshly ground black pepper to taste
½–¾ cup freshly grated Parmesan cheese

1. Bring a large pot of salted water to a boil. Cook pasta according to package directions until al dente. Drain pasta, and return it to the pot.
2. While water heats, place ground beef and sausage in a large, deep skillet. Cook, breaking up lumps with a fork, for 3–5 minutes, or until meats are no longer pink. Remove meats from the skillet with a slotted spoon, and set aside. Discard grease from the skillet.
3. Heat olive oil in the skillet over medium-high heat. Add onion, garlic, celery, and carrot, and cook, stirring frequently, for 3 minutes, or until onion is translucent.

4. Return meats to the skillet, and add tomatoes, wine, milk, parsley, Italian seasoning, and thyme. Bring to a boil, and simmer sauce over medium heat, uncovered, for 20 minutes, stirring occasionally. Stir sauce into pasta, and reheat over low heat, if necessary. Season to taste with salt and pepper, and serve immediately, passing Parmesan cheese separately.

Note: The sauce can be prepared up to 2 days in advance and refrigerated, tightly covered. Reheat it over low heat, covered, stirring frequently. The sauce can also be frozen for up to 3 months.

Variation:
- Substitute ground turkey or turkey sausage for the beef and pork sausage.

> A tenet of food science is that the larger the surface area of a pot, the faster evaporation—called reduction in cooking—will occur. This sauce achieves the same depth of flavor of a Bolognese cooked much longer because it cooks in a skillet rather than in a saucepan.

Beef Lo Mein

While Cantonese lo mein is traditionally made with long egg noodles, spaghetti works just fine. This is not a spicy dish, but one that has lots of flavor, as well as a large amount of healthful cabbage.

Yield: 4–6 servings | **Active time:** 15 minutes | **Start to finish:** 30 minutes

½–⅔ pound thin spaghetti, broken into 2-inch lengths
8 large dried shiitake mushrooms *
½ cup boiling water
1 pound flank steak
1 tablespoon cornstarch
4 tablespoons soy sauce, divided
Freshly ground black pepper to taste
3 tablespoons Asian sesame oil *
12 scallions, white parts and 4 inches of green tops, rinsed, trimmed, and sliced, divided
4 garlic cloves, peeled and minced
2 tablespoons grated fresh ginger
2 celery ribs, rinsed, trimmed, and sliced on the diagonal
2 cups shredded green cabbage
1 carrot, peeled and thinly sliced
⅓ cup oyster sauce *
½ cup Beef Stock (recipe on page 36) or purchased stock

1. Bring a large pot of salted water to a boil. Add spaghetti, and cook according to package directions until al dente. Drain, and set aside. Pour boiling water over dried mushrooms, and push mushrooms down into liquid with the back of a spoon. Allow mushrooms to soak for 10 minutes, then drain, reserving soaking water. Discard mushroom stems, and slice thinly. Strain soaking water through a sieve lined with a paper coffee filter or a paper towel, and set aside.
2. Rinse steak and pat dry with paper towels. Trim steak of all visible fat. Cut steak into thirds lengthwise, and then slice each piece thinly against the grain. Stir cornstarch into 2 tablespoons soy sauce, and stir mixture into steak. Season beef to taste with pepper, and set aside.

* Available in the Asian aisle of most supermarkets and in specialty markets.

3. Heat sesame oil in large skillet over medium-high heat. Add 1/3 of scallions, garlic, and ginger. Cook, stirring constantly, for 30 seconds, or until fragrant. Add beef to the pan, and cook, stirring constantly, for 1–2 minutes, or until beef is brown on both sides. Remove beef from the pan with a slotted spoon, and set aside.

4. Add remaining scallions, celery, cabbage, and carrot to the pan. Cook, stirring constantly, for 2 minutes. Add reserved mushrooms, mushroom soaking liquid, oyster sauce, stock, and remaining soy sauce to pan. Cover and cook 5 minutes, or until vegetables are crisp-tender. Uncover the pan, stir in pasta and beef, and cook an additional 2–3 minutes, or until pasta is hot. Serve immediately.

Note: The dish can be prepped up to 6 hours in advance and refrigerated, tightly covered.

Variations:
- Substitute boneless, skinless chicken thighs, cut into 1/2-inch dice, for the beef, and substitute chicken stock for the beef stock. Do not remove chicken from the pan before cooking vegetables so that chicken will be cooked through and no longer pink.
- Substitute boneless pork loin, cut into thin strips, for the beef, and substitute chicken stock for the beef stock. Cook pork for 3–4 minutes, or until cooked through.
- Substitute mushrooms, wiped with a damp paper towel, trimmed, and sliced, for the beef, and substitute vegetable stock for the beef stock. Cook mushrooms along with other vegetables.

Pasta with Szechwan Pork Sauce

This is one of my favorite dishes, and it's my adaptation of a classic Chinese dish called Ants on a Tree. Rather than rice noodles, this spicy pork sauce with crunchy bean sprouts is served atop spaghetti.

Yield: 4–6 servings | **Active time:** 15 minutes | **Start to finish:** 35 minutes

2/3 pound spaghetti

1 pound lean ground pork

2 tablespoons cornstarch

3 tablespoons soy sauce

2 tablespoons Asian sesame oil *

4 scallions, white parts and 4 inches of green tops, rinsed, trimmed, and sliced

3 tablespoons grated fresh ginger

4 garlic cloves, peeled and minced

2 jalapeño or serrano chiles, rinsed, seeds and ribs removed, and finely chopped

1½ cups Chicken Stock (recipe on page 35) or purchased stock

2 tablespoons dry sherry

2 tablespoons rice vinegar

2 tablespoons firmly packed dark brown sugar

2 tablespoons fermented black beans, chopped *

Salt and freshly ground black pepper to taste

2 cups fresh bean sprouts, rinsed

1. Bring a large pot of salted water to a boil. Add pasta, and cook according to package directions until al dente. Drain, and set aside.

2. Place pork in a mixing bowl. Combine cornstarch with soy sauce, and stir well. Pour mixture over pork and work it into pork with your fingers. Set aside.

* Available in the Asian aisle of most supermarkets and in specialty markets.

3. Heat sesame oil in a heavy 2-quart saucepan over medium-high heat. Add scallions, ginger, garlic, and chiles, and stir-fry for 30 seconds, or until fragrant. Add pork and cook, breaking up lumps with a fork, for 5 minutes, or until pork is no longer pink. Add stock, sherry, rice vinegar, brown sugar, and fermented black beans to the pan. Stir well, and bring to a boil. Reduce the heat to low and simmer sauce, uncovered, for 15 minutes. Season to taste with salt and pepper. Add pasta to sauce, stir in bean sprouts, and cook for 1 minute. Serve immediately.

Note: Up to adding the bean sprouts, the sauce can be prepared up to 2 days in advance and refrigerated, tightly covered. Reheat it over medium heat, stirring occasionally, until simmering before adding the bean sprouts.

Variation:
- Substitute ground turkey for the ground pork.

Fermented black beans are small black soybeans with a pungent flavor that have been preserved in salt before being packed. They should be chopped and soaked in some sort of liquid to soften them and release their flavor prior to cooking. Because they have salt as a preservative, they last for up to 2 years if refrigerated once opened.

Italian Pork "Lo Mein"

Sesame seeds are used in Italian cooking as well as in Asian cooking, and this pasta dish is reminiscent of a Chinese lo mein, although all the flavors are Western.

Yield: 4–6 servings | **Active time:** 15 minutes | **Start to finish:** 30 minutes

- ²/₃ pound angel hair pasta
- 1 pound boneless pork loin
- Salt and freshly ground black pepper to taste
- 3 tablespoons olive oil
- 6 scallions, white parts and 3 inches of green tops, rinsed, trimmed, and thinly sliced, divided
- 3 garlic cloves, peeled and minced
- 1 large green bell pepper, seeds and ribs removed, and thinly sliced
- 2 medium zucchini, rinsed, trimmed, and thinly sliced
- 2 cups shredded green cabbage
- 1½ cups Chicken Stock (recipe on page 35) or purchased stock
- 2 tablespoons chopped fresh parsley
- 1 teaspoon Italian seasoning
- 3 ripe plum tomatoes, rinsed, cored, seeded, and sliced
- 2 tablespoons sesame seeds

1. Bring a large pot of salted water to a boil. Cook pasta according to package directions until al dente. Drain, and return pasta to the pot. Rinse pork and pat dry with paper towels. Cut pork into ½-inch slices, stack slices, and cut into 1½-inch strips. Sprinkle with salt and pepper, and set aside.

2. While water heats, heat oil in a large skillet over medium-high heat. Add pork, ²/₃ of scallions, garlic, and green bell pepper. Cook, stirring frequently, for 3 minutes, or until scallions are translucent. Add zucchini, cabbage, stock, parsley, and Italian seasoning.

3. Bring to a boil over high heat, stirring frequently. Cover the pan, reduce the heat to medium, and cook, stirring occasionally, for 10–12 minutes, or until pork is cooked through and vegetables soften. Add tomato, and cook for 1 minute.

4. Add sauce to the pot with pasta, and heat through. Season to taste with salt and pepper. To serve, mound pork and vegetables into bowls and sprinkle with sesame seeds and remaining scallions. Serve immediately.

Note: The dish can be prepared for cooking up to 6 hours in advance and refrigerated, tightly covered.

Variation:

- Substitute boneless, skinless chicken breast halves for the pork.

Cabbage is a nutritional powerhouse at a very low cost. While ¼ pound contains a mere 30 calories, it's an excellent source of minerals like manganese, calcium, and potassium, as well as an excellent source of vitamin C.

Pasta with Sausage and Greens

Italian sausage could almost be considered a convenience food because its built-in seasoning is really all a dish needs for flavor! As is the case with many authentic Italian pasta dishes, this one includes some greens; bitter escarole adds great character to the recipe.

Yield: 4–6 servings | **Active time:** 15 minutes | **Start to finish:** 30 minutes

> ⅔ pound spaghetti
> 2 tablespoons olive oil
> 1 pound mild or hot bulk Italian sausage
> 6 garlic cloves, peeled and thinly sliced
> 1 large green bell pepper, seeds and ribs removed, and thinly sliced
> 4 tablespoons (½ stick) unsalted butter, diced
> 4 cups chopped escarole, rinsed and dried
> Salt and freshly ground black pepper to taste
> ¾ cup freshly grated Parmesan cheese

1. Bring a large pot of salted water to a boil. Add pasta, and cook according to package directions until al dente. Drain, reserving 1½ cups pasta water. Return pasta to the pot.

2. While water heats, heat olive oil in a large skillet over medium-high heat. Add sausage, breaking up lumps with a fork, and cook for 5–7 minutes, or until sausage is browned. Add garlic, green bell peppers, and ½ cup of reserved pasta water to the skillet. Cook for 5–7 minutes, or until peppers are soft. Add an additional ½ cup pasta water and butter, and heat until butter melts.

3. Add escarole to the skillet, and cook for 3 minutes. Stir sauce into the pot with pasta, and season to taste with salt and pepper; add more pasta water if mixture seems dry. Serve immediately, passing Parmesan cheese separately.

Note: Up to adding the escarole, the sauce can be prepared up to 1 day in advance and refrigerated, tightly covered. Reheat the sauce to a simmer before adding the escarole.

Variations:
- Substitute turkey sausage for the pork sausage.
- Substitute watercress or arugula for the escarole.

Pasta with Ham and Peas

This is a delicate and creamy pasta dish that children adore; the pasta is napped in a Parmesan cream sauce dotted with bright green peas and cubes of baked ham. Serve it with a green salad.

Yield: 4–6 servings | **Active time:** 15 minutes | **Start to finish:** 20 minutes

    2/3 pound linguine
    3 tablespoons unsalted butter
    5 scallions, white parts and 3 inches of green tops, rinsed,
        trimmed, and sliced
    3/4 cup Chicken Stock (recipe on page 35) or purchased stock
    1/2 cup heavy cream
    1 (10-ounce) package frozen peas, thawed
    1 1/2 cups diced ham
    2 tablespoons chopped fresh parsley
    1/2 teaspoon dried thyme
    1 cup freshly grated Parmesan cheese, divided
    Salt and freshly ground black pepper to taste

1. Bring a large pot of salted water to a boil. Cook pasta according to package directions until al dente. Drain, and return pasta to the pot.
2. While water heats, make sauce. Heat butter in a saucepan over medium heat. Add scallions and cook, stirring frequently, for 3 minutes, or until scallions are translucent. Add stock, cream, peas, ham, parsley, and thyme. Bring to a boil over medium-high heat, stirring occasionally. Cook for 4–5 minutes, or until peas are heated through. Stir 1/2 cup Parmesan into sauce.
3. Pour sauce over cooked pasta, and season to taste with salt and pepper. Serve immediately, passing extra cheese separately.

Note: The sauce can be prepared up to 1 day in advance and refrigerated, tightly covered. Reheat it over low heat, covered, stirring occasionally.

Variation:
• Substitute smoked turkey for the ham.

Pasta with Spinach and Salami

Salami is a flavorful and inexpensive Italian sausage that is usually relegated to being a supporting player on sandwiches and occasionally in salads. But its hearty, garlicky flavor is a wonderful addition to this pasta dish napped in a light cheese sauce that also includes spinach for color and nutrition.

Yield: 4–6 servings | **Active time:** 15 minutes | **Start to finish:** 30 minutes

> ²/₃ pound penne or ziti pasta
> 1 (10-ounce) package frozen chopped spinach, thawed
> 4 tablespoons (½ stick) unsalted butter, divided
> 1 large onion, peeled and chopped
> 3 garlic cloves, peeled and minced
> ¼ cup all-purpose flour
> 1 cup Chicken Stock (recipe on page 35) or purchased stock
> 1 cup half-and-half
> 2 tablespoons chopped fresh parsley
> 2 teaspoons Italian seasoning
> ½ cup freshly grated Parmesan cheese
> ¼ pound thinly sliced Genoa salami, chopped
> 3 ripe plum tomatoes, rinsed, cored, seeded, and chopped
> Salt and freshly ground black pepper to taste

1. Bring a large pot of salted water to a boil. Cook pasta according to package directions until al dente. Drain pasta, and return it to the pot. Place spinach in a colander and press with the back of a spoon to extract as much liquid as possible. Set aside.

2. While pasta cooks, heat butter in a saucepan over medium-high heat. Add onion and garlic and cook, stirring frequently, for 3 minutes, or until onion is translucent. Reduce the heat to low, stir in flour, and cook, stirring constantly, for 2 minutes. Whisk in stock, and bring to a boil over medium-high heat, stirring frequently. Add half-and-half, parsley, and Italian seasoning, and return to a boil. Reduce the heat to low, and simmer sauce, stirring occasionally, for 5 minutes.

3. Stir spinach, Parmesan, salami, and tomatoes into sauce, and simmer sauce, stirring occasionally, for an additional 5 minutes. Stir sauce into pasta, and reheat over low heat, if necessary. Season to taste with salt and pepper, and serve immediately.

Note: The sauce can be prepared up to 2 days in advance and refrigerated, tightly covered. Reheat it over low heat, covered, stirring frequently.

Variations:
- Substitute frozen chopped broccoli, cooked according to package directions, for the spinach.
- Substitute smoked turkey or baked ham for the salami.

The reason why frozen spinach needs no further cooking before being added to a dish is that the blanching it receives prior to freezing really cooks it through. The same is true for frozen corn kernels, but not for many other frozen vegetables.

Chapter 6:
Stir-Fries and Sautés

I hope that the recipes in this chapter give you a new definition of "fast food." What unites the dishes, drawn from Asian and Western cuisines, is that they're cooked either by stir-frying—which is cooking small pieces of food by moving them quickly in the pan—or by sautéing—in which the pieces can be larger, but it's still a high-heat cooking method.

These recipes are cooked over high or close to high heat, which means that you have to pay attention every minute that the food is in the pan. So the key to success for the recipes in this chapter is to have *all* of the ingredients prepped before you turn on the stove. While this is especially true for stir-fried dishes, you can't leave a sauté alone either as you hunt down an ingredient. Read these recipes from beginning to end, and have all your slicing and dicing done.

A way to save time on cleanup is to assemble your ingredients on sheets of plastic wrap on the counter; or save the plastic produce bags that held "clean" ingredients like bell peppers or a head of cabbage. You can transfer the ingredients to the pan using the plastic, rather than dirtying bowls or plates.

STIR-FRYING

For stir-frying, advance planning, speed, and control are the keys to success. The ancient Chinese invented stir-frying as one of their more than fifty methods of food preparation. However, many recipes now utilize the technique for non-Asian dishes. It's quick, requires little fat, and leaves food with the crisp-tender texture we enjoy today.

Because the final cooking is a quick process, the food must be sitting in bowls or dishes placed within arm's reach, ready to be cooked. Cut all pieces of the same ingredient the same size, have your seasonings at hand, and make sure that any vegetables requiring partial cooking—such as blanching green beans—have already been done.

Another aspect of Asian presentation that makes the dishes attractive is how the food is sliced, and there's no difference in the time it takes for simple or dramatic. The rationale behind both methods is that these cuts create a larger surface area. And it's contact of the surfaces with the hot pan that produces crisp-tender food the most quickly. Here are the two basic Asian slicing techniques:

- Slicing on the diagonal. This is a "no-brainer." Instead of cutting celery ribs or scallions at a right angle, tilt your knife so that the slices are at a 45-degree angle. Your pieces will be longer and more attractive.

- Roll cutting. This method is sort of like walking and chewing gum at the same time, but it's hardly difficult. This is especially attractive for round vegetables like carrots and asparagus spears. While cutting on the diagonal, turn the vegetable a quarter turn between slices using your other hand. The pieces will be regularly irregular.

The game plan is that when the dish comes to the table all the ingredients are properly cooked, so there are two options: Either cut food that takes longer to cook into smaller pieces and cook everything at the same time, or start with the longer cooking food and keep adding ingredients in their decreasing need of cooking time. Both strategies produce good results. Never place too much food in the wok or skillet at one time. The food must be able to be seared on all sides, without steaming from being buried under a layer of food.

While it's possible to adapt many recipes to stir-frying, oil rather than butter should be used. The dairy solids in butter burn at a very low temperature, 250°F, so it can only be added as a flavoring agent once food is cooked. Oil, on the other hand, does not begin to smoke until it is heated to more than 400°F, so it is the better choice. There is no consensus as to what oil to use; that's why I lump them together as vegetable oil in the ingredient lists. Peanut, corn, soy, or canola all work well. Olive oil will give the dish a pronounced flavor, and it smokes at too low a temperature to be effective in sealing the food.

Place the wok or skillet over a high flame, and heat it very hot. Listen for the sound of sizzles; if a few drops of water evaporate immediately the pan is ready. Add the required amount of oil to the pan, and swirl it around gently to coat all sides.

Add the food, and keep it moving in the pan. If stir-frying in a wok, use a wire mesh spoon designed for the job. If stir-frying in a skillet, use a spoon that will reach to all places on the bottom, and with which you can keep food moving. In some recipes, liquid is added and the pan is covered for a brief time. In other recipes, it's fry and eat.

SAUTÉING

Sauté literally means "to jump" in French. What it means for food is quick cooking with just a little fat over moderate to high heat. You sauté foods all the time and don't even know it. All those times that you cook onions or shallots (with or without garlic) at the beginning of cooking a dish—that's a sauté. The reason for this initial cooking is to soften these ingredients' natural harshness before they're transferred to the finished dish.

And like a stir-fry, these dishes produce a meal in very little time and in one pan. Like broiling, sautéing is reserved for relatively thin and tender pieces of protein. It's not for "stewing meat" that needs both time and moisture to get tender. Nor is it suited to large pieces, because the outer portions would become dry before the interior cooked properly.

As is true with foods for a stir-fry, preparing food is the first step to a great sauté. The pieces of food must be of equal size and thickness so that they cook evenly, regardless of whether they are diced onions or chicken cutlets. Sautéing is not recommended for any pieces of poultry or fish more than 1/2 inch thick, since it is unlikely that the center would be properly cooked before the outside is dried. For beef, the thickness can be up to 1 inch since most people would want the center rare in the end.

The purpose of the fat is to lubricate the pan and keep the food from sticking. The fat selected must be able to reach relatively high temperatures without breaking down or smoking. The best selections are cooking oil or a combination of oil and butter. Foods that are sautéed need room around them, so that they cook from the heat and not from the steam created as juices are released. Also, if too much food is put into the pan at one time it will lower the temperature of the pan so that heat will not be transferred with the proper intensity.

Cantonese Stir-Fried Chicken with Vegetables

Cantonese food was the first true Chinese food to arrive on American shores, and it's characterized by subtle seasoning and a reliance on lots of fresh vegetables. That's what you'll find in this dish, which should be served over rice.

Yield: 6 servings | **Active time:** 25 minutes | **Start to finish:** 25 minutes

  1 pound boneless, skinless chicken breast halves
  2 tablespoons cornstarch
  2 tablespoons dry sherry
  2 tablespoons soy sauce

¾ cup Chicken Stock (recipe on page 35) or purchased stock

2 tablespoons oyster sauce*

3 tablespoons vegetable oil

3 scallions, white parts and 4 inches of green tops, rinsed, trimmed, and sliced

4 garlic cloves, peeled and minced

2 tablespoons grated fresh ginger

1 large carrot, peeled and thinly sliced on the diagonal

¼ pound green beans, trimmed and cut into 2-inch lengths

¼ pound bok choy, including leaves, rinsed and cut into 1½-inch slices

Salt and freshly ground black pepper to taste

1. Rinse chicken and pat dry with paper towels. Trim chicken of all visible fat. Cut chicken into ¾-inch cubes. Place chicken in a mixing bowl, and sprinkle with cornstarch. Toss to coat evenly, and add sherry and soy sauce, tossing again to coat evenly. Set aside. Combine stock and oyster sauce in a small bowl. Stir well, and set aside.

2. Heat vegetable oil in a heavy wok or large skillet over high heat, swirling to coat the pan. Add scallions, garlic, and ginger, and stir-fry for 30 seconds, or until fragrant, stirring constantly. Add chicken and cook for 1 minute, stirring constantly. Add carrot and green beans, and stir-fry vegetables for 2 minutes more, stirring constantly. Add bok choy, and stir-fry for 1 minute.

3. Add sauce mixture and cook, stirring constantly, for 2 minutes, or until chicken is cooked through and no longer pink and sauce is slightly thickened. Season to taste with salt and pepper, and serve immediately.

Note: The chicken, vegetables, and sauce can be prepped up to 6 hours in advance and refrigerated, tightly covered.

Variations:
- Add 1 jalapeño or serrano chile, seeds and ribs removed, and finely chopped, to the pan along with the scallions, garlic, and ginger for a spicy dish.
- Substitute Asian sesame oil for the vegetable oil, and sprinkle the cooked dish with 2 tablespoons toasted sesame seeds.
- Substitute asparagus or broccoli florets for the green beans.
- Substitute boneless pork loin for the chicken.

* Available in the Asian aisle of most supermarkets and in specialty markets.

Southwestern Sweet Potato Pancakes

I think sweet potatoes are one of the more underutilized vegetables; they add so much inherent flavor as well as glorious color to dishes, and they're usually relegated to holiday meals. These crispy pancakes balance the sweetness with fiery chiles.

Yield: 4–6 servings | **Active time:** 25 minutes | **Start to finish:** 25 minutes

- 4 large sweet potatoes (about 2½ pounds total), scrubbed and cut into 1-inch dice
- 1 medium onion, peeled and cut into 1-inch dice
- 2 large eggs
- 3 tablespoons all-purpose flour
- ½ cup chopped fresh cilantro
- 1 jalapeño or serrano chile, seeds and ribs removed, and finely chopped
- 1 tablespoon ground cumin
- Salt and freshly ground black pepper to taste
- ½ cup vegetable oil
- 1 cup sour cream
- 1 cup refrigerated salsa (found in the produce department or refrigerated case of supermarkets)

1. Preheat the oven to 200°F, and line a baking sheet with paper towels.
2. Place 1 cup sweet potato cubes in the work bowl of a food processor fitted with the steel blade. Chop finely using on-and-off pulsing. Scrape potatoes into a colander, and repeat until all sweet potatoes and onion are finely chopped. (You can also shred the vegetables through the large holes of a box grater.) Press on sweet potatoes and onion with the back of a spoon to extract as much liquid as possible.
3. Whisk eggs, flour, cilantro, chile, cumin, salt, and pepper in a large mixing bowl. Add sweet potato mixture, and stir well.

4. Heat oil in a heavy large skillet over medium-high heat. Add batter by ¼-cup measures, and flatten pancakes with a slotted spatula. Cook for 4 minutes, or until browned and crisp. Turn gently with a slotted spatula, and fry other side. Remove pancakes from the skillet, and drain on paper towels. Place pancakes in the warm oven with the door ajar, and repeat with remaining batter.

5. To serve, spread tops of pancakes with sour cream and then top with salsa. Serve immediately.

Note: The batter can be prepared up to 6 hours in advance and refrigerated, tightly covered. Also, the pancakes can be made up to 1 day in advance, and reheated in a 375°F oven for 8–10 minutes, or until hot and crispy.

Variation:

- For more all-American flavor, omit the cilantro, chile, and cumin; add 2 tablespoons firmly packed dark brown sugar and 1 teaspoon ground cinnamon to the recipe. Substitute applesauce for the salsa to top the sour cream.

When using a food processor for pureeing food, never fill it more than ⅔ full, so there's room for the food to move. But when you're chopping food finely, it needs a lot more space than that. Don't fill it more than ¼ full, or the food on the bottom will puree while the food on top does not chop.

Sautéed Tofu Patties with Wasabi Mayonnaise

Tofu, also called bean curd, is a wonderfully healthful and inexpensive form of protein, and these Asian-spiced patties are almost like burgers. The spicy mayonnaise sauce gives them creaminess, along with some bite. Serve them with some fried rice.

Yield: 4–6 servings | **Active time:** 15 minutes | **Start to finish:** 20 minutes

2 (12–14-ounce) packages firm tofu
½ cup blanched slivered almonds
½ cup mayonnaise
1½ teaspoons wasabi paste *
2 large eggs, lightly beaten
5 scallions, white parts and 4 inches of green tops, rinsed, trimmed, and thinly sliced
2 garlic cloves, peeled and minced
1 tablespoon grated fresh ginger
2 tablespoons soy sauce
Salt and freshly ground black pepper to taste
1 cup panko breadcrumbs *
3 tablespoons Asian sesame oil *
2 tablespoons vegetable oil

1. Preheat the oven to 350°F. Drain tofu, cut into 1-inch-thick slices, and wrap in several layers of paper towels. Place a pan on top of tofu, and weight the pan with 5 pounds of food cans. Allow tofu to drain for 5 minutes.

2. Meanwhile, place almonds on a baking sheet, and bake for 5–7 minutes, or until browned. Chop almonds coarsely, and set aside. Combine mayonnaise and wasabi paste in a small bowl, and stir well. Refrigerate until ready to use.

3. Transfer tofu to a medium mixing bowl, and mash into small pieces with a potato masher or a large fork. Add almonds, eggs, scallions, garlic, ginger, and soy sauce to tofu. Season to taste with salt and pepper, and mix well. Form mixture into 4–6 (½-inch-thick) patties. Pat panko crumbs on both sides.

* Available in the Asian aisle of most supermarkets and in specialty markets.

4. Heat sesame oil and vegetable oil in a large skillet over medium heat. Add tofu patties, and cook for 3–4 minutes per side, or until browned. Turn patties gently with a slotted spatula, and cook on the other side. Remove patties from the skillet, and drain on paper towels. Serve immediately, passing wasabi mayonnaise separately.

Note: The tofu mixture can be prepared up to 1 day in advance and refrigerated, tightly covered.

Variations:
- Add 1 tablespoon Chinese chile paste with garlic to the tofu mixture for a spicier dish.
- Substitute 1¼ pounds ground turkey for the tofu. Cook turkey patties over medium heat for 5–7 minutes per side, or until cooked through and no longer pink.

Wasabi, pronounced *wah-sah-bee*, is a Japanese form of horseradish that's light green and has a sharp, fiery flavor. It's sold both as paste and powder; mix the powder with water, like dry mustard, to make a paste. In a pinch you can use bottled Western horseradish.

Eggplant in Spicy Chile Sauce

Eggplant is such a "meaty" vegetable that this Chinese dish, which is relatively low in calories, is hearty enough to please even the most devout carnivore. Serve it with some steamed rice.

Yield: 4–6 servings | **Active time:** 15 minutes | **Start to finish:** 25 minutes

2 (1-pound) eggplants
1 cup Vegetable Stock (recipe on page 37) or purchased stock
2 tablespoons dry sherry
2 tablespoons soy sauce
1–2 tablespoons Chinese chile paste with garlic *
1 tablespoon rice vinegar
1½ teaspoons granulated sugar
¼ cup vegetable oil
4 garlic cloves, peeled and minced
2 tablespoons grated fresh ginger
4 scallions, white parts and 4 inches of green tops, rinsed,
    trimmed, and finely chopped
Salt and freshly ground black pepper to taste
1 tablespoon Asian sesame oil *

1. Rinse eggplant, discard stem end, and cut into ¾-inch dice. In a small bowl, stir together stock, sherry, soy sauce, chile paste, vinegar, and sugar. Set aside.
2. Heat oil in a wok or large skillet pan over high heat, swirling to coat the bottom and sides of the pan. When oil is very hot but not quite smoking, add eggplant. Cook, stirring constantly, for 2–3 minutes, or until lightly browned.
3. Add garlic, ginger, and scallions, and stir-fry 1 minute. Stir sauce and add to the pan. Cook, stirring constantly, for 3 minutes. Reduce the heat to low, cover the pan, and simmer, stirring occasionally, for 10–12 minutes, or until eggplant is tender.
4. Season to taste with salt and pepper, and drizzle with sesame oil. Serve immediately.

* Available in the Asian aisle of most supermarkets and in specialty markets.

Note: The dish can be prepared 1 day in advance and refrigerated, tightly covered. Reheat it over low heat or in a microwave oven. It can also be served at room temperature or chilled.

Variation:
- Substitute ½ pound boneless, skinless chicken breast, cut into ¾-inch cubes, for ½ pound of eggplant. It will cook in the same amount of time.

Many recipes call for eggplant to be salted or soaked, but I've found that for a stir-fried dish that is really not necessary. The high heat from the pan evaporates excess moisture.

Middle Eastern Lentil Patties

Small, lens-shaped lentils are a mainstay for protein in the lands from the Middle East to India. They have a wonderful earthy flavor that is enlivened in this dish with crunchy almonds and spices. Serve these patties with some rice or other grain.

Yield: 4-6 servings | **Active time:** 20 minutes | **Start to finish:** 35 minutes

2 cups lentils, picked over, washed, and drained
1 quart water
Salt and freshly ground black pepper to taste
$^3/_4$ cup slivered almonds
$^1/_4$ cup olive oil, divided
1 medium onion, peeled and chopped
2 garlic cloves, peeled and minced
2 teaspoons ground coriander
1 teaspoon ground cumin

1. Place lentils in a 2-quart saucepan, and cover with water and at least 1 teaspoon salt. Bring to a boil over medium-high heat, then reduce the heat to low and simmer lentils, covered, for 20-25 minutes, or until cooked. Drain lentils, and place in a mixing bowl.

2. While lentils simmer, place almonds in a small, dry skillet over medium-high heat. Toast nuts, shaking the pan frequently, for 2-3 minutes, or until browned. Chop $^1/_4$ cup of almonds, and set aside. Also, while lentils cook, heat 2 tablespoons oil in a small skillet over medium-high heat. Add onion and garlic, and cook, stirring frequently, for 3 minutes, or until onion is translucent. Add coriander and cumin, and cook, stirring constantly, for 1 minute. Add onion mixture to lentils, and stir well.

3. Puree $^1/_2$ cup unchopped almonds and 1 cup lentil mixture in a food processor fitted with the steel blade or in a blender. Scrape mixture back into mixing bowl, and add chopped almonds. Season to taste with salt and pepper. Form mixture into 4-6 patties that are $^1/_2$ inch thick.

4. Heat remaining oil in a large skillet over medium-high heat. Add patties and cook for 3–4 minutes per side, or until crisp, turning them gently with a spatula. Drain on paper towels, and serve immediately.

Note: The lentil mixture can be prepared up to 1 day in advance and refrigerated, tightly covered. However, do not stir the chopped almonds in until just prior to frying.

Variation:
- Add 1½ cups shredded cooked chicken to the lentil mixture.

Lentils are tiny lens-shape pulses and one of the oldest foods in the world. We commonly find brownish gray lentils, but they also come in bright red, green, and yellow.

Southern Fish

Catfish is the species used most commonly for this simple sautéed fish dish in the South, but you can use tilapia or whatever thin fish is fresh and the best buy. I serve it with coleslaw and biscuits to complete the theme.

Yield: 4–6 servings | **Active time:** 15 minutes | **Start to finish:** 15 minutes

1¼ pounds thin white-fleshed fish fillets
½ cup yellow cornmeal
⅓ cup pecans
2 large eggs
2 tablespoons milk
2 tablespoons Cajun seasoning
⅓ cup vegetable oil, divided

1. Rinse fish and pat dry with paper towels. Cut fish into serving pieces, if necessary.
2. Combine cornmeal and pecans in a food processor fitted with the steel blade, and chop very finely, using on-and-off pulsing. Transfer mixture to a sheet of plastic wrap. Beat eggs with milk and Cajun seasoning in a shallow bowl.
3. Heat ½ of oil in a large skillet over medium-high heat. Dip ½ of fish fillets in egg mixture, and then into crumbs, pressing crumbs to adhere to both sides. Cook for 1½–2 minutes per side, turning fish gently with a slotted spatula, or until crisp and flakes easily. Discard fat from skillet, and wipe it out with paper towels. Repeat with remaining fish and oil.

Note: The fish can be prepared for frying up to 6 hours in advance and refrigerated, tightly covered.

Variation:

- Substitute boneless, skinless chicken breast halves, pounded to an even thickness of ½ inch between 2 sheets of plastic wrap, for the fish. Cook chicken for 3–4 minutes per side, or until chicken is cooked through and no longer pink.

It's not being wasteful to discard the fat and wipe out the pan between batches of fish. Foods such as cornmeal and nuts tend to burn easily, and the second batch of fish would be in danger of tasting burnt if cooked in the original oil.

Fish Scampi

While *scampo* is the Italian word for prawn, scampi has become the term used for any Italian fish preparation that includes butter and wine. Serve this easy dish with a tossed salad and some garlic bread.

Yield: 4–6 servings | **Active time:** 15 minutes | **Start to finish:** 15 minutes

1¼ pounds thick white-fleshed fish fillets
5 tablespoons unsalted butter
2 tablespoons olive oil
4 garlic cloves, peeled and minced
1 small onion, peeled and chopped
½ cup dry white wine
¼ cup chopped fresh parsley
1 teaspoon Italian seasoning
Salt and crushed red pepper flakes to taste

1. Rinse fish and pat dry with paper towels. Cut fish into 1-inch cubes, and set aside.
2. Heat butter and oil in a large skillet over medium-high heat. When butter foam starts to subside add garlic, onion, and fish. Cook, stirring frequently, for 3 minutes, or until onion is translucent.
3. Add wine, parsley, and Italian seasoning to the skillet. Stir well, and season to taste with salt and red pepper flakes. Cook for 2 minutes. Serve immediately.

Note: The fish can be prepared for cooking up to 6 hours in advance and refrigerated, tightly covered.

Variation:
- Substitute boneless, skinless chicken breast halves, cut into ½-inch cubes, for the fish. Cook chicken for 3–4 minutes, or until chicken is cooked through and no longer pink.

While butter gives food a delicious flavor, it should never be used alone when sautéing food. The reason is that all fats burn at a certain temperature, and the dairy solids in butter make that temperature rather low. That's why in these recipes there is always some sort of oil added to raise the smoke point.

Fish with Tomatoes and Herbs

Here's another fish dish that relies mainly on items you probably stock on a regular basis. The aromatic white wine and tomato sauce enhances the delicacy of the fish, and it's great served over rice or couscous.

Yield: 4–6 servings | **Active time:** 10 minutes | **Start to finish:** 20 minutes

1¼ pounds thick white-fleshed fish fillets
Salt and freshly ground black pepper to taste
3 tablespoons olive oil
1 small onion, peeled and chopped
3 garlic cloves, peeled and minced
1 (14.5-ounce) can petite diced tomatoes, undrained
⅓ cup dry white wine
3 tablespoons chopped fresh parsley
2 teaspoons herbes de Provence

1. Rinse fish and pat dry with paper towels. Cut fish into 1-inch cubes, and sprinkle to taste with salt and pepper. Set aside.
2. Heat oil in a large skillet over medium-high heat. Add onion and garlic, and cook, stirring frequently, for 3 minutes, or until onion is translucent. Stir in tomatoes, wine, parsley, and herbes de Provence. Bring to a boil, and cook, stirring frequently, for 3 minutes.
3. Add fish, reduce the heat to medium, and cook for 5 minutes, stirring occasionally very gently, until fish is cooked through and flakes easily. Season to taste with salt and pepper, and serve immediately.

Note: The dish can be prepared for cooking up to 6 hours in advance and refrigerated, tightly covered.

Variation:
• Substitute 1-inch cubes of firm tofu for the fish.

Petite diced tomatoes are relatively new to the market, and they are great for certain dishes. They're no more expensive than the larger version, and they save the time that was formerly spent chopping larger tomatoes into smaller pieces.

Chicken with Summer Squash and Mushrooms

One of the tenets of a sautéed dish is that the vegetables used all have to be ones that are cooked quickly, and both summer squash and mushrooms qualify. The dish is lightly seasoned, so the flavors of the food become the stars. Serve this over some egg noodles.

Yield: 4–6 servings | **Active time:** 15 minutes | **Start to finish:** 30 minutes

> 1 pound boneless, skinless chicken breast halves
> Salt and freshly ground black pepper to taste
> 1/4 cup olive oil, divided
> 1 small onion, peeled and chopped
> 2 garlic cloves, peeled and minced
> 3 small yellow summer squash, rinsed, trimmed, and thinly sliced
> 1/4 pound mushrooms, wiped with a damp paper towel, trimmed, and thinly sliced
> 3/4 cup Chicken Stock (recipe on page 35) or purchased stock
> 2 tablespoons chopped fresh parsley
> 1 teaspoon Italian seasoning

1. Rinse chicken and pat dry with paper towels. Trim chicken of all visible fat, and cut into 3/4-inch cubes. Sprinkle chicken with salt and pepper.

2. Heat 2 tablespoons oil in a large skillet over medium-high heat. Add chicken, and cook, stirring constantly, for 2 minutes, or until chicken is opaque. Remove chicken from the pan with a slotted spoon, and set aside. Heat remaining oil in the skillet, and add onion, garlic, yellow squash, and mushrooms. Cook over medium-high heat, stirring frequently, for 3 minutes, or until onion is translucent.

3. Return chicken to the pan, and add stock, parsley, and Italian seasoning. Reduce the heat to medium, and cook, stirring occasionally, 7–10 minutes, or until chicken is cooked through and no longer pink. Season to taste with salt and pepper, and serve immediately.

Note: The dish can be prepared for cooking up to 6 hours in advance and refrigerated, tightly covered.

Variation:

- Substitute 1-inch cubes of thick white-fleshed fish fillets for the chicken. Add fish along with stock.

Chicken with Parsley Butter Sauce

Classic French cooking includes a whole category of sauces called compound butters; all they are is unsalted butter flavored in different ways. This is a fast and refreshing dish, with some tangy lemon juice added to balance the richness of the other flavors.

Yield: 4–6 servings | **Active time:** 20 minutes | **Start to finish:** 20 minutes

> 1¼ pounds boneless, skinless chicken thighs
> 3 tablespoons all-purpose flour
> Salt and freshly ground black pepper to taste
> ¼ cup olive oil
> 4 garlic cloves, peeled and minced
> ⅓ cup chopped fresh parsley
> 4 tablespoons (½ stick) unsalted butter
> 2 tablespoons lemon juice

1. Rinse chicken and pat dry with paper towels. Trim chicken of all visible fat. Cut chicken into ½-inch cubes. Toss chicken with flour, salt, and pepper in a bowl. Heat oil in a 12-inch skillet over high heat, add chicken cubes, and cook, stirring frequently, for 4–5 minutes, or until chicken is cooked through and no longer pink.

2. Add garlic, parsley, and butter to the skillet and cook for 1 minute, shaking the skillet occasionally to coat chicken. Add lemon juice, and season to taste with salt and pepper. Serve immediately.

Note: The dish can be prepared for cooking up to 6 hours in advance, and refrigerated, tightly covered.

Variation:
- Substitute cubes of thick firm-fleshed white fish fillets, cut into 1-inch cubes, for the chicken.

Garlicky Spanish Chicken

It doesn't get much easier than this recipe; there are just a few ingredients and it's on the table in a matter of minutes. I usually serve it with a loaf of crusty bread, along with a tossed salad, to enjoy every drop of the garlicky sauce.

Yield: 4-6 servings | **Active time:** 10 minutes | **Start to finish:** 20 minutes

1¼ pounds boneless, skinless chicken breast halves
½ cup olive oil
8 garlic cloves, peeled and minced
2 tablespoons smoked Spanish paprika
3 tablespoons chopped fresh parsley
Salt and red pepper flakes to taste

1. Rinse chicken and pat dry with paper towels. Trim chicken of all visible fat, and cut into ¾-inch cubes.
2. Heat oil in a large skillet over medium-high heat. Add garlic and paprika, and cook for 1 minute, stirring constantly. Add chicken and parsley, and cook, stirring constantly, for 3-4 minutes, or until chicken is cooked through and no longer pink. Season to taste with salt and red pepper flakes, and serve immediately.

Note: The chicken can be prepared up to 3 hours in advance and served at room temperature.

Variation:
- Substitute thick white-fleshed fish fillets, cut into ¾-inch cubes, for the chicken. Cook for 2-3 minutes, or until fish is opaque and flakes easily.

Beef Stroganoff

Few women who learned how to cook in the 1960s didn't list beef Stroganoff, named for an Eastern European count, as dinner party fare. It went out of fashion, but it's truly delicious, with sour cream enriching the tomato-scented sauce. Serve it over buttered egg noodles.

Yield: 4–6 servings | **Active time:** 25 minutes | **Start to finish:** 25 minutes

> 1 pound sirloin tips
> Salt and freshly ground black pepper to taste
> 3 tablespoons unsalted butter, divided
> 2 tablespoons all-purpose flour
> 1½ cups Beef Stock (recipe on page 36) or purchased stock
> 2 tablespoons tomato paste
> 4 tablespoons olive oil, divided
> 1 small onion, peeled and diced
> 2 garlic cloves, peeled and minced
> ¾ pound mushrooms, wiped with a damp paper towel, trimmed, and sliced
> ⅓ cup sour cream
> 2 teaspoons Dijon mustard
> 2 tablespoons chopped fresh parsley

1. Rinse beef and pat dry with paper towels. Slice beef into ½-inch slices against the grain. Season to taste with salt and pepper, and set aside.

2. Melt 2 tablespoons butter in a small saucepan over medium heat. Stir in flour, and cook, stirring constantly, for 1 minute. Add stock in a slow stream, whisking constantly, and bring to a boil. Whisk in tomato paste. Reduce the heat and simmer, whisking occasionally, for 3 minutes. Remove the pan from the heat, and cover to keep warm.

3. While sauce simmers, heat 2 tablespoons olive oil in a large skillet over medium-high heat. Add beef and cook, turning gently with a spatula, until browned on both side but still pink inside, about 1 minute total time. Remove meat from the skillet. Set aside.

4. Heat remaining butter and remaining oil in the skillet over medium-high heat. Add onion, garlic, and mushrooms, and cook, stirring frequently, for 5–7 minutes, or until mushrooms are soft.

5. Return meat to the skillet, along with any juices that have accumulated. Add sauce, and bring to a boil. Remove the pan from the heat, and whisk in sour cream, mustard, and parsley. *Do not allow sauce to boil.* Season to taste with salt and pepper, and serve immediately.

Note: The dish can be prepared 1 day in advance and refrigerated, tightly covered. Reheat it over low heat, covered, until hot.

Variation:
- Substitute boneless pork loin for the beef, and substitute chicken stock for the beef stock.

A substitute for sour cream, that does not curdle when it boils, is crème fraîche. While it's far more expensive than sour cream at the supermarket, you can make it at home by adding 1–2 tablespoons of cultured buttermilk to 2 cups of pasteurized (not ultra-pasteurized) heavy cream and letting the mixture stand at room temperature for 8–24 hours until thick.

Pepper Steak

Here's a Chinese-American dish that always pleases a crowd. The beef is quickly stir-fried with onion and bell peppers in a mild sauce. Serve it with steamed rice or fried rice, and the meal is complete.

Yield: 4–6 servings | **Active time:** 30 minutes | **Start to finish:** 30 minutes

1 pound flank steak
¼ cup soy sauce, divided
2 tablespoons dry sherry
2 tablespoons Asian sesame oil *
½ cup Beef Stock (recipe on page 36) or purchased stock
2 tablespoons Chinese fermented black beans, finely chopped *
1 tablespoon cornstarch
2 teaspoons granulated sugar
5 tablespoons vegetable oil, divided
4 garlic cloves, peeled and minced
2 tablespoons grated fresh ginger
½ teaspoon crushed red pepper flakes or to taste
1 large sweet onion, such as Vidalia or Bermuda, peeled, halved lengthwise, and thinly sliced
2 large green bell peppers, seeds and ribs removed, and thinly sliced

1. Rinse steak and pat dry with paper towels. Trim steak of all visible fat. Cut steak in into thirds lengthwise, and then slice each piece thinly against the grain. Toss beef with 3 tablespoons soy sauce, sherry, and sesame oil. Combine remaining soy sauce, stock, black beans, cornstarch, and sugar in a small bowl. Stir well, and set aside.

2. Heat 3 tablespoons vegetable oil in a heavy wok or skillet over high heat, swirling to coat the pan. Add beef and stir-fry for 2 minutes, or until slices separate and are no longer red. Remove beef from the pan with a slotted spoon, and set aside. Discard grease from the pan, and wipe out the pan with paper towels.

* Available in the Asian aisle of most supermarkets and in specialty markets.

3. Heat remaining oil over high heat, swirling to coat. Add garlic, ginger, and red pepper flakes, and stir-fry for 15 seconds, or until fragrant. Add onion and bell peppers and stir-fry for 2 minutes. Add sauce, and stir-fry for 2 minutes, or until slightly thickened.
4. Return beef to the pan, and stir-fry until heated through. Serve immediately.

Note: The dish can be prepared for cooking up to 6 hours in advance and refrigerated, tightly covered.

Variation:
• Substitute boneless pork loin for the beef.

Cutting meats and chicken breasts against the grain is a key to success. Shreds are cut with the grain to become like matchsticks, while thin slices cut against the grain are much more tender because the length of the muscle filaments is so short.

Curried Beef and Vegetables

This recipe is a hybrid of Asian and Caribbean cuisines, which are united by their use of curry powder. Some chopped dried apricots add a sweet nuance, and healthful vegetables complement the hearty beef. Serve it over rice or egg noodles.

Yield: 4–6 servings | **Active time:** 15 minutes | **Start to finish:** 30 minutes

1 pound sirloin tips
3 tablespoons vegetable oil
6 scallions, white parts and 4 inches of green tops, rinsed, trimmed, and sliced, divided
3 garlic cloves, peeled and minced
2 tablespoons grated fresh ginger
2 tablespoons curry powder, or to taste
1 cup coconut milk
$\frac{1}{4}$ cup dry sherry
$\frac{1}{4}$ cup soy sauce
2 large carrots, peeled and thinly sliced on the diagonal
2 celery ribs, rinsed, trimmed, and thinly sliced on the diagonal
1 cup shredded green cabbage
$\frac{1}{2}$ cup chopped dried apricots
1 tablespoon cornstarch
2 tablespoons cold water
Salt and freshly ground black pepper to taste

1. Rinse beef and pat dry with paper towels. Cut beef into $\frac{1}{2}$-inch slices against the grain, and set aside.
2. Heat oil in a wok or large skillet over high heat. Add beef, and stir-fry for 1–2 minutes, or until no longer red. Remove beef from the pan with a slotted spoon, and set aside. Add $\frac{2}{3}$ of scallions, garlic, and ginger to the pan, and stir-fry for 30 seconds, or until fragrant. Stir in curry powder, and cook for 30 seconds.
3. Stir coconut milk, sherry, and soy sauce into the skillet, and bring to a boil, stirring frequently. Add carrots, celery, cabbage, and dried apricots. Bring to a boil, reduce the heat to medium-low, and simmer mixture, stirring occasionally, for 5–7 minutes, or until vegetables are crisp-tender.

4. Mix cornstarch and water in a small cup. Return beef to the pan, and stir in cornstarch mixture. Cook for 2 minutes, or until slightly thickened. Season to taste with salt and pepper, and serve immediately, sprinkled with remaining scallions.

Note: The dish can be prepared for cooking up to 6 hours in advance and refrigerated, tightly covered.

Variations:
- Substitute 1 pound boneless, skinless chicken breast, cut into 3/4-inch cubes, for the beef. Add chicken back into the pan along with vegetables, and cook until chicken is cooked through and no longer pink.
- Substitute 2 (12–14-ounce) packages firm tofu, drained and cut into 1-inch cubes, for the beef.

While it's a good idea to toss out any dried herb or spice that's been opened for more than 6 months, abbreviate the life of curry powder to 2 months. This ground blend, made of up to 20 herbs and spices, loses its flavor and aroma very quickly.

Spicy Korean Beef

Koreans frequently serve this sweet and spicy dish in cups made from lettuce leaves, and if you want to do that, it adds another vegetable to the meal. Otherwise, serve it over rice.

Yield: 4–6 servings | **Active time:** 20 minutes | **Start to finish:** 20 minutes

> 1 pound sirloin tips
> ¼ cup soy sauce
> 2 tablespoons Asian sesame oil *
> 2 tablespoons firmly packed dark brown sugar
> 6 garlic cloves, peeled and minced
> 1 tablespoon grated fresh ginger
> ½–1 teaspoon crushed red pepper flakes, or to taste
> 1 tablespoon cornstarch
> 3 tablespoons vegetable oil, divided
> 1 medium sweet onion, such as Vidalia or Bermuda, peeled, halved, and cut into ½-inch slices
> 1 green bell pepper, seeds and ribs removed, and cut into ½-inch strips

1. Rinse beef and pat dry with paper towels. Cut beef into ½-inch slices against the grain. Place beef in a mixing bowl. Combine soy sauce, sesame oil, brown sugar, garlic, ginger, and red pepper flakes in a small bowl, and stir well. Toss beef with ½ of mixture and cornstarch.
2. Heat 1 tablespoon oil over high heat, swirling to coat the pan. Add onion and green bell pepper, and stir-fry for 3 minutes. Remove vegetables from the pan with a slotted spoon, and set aside.
3. Heat remaining oil in the pan, swirling to coat the pan. Add beef, and stir-fry for 1–2 minutes, or until no pink remains. Return vegetables to the pan, and add remaining sauce mixture. Cook for 1 minute, or until slightly thickened. Serve immediately.

Note: The dish can be prepared for cooking up to 6 hours in advance, and refrigerated, tightly covered.

Variation:
- Substitute boneless pork loin for the beef.

* Available in the Asian aisle of most supermarkets and in specialty markets.

Spicy Orange Beef and Broccoli

Using orange marmalade gives this fast and easy stir-fry a slightly fruity flavor. Serve it with rice.

Yield: 4–6 servings | **Active time:** 25 minutes | **Start to finish:** 25 minutes

        1 pound sirloin tips
        1 pound head broccoli
        ³/₄ cup Beef Stock (recipe on page 36) or purchased stock, divided
        3 tablespoons orange marmalade
        2 tablespoons soy sauce
        2 tablespoons oyster sauce*
        1 tablespoon rice vinegar
        2 teaspoons Chinese chile paste with garlic*
        1 tablespoon cornstarch
        2 tablespoons vegetable oil
        6 scallions, white parts and 4 inches of green tops, rinsed,
            trimmed, and cut into 1-inch lengths
        Salt and freshly ground black pepper to taste

1. Rinse beef and pat dry with paper towels. Cut beef against the grain into ¹/₂-inch slices, and set aside. Cut florets off broccoli spears, peel stems, and slice stems. Combine ¹/₄ cup stock, marmalade, soy sauce, oyster sauce, vinegar, chile paste, and cornstarch in a small bowl, and stir well.

2. Heat oil in a large, covered skillet over high heat, swirling to coat the pan. Add beef, and stir-fry for 1 minute, or until both sides are browned. Remove beef from the skillet with a slotted spoon, and set aside. Add scallions and broccoli to the skillet, and stir-fry for 1 minute. Add remaining stock, cover the skillet, and steam vegetables for 2–4 minutes, or until broccoli is crisp-tender.

3. Return beef to the skillet; add sauce mixture. Cook for 1¹/₂–2 minutes, or until slightly thickened. Season to taste with salt and pepper, and serve immediately.

Note: The dish can be prepped up to 6 hours in advance and refrigerated, tightly covered. Do not cook it until just prior to serving.

Variation:
*   Substitute asparagus for the broccoli.
*   Substitute boneless pork loin for the beef, and substitute chicken stock for the beef stock.

* Available in the Asian aisle of most supermarkets and in specialty markets.

Pork Scaloppine

This fast and easy meal is an adaptation of a classic Italian recipe made with veal. Pork has the same delicacy—at a fraction of the cost. It's breaded with crumbs seasoned with herbs and cheese and then topped with sautéed mushrooms.

Yield: 4–6 servings | **Active time:** 25 minutes | **Start to finish:** 25 minutes

1¼ pounds boneless pork loin
Salt and freshly ground black pepper to taste
2 large eggs
2 cups Italian breadcrumbs
⅓ cup freshly grated Parmesan cheese
2 teaspoon Italian seasoning
⅓ cup olive oil, divided
3 tablespoons unsalted butter
1 small onion, peeled and chopped
2 garlic cloves, peeled and minced
½ pound mushrooms, wiped with a damp paper towel, trimmed, and sliced
⅓ cup lemon juice
2 tablespoons chopped fresh parsley

1. Preheat the oven to 150°F, and line a baking sheet with aluminum foil. Rinse pork and pat dry with paper towels. Cut pork into ¼-inch slices, and sprinkle with salt and pepper.
2. Beat eggs with a fork in a shallow bowl. Combine breadcrumbs, cheese, and Italian seasoning in another shallow bowl. Dip meat slices into egg, letting any excess drip off, then dip meat into crumb mixture, pressing crumbs into meat on both sides.
3. Heat ¼ cup olive oil in a large skillet over medium-high heat. Cook pork for 1½ minutes, or until nicely browned. Turn gently with tongs, and cook the second side. Drain slices on paper towels. Transfer pork to the baking sheet, and place it in the oven to keep warm.

4. Discard oil from the skillet, and wipe it with paper towels. Heat remaining olive oil and butter over medium-high heat. Add onion and garlic, and cook, stirring frequently, for 3 minutes, or until onion is translucent. Add mushrooms and cook, stirring frequently, for 5–7 minutes, or until mushrooms are lightly browned and most of liquid has evaporated. Stir in lemon juice and parsley, and season to taste with salt and pepper.
5. Remove pork from the oven. Spoon mushrooms over pork, and serve immediately.

Note: The pork can be prepared up to frying up to 6 hours in advance and refrigerated, tightly covered. The mushroom mixture can be made 1 day in advance and refrigerated, tightly covered. Reheat the mushrooms over medium heat, stirring occasionally.

Variation:
- Substitute chicken breasts, pounded to a thickness of ¼ inch, for pork. The chicken should be cooked for 2 minutes per side, or until cooked through and no longer pink.

These breadcrumbs have already been seasoned, and you can add ¼ cup freshly grated Parmesan cheese, 1 tablespoon Italian seasoning, and ½ teaspoon salt to each 1 cup plain breadcrumbs to replicate the flavor.

Stir-Fried Pork and Oranges

Sweet oranges, colorful broccoli, and traditional Asian seasonings are joined in this dish. All you need to complete the meal is some rice; the vegetables are right in the dish.

Yield: 4–6 servings | **Active time:** 20 minutes | **Start to finish:** 20 minutes

> 2 navel oranges, rinsed in warm soapy water
> 3 tablespoons soy sauce
> ½–1 teaspoon crushed red pepper flakes
> 1 pound boneless pork loin
> 3 tablespoons Asian sesame oil *
> 6 scallions, white parts and 4 inches of green tops, rinsed, trimmed, and chopped, divided
> 2 garlic cloves, peeled and minced
> 1 tablespoon grated fresh ginger
> 2 cups broccoli florets
> 1 tablespoon cornstarch
> 2 tablespoons cold water

1. Grate zest of 1 orange into a mixing bowl, and squeeze juice from orange. Add soy sauce and red pepper flakes to the mixing bowl, and set aside. Peel and cut white pith from other orange, and dice flesh into ¾-inch cubes. Set aside. Cut pork into ½-inch slices, then stack slices, and cut into thin strips. Set aside.

2. Heat oil in a wok or large, heavy skillet over high heat, swirling to coat the pan. Add pork, and stir-fry for 1–2 minutes, or until pork is no longer pink. Remove pork from the pan with a slotted spoon, and set aside.

3. Add ⅔ of scallions, garlic, and ginger to the pan, and stir-fry for 30 seconds, or until fragrant. Add broccoli, and stir-fry for 2 minutes. Return pork to the pan and add orange and orange juice mixture. Cook for 3 minutes, or until broccoli is crisp-tender.

* Available in the Asian aisle of most supermarkets and in specialty markets.

4. Mix cornstarch with water in a small cup. Add to the pan, and cook for 1 minute, or until slightly thickened. Stir in remaining scallions, and serve immediately.

Note: The dish can be prepared for cooking up to 6 hours in advance and refrigerated.

Variation:
- Substitute flank steak or sirloin tips for the pork.

Many times citrus fruits are coated with wax before being shipped to keep them fresh longer. If using the zest of a citrus fruit, such as in this recipe, it's always a good idea to wash the fruit with soapy water to remove the wax coating.

Chapter 7:
Simmer and Skillet Suppers

Long before there were mixes on the market into which you had to add the protein, there were dishes termed "skillet suppers" that were essentially the same thing—whole meals, perhaps minus a salad, that were cooked in one pan. Those are the recipes you'll find in this chapter.

The other category of dishes in this chapter is stove-cooked stews in sauce. For these you'll have to come up with a quick-cooking carbohydrate to enjoy the sauce. One way to save time (and pot washing) is to make large batches of foods like steamed rice, brown rice, and grains. Freeze them in packages the right size for your family, and thaw them in the microwave while dinner cooks.

The reason why foods cook faster on top of the stove compared with in the oven is that the direct heat of the burner heats the metal of the pot, instead of the indirect heat of the oven. Think of it this way: if you're standing on a hot sidewalk, the bottoms of your feet are getting direct heat, but if you're lounging in a chair in the shade on a summer day, your whole body is feeling indirect heat.

The direct heat is why these dishes need tending on the stove, but not for very long. In Chapter 8 you'll find dishes that take a bit longer to cook because they're in the oven, but they don't require your constant attention.

Curried Rice with Cauliflower

Cauliflower, a member of the cabbage family, is frequently the star player in Indian cuisine, as in this one-dish meal with vibrant curry flavor. The rice is cooked right along with the vegetable, too.

Yield: 6–8 servings | **Active time:** 15 minutes | **Start to finish:** 35 minutes

> 3 tablespoons olive oil
> 1/2 green bell pepper, seeds and ribs removed, and finely chopped
> 1 small onion, peeled and diced
> 3 garlic cloves, peeled and minced
> 2 tablespoons grated fresh ginger
> 1–2 tablespoons curry powder
> 1 1/2 cups long-grain white rice
> 2 cups small cauliflower florets
> 3 cups Vegetable Stock (recipe on page 37) or purchased stock
> Salt and freshly ground black pepper to taste

1. Heat oil in a large saucepan over medium-high heat. Add green pepper, onion, and garlic, and cook, stirring frequently, for 3 minutes, or until onion is translucent. Add ginger and curry powder, and cook 30 seconds, stirring constantly. Add rice, and cook for 1 minute, stirring constantly.

2. Add cauliflower and stock, and bring to a boil, stirring occasionally. Reduce the heat to low, cover the pan, and simmer for 15–20 minutes, or until water is absorbed and rice is tender. Remove the pan from heat, and let it stand covered for 5 minutes. Fluff rice with a fork, season to taste with salt and pepper, and serve immediately.

Note: The dish can be prepared up to 2 days in advance and refrigerated, tightly covered. Reheat it, covered, in a 350°F oven for 20–25 minutes, or until hot.

Spicy Garbanzo Bean and Kale Stew

Iron-rich kale adds texture, and color, to this bean stew flavored with chili powder. Kale is the renegade cousin of the cabbage family. Its flavor is very mild, and it has frilly, deep-green leaves that look like a bouquet of flowers rather than a tight head. For best results, buy small heads that are perky and not limp.

Yield: 4–6 servings | **Active time:** 15 minutes | **Start to finish:** 40 minutes

1¼ pounds kale
¼ cup olive oil
2 medium onions, peeled and diced
3 garlic cloves, peeled and minced
2 green bell peppers, seeds and ribs removed, and chopped
2 tablespoons chili powder
1 teaspoon dried thyme
1 teaspoon dried oregano
1 teaspoon ground cumin
1 teaspoon granulated sugar
½ teaspoon crushed red pepper flakes, or to taste
1 bay leaf
2 (15-ounce) cans garbanzo beans, drained and rinsed
1 (28-ounce) can diced plum tomatoes, undrained
2 cups Vegetable Stock (recipe on page 37) or purchased stock
1 (6-ounce) can tomato paste
Salt and freshly ground black pepper to taste

1. Discard coarse stems from kale and rinse well. Chop leaves, and set aside.
2. Heat olive oil in a large saucepan over medium-high heat. Add onions and garlic, and cook, stirring frequently, for 3 minutes, or until onions are translucent. Add green bell peppers, and cook for an additional 2 minutes. Add chili powder, thyme, oregano, cumin, sugar, red pepper flakes, and bay leaf. Cook, stirring constantly, for 1 minute.
3. Add garbanzo beans, tomatoes, stock, and tomato paste, and bring to a boil, stirring occasionally. Reduce the heat to low, and cook, covered, for 25–30 minutes, or until kale is tender.

4. Remove and discard bay leaf, and season to taste with salt and pepper. Serve immediately.

Note: The dish can be made up to 2 days in advance and refrigerated, tightly covered. Reheat it over low heat, covered, until hot, stirring occasionally.

Variations:
- Substitute black beans for the garbanzo beans.
- Add ¾ pound boneless, skinless chicken thighs, cut into ½-inch dice, and substitute chicken stock for the vegetable stock.

The antioxidant phytonutrients in kale and other members of the cabbage family have been found to actually signal our genes to increase production of enzymes involved in detoxification, the cleansing process through which our bodies eliminate harmful compounds.

Asian Black Bean "Chili"

This is as hearty a bean dish as you could find in any cuisine; the black beans are flavored with a wide range of Asian flavors. Serve it over aromatic jasmine rice to form a complete protein.

Yield: 4–6 servings | **Active time:** 15 minutes | **Start to finish:** 30 minutes

2 tablespoons Asian sesame oil *
8 scallions, white parts and 3 inches of green tops, rinsed, trimmed, and sliced
3 garlic cloves, peeled and minced
2 tablespoons grated fresh ginger
3 (15-ounce) cans black beans, drained and rinsed
1¼ cups Vegetable Stock (recipe on page 37) or purchased stock
½ cup dry sherry
¼ cup hoisin sauce *
¼ cup soy sauce
3 tablespoons rice vinegar
2 tablespoons Chinese black bean sauce *
2 teaspoons Chinese chile paste with garlic *
2 teaspoons granulated sugar
Salt and freshly ground black pepper to taste
½ cup chopped fresh cilantro

1. Heat sesame oil in a 3-quart saucepan over medium-high heat. Add scallions, garlic, and ginger, and cook, stirring constantly, for 30 seconds, or until fragrant. Add beans, stock, sherry, hoisin sauce, soy sauce, vinegar, black bean sauce, chile paste, and sugar, and bring to a boil over high heat, stirring occasionally.
2. Reduce the heat to low, and cook mixture, covered, for 15 minutes. Season to taste with salt and pepper, and stir in cilantro. Serve immediately over rice.

* Available in the Asian aisle of most supermarkets and in specialty markets.

Note: The dish can be made up to 2 days in advance and refrigerated, tightly covered. Reheat it over low heat, covered, until hot, stirring occasionally.

Proper storage can give extra life to leafy herbs like cilantro, parsley, and dill. Treat them like a bouquet of flowers; trim the stems when you get home from the market and then stand the bunch in a glass with its roots—but not its leaves—in water in the refrigerator.

Zucchini Chili

Cubes of tender zucchini take the place of meat or poultry in this authentically seasoned Texas chili, which should be served over rice with a tossed salad. Because it calls for canned beans, it's on the table in a matter of minutes.

Yield: 4–6 servings | **Active time:** 15 minutes | **Start to finish:** 35 minutes

    1 pound small zucchini
    2 tablespoons olive oil
    1 large onion, peeled and diced
    ½ green bell pepper, seeds and ribs removed, and chopped
    3 garlic cloves, peeled and minced
    3 tablespoons chili powder
    1 tablespoon ground cumin
    2 teaspoon dried oregano
    1 (15-ounce) can red kidney beans, drained and rinsed
    1 (28-ounce) can crushed tomatoes in tomato puree
    1 (4-ounce) can diced mild green chiles, drained
    2 tablespoons tomato paste
    1 tablespoon granulated sugar
    Salt and cayenne to taste

1. Rinse and trim zucchini. Cut zucchini lengthwise into quarters and then into ½-inch slices. Soak zucchini in a bowl of salted cold water for 10 minutes. Drain, and set aside.

2. While zucchini soaks, heat oil in a medium saucepan over medium-high heat. Add onion, green bell pepper, and garlic, and cook, stirring frequently, for 3 minutes, or until onion is translucent. Reduce the heat to low, and stir in chili powder, cumin, and oregano. Cook for 1 minute, stirring constantly.

3. Add zucchini, kidney beans, tomatoes, green chiles, tomato paste, and sugar to the pan, and bring to a boil over medium-high heat, stirring occasionally. Reduce the heat to low, and cook, partially covered, stirring occasionally, for 15 minutes, or until zucchini is tender. Season to taste with salt and cayenne, and serve immediately.

Note: The dish can be made up to 2 days in advance and refrigerated, tightly covered. Reheat it over low heat, covered, until hot, stirring occasionally.

Variations:
- Substitute yellow squash, and prepare it exactly like the zucchini.
- Substitute thinly sliced carrots; they will not need soaking but will cook in the same amount of time as the zucchini.

You might think it's wasting time to allow the zucchini to soak in salted water, but here is the reason to do it: It keeps the squash from becoming mushy when it cooks with the other ingredients.

Fish with Lemon Sauce

This simple poached fish is incredibly elegant to serve guests, and they'll never know how easy it was to make. Serve it with some sautéed zucchini and steamed rice.

Yield: 4-6 servings | **Active time:** 10 minutes | **Start to finish:** 20 minutes

1¼ pounds thin white-fleshed fish fillets
1 lemon
Salt and freshly ground black pepper to taste
¾ cup dry white wine
½ teaspoon dried thyme
3 tablespoons lemon juice
3 tablespoons unsalted butter, cut into tiny bits

1. Rinse fish and pat dry with paper towels. Cut into serving pieces, if necessary. Grate 1 teaspoon lemon zest off ends of lemon. Then thinly slice lemon, discarding seeds. Fold each fillet in half, and top with lemon slices. Sprinkle fish with salt and pepper.
2. Arrange fish in a medium skillet, and add lemon zest, wine, and thyme. Bring to a boil over medium heat, covered. Reduce the heat to low, and simmer fish for 3 minutes. Turn gently with a slotted spatula, and cook for an additional 3 minutes, or until fish is opaque and flakes easily. Remove fish from the skillet, and keep warm.
3. Cook wine over high heat until reduced by ½. Stir in lemon juice, and remove the pan from the stove. Whisk in butter, a few bits at a time, whisking until butter melts before adding next bits. Season sauce to taste with salt and pepper, and spoon sauce over fish. Serve immediately.

Note: If the sauce cools off so that the butter is not melting, place the pan back on the stove over very low heat. But do not allow sauce to boil.

Variation:

- Substitute 1 lime and lime juice for the lemon and lemon juice.

This easy sauce is called a *beurre blanc* in French cooking, and it's one of the hallmarks of French *nouvelle cuisine*. The sauce becomes thickened by an emulsion with the butter so it has a satiny quality to it.

Creole Fish

Those wonderful flavors of tomato, vegetables, and Creole herbs and spices make this dish special. Serve it with some rice and stewed red beans for a true Louisiana experience.

Yield: 4–6 servings | **Active time:** 25 minutes | **Start to finish:** 30 minutes

1¼ pounds thick white-fleshed fish fillets, cut into serving pieces
2 tablespoons olive oil
1 medium onion, peeled and finely chopped
2 celery ribs, rinsed, trimmed, and finely chopped
3 garlic cloves, peeled and minced
1 green bell pepper, seeds and ribs removed, finely chopped
½ cup Seafood Stock (recipe on page 38), purchased stock, or bottled clam juice
½ cup dry white wine
1 (14.5-ounce) can diced tomatoes, undrained
1 (8-ounce) can tomato sauce
½–1 teaspoon hot red pepper sauce, or to taste
3 tablespoons chopped fresh parsley
1 bay leaf
½ teaspoon dried thyme
Salt and freshly ground black pepper to taste

1. Rinse fish, and pat dry with paper towels. Set aside. Heat oil in a large skillet over medium-high heat. Add onions, celery, garlic, and green pepper. Cook, stirring frequently, for 3 minutes, or until onion is translucent.

2. Add stock, wine, tomatoes, tomato sauce, red pepper sauce, parsley, bay leaf, and thyme. Bring to a boil over medium heat, stirring occasionally. Add fish, reduce the heat to low, and poach fish, partially covered, for 4–6 minutes, depending on thickness. Turn fish gently with a slotted spatula, and poach an additional 4–6 minutes, or until cooked through and flakes easily.

3. Remove fish from the pan with a slotted spatula, and keep warm. Raise the heat to high and reduce sauce by ⅓, stirring frequently. Remove and discard bay leaf, and season sauce to taste with salt and pepper. To serve, spoon sauce over fish.

Note: The sauce can be prepared up to 2 days in advance and refrigerated, tightly covered. The fish is best cooked just prior to serving, but it can be served at room temperature or cold as well as hot.

Variation:

- Substitute 4–6 boneless, skinless chicken thighs for the fish, and substitute chicken stock for the seafood stock. Poach chicken for a total of 15 minutes, or until cooked through and no longer pink.

> To poach is to cook food gently in liquid that is barely simmering, just at the boiling point. This way of cooking preserves tenderness of what's being cooked, be it an egg or a fish steak.

Chicken and Rice in Mustard Sauce

Here's an easy one-skillet meal in which the chicken, dried fruit, and rice are cooked in apricot nectar enlivened with sharp Dijon mustard. Serve it with a tossed salad.

Yield: 4–6 servings | **Active time:** 15 minutes | **Start to finish:** 35 minutes

  1 pound boneless, skinless chicken breast halves
  Salt and freshly ground black pepper to taste
  2 tablespoons vegetable oil
  1 small onion, peeled and minced
  2 garlic cloves, peeled and minced
  1 green bell pepper, seeds and ribs removed, and thinly sliced
  1½ cups long-grain rice
  2 cups apricot nectar
  ¾ cup Chicken Stock (recipe on page 35) or purchased stock
  3 tablespoons Dijon mustard
  ⅓ cup chopped dried apricots
  ⅓ cup raisins, preferably golden raisins
  1 (10-ounce) package frozen peas, thawed

1. Rinse chicken and pat dry with paper towels. Cut chicken into 1-inch cubes, and sprinkle chicken with salt and pepper. Heat oil in a large, deep skillet over medium-high heat. Add chicken, and cook, stirring frequently, for 2 minutes, or until chicken is opaque. Remove chicken from the pan with a slotted spoon, and set aside.

2. Add onion and garlic, and cook, stirring frequently, for 3 minutes, or until onion is translucent. Add green pepper and rice, and cook, stirring frequently, for 2 minutes. Return chicken to pan, and add apricot nectar, chicken stock, mustard, dried apricots, and raisins. Bring to a boil, stirring occasionally. Cover the pan, reduce the heat to low, and simmer 15 minutes.

3. Stir in peas, cover the pan again, and cook for 3–5 minutes, or until chicken is tender and no longer pink, and rice has absorbed all liquid. Serve immediately.

Note: The dish can be prepared up to 2 days in advance and refrigerated, tightly covered. Reheat it, covered, in a 350°F oven for 20–25 minutes, or until hot.

Variation:

- Substitute boneless pork loin for the chicken.

Dijon mustard is made from a combination of brown and black mustard seeds, and the essential ingredients are white wine and unfermented grape juice. While Grey Poupon is a best known American brand, there are dozens of French producers, many of which also flavor their mustard.

Spicy Southwestern Chicken with Black Beans

Chicken is cooked with chiles and spices, and then turned into a healthful stew with black beans. Serve this quick and easy stew over rice, with a tossed salad alongside.

Yield: 4–6 servings | **Active time:** 15 minutes | **Start to finish:** 30 minutes

> ³/₄ pound boneless, skinless chicken breast halves
> 2 tablespoons olive oil
> 2 medium onions, peeled and diced
> 5 garlic cloves, peeled and minced
> 2 jalapeño or serrano chiles, seeds and ribs removed, and finely chopped
> 1 tablespoon ground cumin
> 1 teaspoon dried oregano
> 1 (14.5-ounce) can diced tomatoes, drained
> 2 (15-ounce) cans black beans, drained and rinsed
> 1¹/₂ cups Chicken Stock (recipe on page 35) or purchased stock
> 3 tablespoons chopped fresh cilantro
> ¹/₂ teaspoon dried thyme
> Salt and freshly ground black pepper to taste

1. Rinse chicken and pat dry with paper towels. Trim chicken of all visible fat, and cut into ³/₄-inch cubes.
2. Heat oil in a large, deep skillet over medium-high heat. Add chicken, onion, garlic, and chiles, and cook, stirring frequently, for 3 minutes, or until onions are translucent. Add cumin and oregano, and cook for 1 minute, stirring constantly.
3. Add tomatoes, beans, stock, cilantro, and thyme to the pan. Bring to a boil, reduce the heat to low, and simmer, uncovered, for 10–12 minutes, or until chicken is cooked through and no longer pink. Season to taste with salt and pepper, and serve immediately.

Note: The dish can be prepared 1 day in advance and refrigerated, tightly covered. Reheat it over low heat in a saucepan.

Variation:

- Substitute 1-inch cubes of firm tofu for the chicken, and use vegetable stock in the bean mixture.

Be careful when cooking hot chiles that the steam from the pan doesn't get in your eyes. The potent oils in the peppers can be transmitted in the vapor.

Skillet Chicken and Broccoli with Orzo

Orzo, a small rice-shaped pasta, looks very much like Arborio rice, and it functions like it in this dish, which is like a cross between risotto and baked mac and cheese. A tossed salad is all you need to complete the meal.

Yield: 4–6 servings | **Active time:** 10 minutes | **Start to finish:** 30 minutes

> 1 pound boneless, skinless chicken breast halves
> Salt and freshly ground black pepper to taste
> 3 tablespoons unsalted butter
> 1 large onion, peeled and chopped
> 3 garlic cloves, peeled and chopped
> 2 cups orzo
> 3 cups Chicken Stock (recipe on page 35) or purchased stock
> 1 teaspoon dried thyme
> 2 (10-ounce) packages frozen broccoli spears, thawed and sliced
>   into 1-inch pieces
> 1½ cups grated sharp cheddar cheese

1. Rinse chicken and pat dry with paper towels. Cut chicken into 1-inch cubes, and sprinkle with salt and pepper.
2. Heat butter in large deep skillet over medium-high heat. Add chicken and cook, stirring frequently, for 3–4 minutes, or until chicken is opaque. Remove chicken from the pan with a slotted spoon, and set aside.
3. Add onion, garlic, and orzo to skillet, and cook, stirring frequently, for 3 minutes, or until onion is translucent. Add stock and thyme to the pan. Bring to a boil, then reduce heat to low, and cook for 5 minutes. Return chicken to the pan and stir in broccoli. Cover the pan, and cook, stirring occasionally, for 12–14 minutes, or until chicken is cooked through and no longer pink and orzo is soft.
4. Stir cheese into the skillet, and cook for 2 minutes, stirring occasionally, or until cheese melts. Season to taste with salt and pepper, and serve immediately.

Note: The dish can be prepared up to 2 days in advance and refrigerated, tightly covered. Reheat it, covered, in a 350°F oven for 20–25 minutes, or until hot.

Variation:
- Substitute Swiss cheese for the cheddar cheese.

It's important not to stir cheese into a dish until the very end of the cooking time. The dairy solids in cheese cause it to scorch very quickly, and that flavor can ruin an entire dish. Unless otherwise directed, cheese is the final enrichment right before a dish is served.

Balsamic Sweet and Sour Chicken

Dishes such as this one that are inherently low in fat are great candidates to be served at room temperature or chilled as well as hot. You wouldn't want to eat butter that's been chilled, but this light sauce works fine.

Yield: 4–6 servings | **Active time:** 15 minutes | **Start to finish:** 20 minutes

1¼ pounds boneless, skinless chicken breast halves
⅔ cup dry white wine
½ cup orange juice
½ cup balsamic vinegar
1 cup raisins, preferably golden raisins
2 tablespoons olive oil
½ teaspoon dried thyme
Salt and freshly ground black pepper to taste

1. Rinse chicken and pat dry with paper towels. Trim chicken of all visible fat. Place chicken between 2 sheets of plastic wrap and pound to a uniform thickness of ½ inch. Cut into 2-inch strips, and set aside.

2. Pour wine into a large skillet and bring to a boil over medium-high heat. Add chicken breasts, reduce the heat to a simmer, and poach chicken for 5–7 minutes, or until chicken is cooked through and no longer pink. Remove chicken from the skillet with a slotted spoon, and set aside.

3. While wine heats, bring orange juice and vinegar to a boil in a saucepan. Remove the pan from the heat and add raisins. Plump fruit for 10 minutes.

4. Add reserved wine, olive oil, and thyme to the saucepan. Bring to a boil over high heat. Reduce the heat to medium-high, and boil sauce for 5–10 minutes, or until the mixture is reduced by ½. Add chicken to the saucepan to reheat, season to taste with salt and pepper, and serve immediately.

Note: The dish can be prepared up to 1 day in advance and refrigerated, tightly covered. Reheat it, covered, over low heat, stirring occasionally.

Variation:

- Substitute thinly sliced boneless pork loin for the chicken.

Tarragon Chicken Stew

Tarragon is a fragrant herb and has a mild anise flavor that goes so well with the chicken and delicate vegetables in this stew. Serve it over buttered egg noodles.

Yield: 4–6 servings | **Active time:** 15 minutes | **Start to finish:** 35 minutes

    1¼ pounds boneless, skinless chicken breast halves
    Salt and freshly ground black pepper to taste
    3 tablespoons unsalted butter
    1 medium onion, peeled and diced
    2 garlic cloves, peeled and minced
    1 cup Chicken Stock (recipe on page 35) or purchased stock
    ⅔ cup dry white wine
    ⅔ cup heavy cream
    2 teaspoons dried tarragon
    2 carrots, peeled and thinly sliced
    2 celery ribs, rinsed, trimmed, and thinly sliced
    2 small zucchini, rinsed, trimmed, and sliced
    1 (10-ounce) package frozen peas, thawed

1. Rinse chicken and pat dry with paper towels. Trim chicken of all visible fat. Cut chicken into 1-inch cubes. Sprinkle chicken with salt and pepper to taste.
2. Heat butter in a large skillet over medium heat. Add chicken cubes, and cook for 3 minutes, or until chicken is opaque. Add onion and garlic, and cook, stirring occasionally, for 3 minutes, or until onion is translucent.
3. Stir stock, wine, cream, tarragon, carrots, and celery into the skillet. Bring to a boil, reduce the heat to medium-low, and simmer, uncovered, for 10 minutes. Add zucchini, and peas, and simmer for an additional 5–7 minutes, or until chicken is cooked through and no longer pink. Season to taste with salt and pepper. Serve immediately.

Note: The dish can be prepared up to 2 days in advance and refrigerated, tightly covered.

Variation:
- Substitute thick white-fleshed fish fillets for the chicken, and seafood stock for the chicken stock.

Chicken Piccata

This is an Italian classic, with chicken breast strips quickly sautéed, and then sauced with lemon juice, parsley, and capers. Serve it over pasta to enjoy the sauce, and with a tossed salad.

Yield: 4–6 servings | **Active time:** 10 minutes | **Start to finish:** 25 minutes

> 1¼ pounds boneless, skinless chicken breast halves
> ⅓ cup all-purpose flour
> Salt and freshly ground black pepper to taste
> ⅓ cup olive oil
> 1½ cups Chicken Stock (recipe on page 35) or purchased stock
> ½ cup lemon juice
> ⅓ cup chopped fresh parsley
> 2 tablespoons capers, drained and rinsed

1. Rinse chicken and pat dry with paper towels. Trim chicken of all visible fat. Place chicken between 2 sheets of plastic wrap, and pound to an even thickness of ½ inch. Cut breasts into 2-inch strips. Season flour to taste with salt and pepper. Dust chicken with seasoned flour, shaking off any excess.
2. Heat olive oil in a large skillet over medium-high heat. Add chicken and cook for 2 minutes per side, turning with tongs.
3. Add stock, lemon juice, parsley, and capers to the skillet. Bring to a boil, reduce the heat to low, cover the pan, and simmer chicken for 5 minutes. Turn chicken over, and simmer for an additional 5 minutes, or until chicken is cooked through and no longer pink. Season to taste with salt and pepper. Serve immediately.

Note: The dish can be prepared up to 2 days in advance and refrigerated, tightly covered.

Variation:
- Substitute thick white-fleshed fish fillets for the chicken, and seafood stock for the chicken stock.

Capers are the flower bud of a low bush native to the Mediterranean. After harvest they're sun-dried and pickled in vinegar. The best capers are the tiny ones from France, and while they are customarily packed in brine they can also be bought packed in coarse salt. However you buy them, rinse them well before using them.

Dilled Swedish Turkey Meatballs

Allspice and nutmeg, in addition to a combination of meats and a creamed sauce, are what define the quintessential Swedish meatball, called *köttbullar* in Sweden. Variations on this recipe have been served at American cocktail parties for generations, and they're still delicious.

Yield: 4–6 servings | **Active time:** 20 minutes | **Start to finish:** 45 minutes

> Vegetable oil spray
> 4 tablespoons unsalted butter, divided
> 1 small onion, peeled and chopped
> ¼ cup whole milk
> 1 large egg
> 1 large egg yolk
> 3 slices white bread
> ¼ teaspoon ground allspice
> ¼ teaspoon freshly grated nutmeg
> 1¼ pounds ground turkey
> Salt and freshly ground black pepper to taste
> ¼ cup all-purpose flour
> 2½ cups Chicken Stock (recipe on page 35) or purchased stock
> ½ cup heavy cream
> ¼ cup chopped fresh dill

1. Preheat the oven broiler, line a rimmed baking sheet with heavy-duty aluminum foil, and grease the foil with vegetable oil spray.
2. Heat 2 tablespoons butter in a large skillet over medium-high heat. Add onion, and cook, stirring frequently, for 3 minutes, or until onion is translucent. Combine milk, egg, and egg yolk in a mixing bowl, and whisk until smooth. Break bread into tiny pieces and add to mixing bowl along with allspice and nutmeg, and mix well.
3. Add onion and turkey, season to taste with salt and pepper, and mix well again. Make mixture into 1½-inch meatballs, and arrange meatballs on the prepared pan. Spray tops of meatballs with vegetable oil spray.

4. Broil meatballs 6 inches from the broiler element, turning them with tongs to brown all sides. While meatballs brown, add remaining butter to the skillet and heat over low heat. Stir flour into the skillet, and cook over low heat for 2 minutes, stirring constantly. Raise the heat to medium-high, whisk in stock and cream, and bring to a boil over medium-high heat, whisking constantly.

5. Remove meatballs from the baking pan with a slotted spoon, and add meatballs and dill to sauce. Bring to a boil, and simmer meatballs, covered, over low heat, turning occasionally with a slotted spoon, for 15 minutes. Season to taste with salt and pepper, and serve immediately.

Note: The meatball mixture can be prepared up to 1 day in advance and refrigerated, tightly covered. Also, the dish can be cooked up to 2 days in advance and refrigerated, tightly covered. Reheat in a 350°F oven, covered, for 15–20 minutes, or until hot.

Variations:
- Substitute a combination of ground pork and ground veal for the turkey.
- Substitute 2 tablespoons chopped fresh parsley and ³⁄₄ teaspoon dried thyme for the dill.

Nutmeg was one of the reasons Columbus discovered America. Nutmeg is the seed of a tropical evergreen native to the Spice Islands that was most popular with European aristocracy beginning in the fifteenth century. When the fruit of the tree is split, it reveals the inch-long nutmeg seed surrounded by a lacy membrane that is ground into mace, a spice similar in flavor.

Spicy Chili

Here's a wonderful rendition of this American favorite; it's made with spicy chiles as well as other herbs and spices. Serve it over rice, with the typical garnishes of cheddar and onions.

Yield: 4–6 servings | **Active time:** 15 minutes | **Start to finish:** 40 minutes

3 tablespoons olive oil, divided
1 pound lean ground beef
1 large onion, peeled and diced
3 garlic cloves, peeled and minced
1 large green bell pepper, seeds and ribs removed, and chopped
2 jalapeño or serrano chiles, seeds and ribs removed, and finely chopped
2 tablespoons all-purpose flour
3 tablespoons chili powder
2 tablespoons ground cumin
2 teaspoons dried oregano
2 teaspoons unsweetened cocoa powder
1 (28-ounce) can diced tomatoes, undrained
1 (15-ounce) can kidney beans, drained and rinsed
Salt and cayenne to taste

1. Heat 1 tablespoon oil in a large saucepan over medium-high heat. Add beef, breaking up lumps with a fork. Cook beef, stirring frequently, for 3 minutes, or until browned. Remove beef from the pan with a slotted spoon, and set aside. Discard fat from the saucepan.
2. Heat remaining oil in the saucepan. Add onion, garlic, bell pepper, and chiles. Cook, stirring frequently, for 3 minutes, or until onion is translucent. Stir in flour, chili powder, cumin, oregano, and cocoa. Cook over low heat, stirring frequently, for 1 minute.
3. Return beef to the pan, add tomatoes, and bring to a boil over medium heat. Simmer chili, uncovered, stirring occasionally, for 20 minutes, or until thick. Add beans, and cook for an additional 5 minutes. Season to taste with salt and cayenne, and serve immediately.

Note: The dish can be prepared up to 2 days in advance and refrigerated, tightly covered. Reheat it, covered, in a saucepan over low heat.

Variations:
- Substitute ground turkey or ground pork for the beef.
- There's a related dish in Mexican cooking called *picadillo*. Omit the oregano, and add ½ teaspoon ground cinnamon, ½ cup raisins, and 1 tablespoon cider vinegar to the chili.

Any chili can become a finger food if you turn it into nachos. Pile the chili on large nacho corn chips, top with some grated Monterey Jack cheese, and pop it under the broiler until the cheese is melted.

Mexican Spaghetti and Meatballs

There's no reason that spaghetti and meatballs can't have a Mexican accent, and the chipotle chiles in the tomato sauce give it just that. Serve this with a tossed salad.

Yield: 4–6 servings | **Active time:** 25 minutes | **Start to finish:** 35 minutes

Vegetable oil spray
²/₃ pound spaghetti
¼ cup olive oil
2 large onions, peeled and chopped
4 garlic cloves, peeled and minced
1 large egg
2 tablespoons whole milk
½ cup plain breadcrumbs
²/₃ cup chopped fresh cilantro, divided
1 tablespoon chili powder
1 tablespoon dried oregano
½ pound ground pork
½ pound ground chuck
Salt and cayenne to taste
1 (15-ounce) can tomato sauce
2 teaspoons ground cumin
2 chipotle chiles in adobo sauce, drained and finely chopped
Salt and freshly ground black pepper to taste

1. Preheat the oven broiler. Line a rimmed baking sheet with heavy-duty aluminum foil, and spray the foil with vegetable oil spray. Bring a large pot of salted water to a boil. Cook pasta according to package directions until al dente. Drain, and return pasta to the pot.
2. While water heats, heat oil in a skillet over medium-high heat. Add onions and garlic and cook, stirring frequently, for 3 minutes, or until onions are translucent. While vegetables cook, combine egg and milk in a mixing bowl, and whisk until smooth. Add breadcrumbs, ½ of cilantro, chili powder, and oregano, and mix well.
3. Add ½ of onion mixture, pork, and beef. Season to taste with salt and cayenne, and mix well again. Make mixture into 2-inch meatballs, and arrange meatballs on the prepared pan. Spray tops of meatballs with vegetable oil spray.

4. Broil meatballs 6 inches from the broiler element, turning them with tongs to brown all sides. While meatballs brown, add tomato sauce, cumin, and chipotle to the skillet containing remaining onions and garlic. Bring to a boil over medium-high heat, stirring occasionally.
5. Remove meatballs from the baking pan with a slotted spoon, and add meatballs to sauce. Bring to a boil, and simmer the meatballs, covered, over low heat, turning occasionally with a slotted spoon, for 10 minutes. Season to taste with salt and pepper, spoon sauce over pasta, and serve immediately.

Note: The meatball mixture can be prepared up to 1 day in advance and refrigerated, tightly covered. Also, the meatballs can be cooked up to 2 days in advance and refrigerated, tightly covered. Reheat them in a 350°F oven, covered, for 15 to 20 minutes, or until hot. Cook the pasta just prior to serving.

Variation:
- Make the meatballs from ground chicken or turkey.

Ham Hash

Hash comes from the French verb *hacher*, which means "to chop." The only constant is that the food is in small pieces. Ham gives this hash a smoky flavor and the vegetables add texture too.

Yield: 4–6 servings | **Active time:** 25 minutes | **Start to finish:** 35 minutes

- 1 small rutabaga, peeled and cut into ½-inch cubes
- 3 large redskin potatoes, scrubbed and cut into ½-inch cubes
- 3 tablespoons olive oil
- 1 medium red onion, peeled and coarsely chopped
- 3 garlic cloves, peeled and minced
- 1 green bell pepper, seeds and ribs removed, and cut into ¼-inch dice
- 1 pound baked ham, thinly sliced and cut into ½-inch squares
- 2 tablespoons unsalted butter
- ¼ cup dry white wine
- 1 teaspoon Worcestershire sauce
- Salt and freshly ground black pepper to taste
- ½ cup chopped fresh parsley
- 1 tablespoon grainy Dijon mustard

1. Bring a large pot of salted water to a boil. Add rutabaga and potato cubes, and cook for about 8–10 minutes, or until crisp-tender. Drain and set aside.

2. Heat olive oil in a large skillet over medium-high heat. Add onion, garlic, and green bell pepper and cook, stirring frequently, for 3 minutes, or until onion is translucent. Stir in rutabaga, potatoes, ham, butter, white wine, and Worcestershire sauce; season to taste with salt and pepper. Cook over medium heat, stirring frequently, for 10–12 minutes, or until all liquid has evaporated and mixture is lightly browned and crisp.

3. Stir in parsley and Dijon mustard and cook for 2 minutes more. Serve immediately.

Note: The hash can be prepared up to 2 days in advance and refrigerated, tightly covered. Reheat it, uncovered, in a 350°F oven for 20–25 minutes, or until hot.

Variation:
- Chicken or turkey can be substituted for the ham.

Cajun Stewed Red Beans and Ham

Red beans and rice are so much a part of Louisiana's culinary heritage that famed jazz musician Louis Armstrong used to sign his letters, "Red beans and ricely yours." That should also be your clue to serve this dish, along with some coleslaw, on top of rice.

Yield: 4–6 servings | **Active time:** 15 minutes | **Start to finish:** 30 minutes

> 2 tablespoons bacon grease or vegetable oil
> 2 medium onions, peeled and finely chopped
> 2 celery ribs, rinsed, trimmed, and finely chopped
> 1 green bell pepper, seeds and ribs removed, and finely chopped
> 2 garlic cloves, peeled and minced
> 1 tablespoon paprika
> 2 bay leaves
> 2 teaspoons dried thyme
> 1½ cups Chicken Stock (recipe on page 35) or purchased stock
> 2 (15-ounce) cans red kidney beans, drained and rinsed
> ¾ pound baked ham, trimmed and cut into ½-inch dice
> Salt and freshly ground black pepper to taste
> Hot red pepper sauce to taste

1. Heat bacon grease in a 3-quart saucepan over medium-high heat. Add onions, celery, green pepper, and garlic, and cook, stirring frequently, for 3 minutes, or until onions are translucent. Add paprika, bay leaves, and thyme, and cook over low heat for 1 minute, stirring constantly.
2. Add stock, beans, and ham to the pan, and bring to a boil, stirring occasionally. Reduce the heat to low, cover the pan, and simmer 15 minutes. Remove and discard bay leaves, and season to taste with salt, pepper, and hot red pepper sauce. Serve immediately.

Note: The dish can be made up to 2 days in advance and refrigerated, tightly covered. Reheat it over low heat or in a 350°F oven for 30 minutes, or until hot.

Variation:
- Omit the ham, use vegetable oil, and add 1 additional can kidney beans for a vegetarian dish.

Fast Black-Eyed Pea, Ham, and Spinach Stew

With canned beans in the pantry and vegetables in the freezer you'll never go hungry, and this flavorful stew is a great showcase for leftover ham. Serve it over rice with a tossed salad.

Yield: 4–6 servings | **Active time:** 15 minutes | **Start to finish:** 30 minutes

1/4 cup olive oil, divided
1 medium onion, peeled and diced
2 garlic cloves, peeled and minced
1 carrot, peeled and thinly sliced
2 cups Chicken Stock (recipe on page 35) or purchased stock
2 (15-ounce) cans black-eyed peas, drained and rinsed
1 (14.5-ounce) can diced stewed tomatoes, undrained
3/4 pound baked ham, trimmed of fat and cut into 1/2-inch dice
1 tablespoon tomato paste
2 tablespoons chopped fresh parsley
1 teaspoon herbes de Provence
1 (10-ounce) package frozen leaf spinach, thawed
Salt and freshly ground black pepper to taste
4–6 (3/4-inch) slices French or Italian bread
1/4 cup freshly grated Parmesan cheese

1. Preheat the oven broiler, and cover a baking sheet with aluminum foil. Heat 2 tablespoons olive oil in a heavy saucepan over medium-high heat. Add onion, garlic, and carrot, and cook, stirring frequently, for 3 minutes, or until onion is translucent.
2. Add stock, black-eyed peas, tomatoes, ham, tomato paste, parsley, and herbes de Provence to the pan, and stir well to dissolve tomato paste. Bring mixture to a boil over medium-high heat, stirring occasionally. Reduce the heat to low, and simmer stew, uncovered, for 10 minutes.
3. Place spinach in a colander, and press with the back of a spoon to extract as much liquid as possible. Add spinach to stew, season to taste with salt and pepper, and simmer for an additional 5 minutes.
4. While stew simmers, brush both sides of bread with remaining olive oil. Arrange bread on baking sheet and broil 6 inches from the broiler element for 1 minute. Turn slices over, and sprinkle with Parmesan. Broil for an additional 1–2 minutes, or until browned.

5. To serve, place toast slices in the bottoms of shallow bowls, and ladle stew over toast. Serve immediately.

Note: The stew can be made up to 2 days in advance and refrigerated, tightly covered. Reheat it, covered, over low heat, stirring occasionally. The toast can be made up to 1 day in advance and kept at room temperature.

Variations:
- Substitute kidney beans, garbanzo beans, or cannellini beans for the black-eyed peas.
- Substitute smoked turkey for the ham.

> While I like to serve this stew over toast because it absorbs all the luscious flavor from the liquid, you can basically use any carbohydrate in place of another. Have some leftover pasta or rice? Don't let it go to waste! Use it in place of the toast.

Mexican Scrambled Eggs (*Migas*)

While the chiles were a bit much for me to handle at 7 a.m. when I was served this dish in Mexico, I immediately tucked this concept away for a quick supper idea. Serve it with a tossed salad.

Yield: 4–6 servings | **Active time:** 25 minutes | **Start to finish:** 25 minutes

4 (6-inch) corn tortillas
½ pound bacon, cut into 1-inch pieces
½ small red onion, peeled and finely chopped
2 garlic cloves, peeled and minced
1 small jalapeño or serrano chile, seeds and ribs removed, and finely chopped
½ green bell pepper, seeds and ribs removed, and finely chopped
4 ripe plum tomatoes, rinsed, cored, seeded, and coarsely chopped
½ teaspoon ground cumin
4 large eggs, lightly beaten
½ cup grated Monterey Jack or mild cheddar cheese
Salt and freshly ground black pepper to taste

1. Tear tortillas into 1-inch pieces, and set aside. Cook bacon in a heavy skillet over medium-high heat, turning occasionally, for 5–7 minutes, or until bacon is crisp. Remove bacon from the pan with a slotted spoon and drain on paper towels. Discard all but 3 tablespoons bacon grease from the skillet.

2. Add tortilla pieces a handful at a time to the skillet and fry them, turning them frequently with tongs, for 2–3 minutes, or until pale golden. Transfer to paper towels to drain.

3. Add onion, garlic, chile, and bell pepper to the skillet and cook, stirring frequently, for 5 minutes, or until onion is soft. Add bacon, tomatoes, and cumin. Cook, stirring occasionally, for 2–3 minutes, or until tomatoes have begun to soften.

4. Add tortilla pieces and stir until well combined. Pour eggs over tortilla mixture and stir in cheese. Season to taste with salt and pepper. Reduce heat to low, and cover pan. Cook for 2 minutes, then stir, recover pan, and cook for an additional 1–2 minutes, or until eggs are just set and cheese is melted. Serve immediately.

Note: The dish can be prepared up to the end of Step 3 up to 1 day in advance and refrigerated, tightly covered. Reheat it in the skillet before completing Step 4.

Variations:
- Substitute jalapeño Jack cheese for the Monterey Jack for a spicier dish.
- Substitute bulk chorizo sausage for the bacon.

This method for making scrambled eggs will produce very light and fluffy eggs, and can be used for all scrambled dishes. For scrambled eggs for a crowd, bake the pan, covered with aluminum foil, in a 350°F oven for 15 minutes. Stir, recover the pan, and cook at 10 minute intervals until the eggs reach the proper consistency.

Chapter 8:
Quick Casseroles and
Oven-Baked Dishes

Here's the tradeoff when you bake dishes in the oven rather than cook them on top of the stove. The total time it takes to complete the dish is longer, but you don't have to be near it to watch it. If you look through these recipes the start to finish time is about 30 minutes, give or take 10 minutes. But if you look at the notation for "active time," it's rarely even 15 minutes. You can't fix these dishes and then forget about them; for dishes that cook while you're at work all day, see my *$3 Slow-Cooked Meals*.

But what you can do is put them into the oven, and spend the 15 or 20 minutes making a salad to accompany the meal. Or you can read a book or answer your e-mail.

The reason why ovens, even hot ovens, are not as fast as a pot on top of the stove is that ovens cook with hot air, which is not as efficient a cooking medium as oil or water. The heat from the oven radiates off the walls and then penetrates the food.

There is one term you'll see reading the recipes in this chapter that I doubt you've seen before, and that's because I made it up writing this book. I'm calling it a "quasi-quiche"; or you could also call it a "crustless quiche." It's quiche filling baked in a breadcrumb-coated and greased quiche pan or pie plate. You get all the protein from the eggs, and all the flavor from the other ingredients. But what you don't get is the crust, which is high in calories and fat, and which must be baked at a relatively low temperature for a longer period of time than the filling.

If you have a favorite quiche recipe, feel free to adapt it to this method. Use the same number of eggs, and the same amount of additional ingredients.

Quasi-Quiche Mexicana

While quiche is a French dish, there are many similar custards in Mexican cooking. The herbs, spices, and vegetables give vibrant flavor to this dish.

Yield: 4–6 servings | **Active time:** 10 minutes | **Start to finish:** 30 minutes

3 tablespoons unsalted butter, divided
3 tablespoons plain breadcrumbs
1 medium onion, peeled and chopped
1 teaspoon ground cumin
½ teaspoon dried oregano
4 large eggs
2 cups half-and-half
1½ cups grated jalapeño Jack cheese
2 tablespoons chopped fresh cilantro
Salt and freshly ground black pepper to taste
1 (10-ounce) package frozen corn kernels, cooked according to package directions and drained well
¼ cup sliced pimiento-stuffed green olives

1. Preheat the oven to 425°F. Grease a 10-inch quiche pan or 10-inch-diameter deep-dish pie plate with 1 tablespoon butter and sprinkle with breadcrumbs. Set aside.
2. Heat remaining butter in a small skillet over medium heat. Add onion, and cook, stirring frequently, for 5 minutes, or until onion is soft. Stir in cumin and oregano, and cook for 1 minute, stirring constantly.
3. While onion cooks, whisk eggs with half-and-half in a mixing bowl. Stir in cheese and cilantro, and season to taste with salt and pepper. Stir corn, olives, and onion mixture into custard. Pour custard into the prepared pan.
4. Bake custard in the center of the oven for 20–25 minutes, or until top is brown and custard is set in the center. Remove the pan from the oven, and cut into wedges. Serve immediately.

Note: The custard can be prepared for baking up to 1 day in advance and refrigerated, tightly covered. The custard can also be baked up to 1 day in advance; serve it at room temperature or chilled.

Variation:
- Substitute Monterey Jack for all or some of the jalapeño Jack for a milder flavor.

Quasi-Quiche Provençale

Tomatoes, olives, and herbs are all part of the wonderful flavors from the Provence region of France. This dish is wonderful to take on a picnic, too.

Yield: 4–6 servings | **Active time:** 10 minutes | **Start to finish:** 30 minutes

3 tablespoons unsalted butter, divided
3 tablespoons plain breadcrumbs
1 medium onion, peeled and chopped
4 large eggs
2 cups half-and-half
2 tablespoons all-purpose flour
1 cup grated Swiss cheese
½ cup grated Monterey Jack cheese
1 tablespoon chopped fresh parsley
1 teaspoon herbes de Provence
Salt and freshly ground black pepper to taste
2 cups grape tomatoes, rinsed, stemmed if necessary, and patted dry with paper towels
½ cup sliced kalamata olives

1. Preheat the oven to 425°F. Grease a 10-inch quiche pan or 10-inch-diameter deep-dish pie plate with 1 tablespoon butter and sprinkle with breadcrumbs. Set aside.
2. Heat remaining butter in a small skillet over medium heat. Add onion, and cook, stirring frequently, for 5 minutes, or until onion is soft.
3. While onion cooks, whisk eggs with half-and-half and flour in a mixing bowl. Stir in Swiss cheese, Monterey Jack cheese, parsley, and herbes de Provence, and season to taste with salt and pepper.
4. Arrange onions, tomatoes, and olives in the prepared pan, and pour custard on top. Bake in the center of the oven for 20–25 minutes, or until top is brown and custard is set in the center. Remove the pan from the oven, and cut into wedges. Serve immediately.

Note: The custard can be prepared for baking up to 1 day in advance and refrigerated, tightly covered. The custard can also be baked up to 1 day in advance; serve it at room temperature or chilled.

Variation:
- Substitute cheddar cheese for the Swiss and Monterey Jack, and omit the olives.

The reason to add flour to this recipe is that the tomatoes will give off liquid as they cook, and the flour prevents the custard from becoming watery.

Greek-Style Baked Fish with Orzo

Orzo is a tiny pasta the size and shape of a grain of cooked rice, and it's used frequently in Greek cooking. In this sumptuous dish the cooked pasta is in a tomato sauce flavored with aromatic dill, and then the fish above it is topped with sharp feta cheese, another hallmark of Greek cuisine.

Yield: 6–8 servings | **Active time:** 15 minutes | **Start to finish:** 35 minutes

2 cups orzo
2 tablespoons olive oil
1 large onion, peeled and diced
3 garlic cloves, peeled and minced
1 (14.5-ounce) can diced tomatoes, undrained
⅓ cup chopped fresh dill
2 teaspoons dried basil
Freshly ground black pepper to taste
1½ pounds white firm-fleshed fish fillets, cut into ¾-inch cubes
⅔ cup crumbled feta cheese

1. Preheat the oven to 450°F, and grease a 9 x 13-inch baking pan.
2. Bring a large pot of salted water to a boil over high heat. Add orzo, and boil for 7 minutes, or until orzo is double in size but still slightly hard. (The amount of time depends on the brand of orzo.) Drain.
3. While orzo boils, heat olive oil in medium skillet over medium-high heat. Add onion and garlic, and cook, stirring frequently, for 3 minutes, or until onion is translucent. Add tomatoes, dill, basil, and pepper to the skillet. Bring to a boil, reduce the heat to low, and simmer 3 minutes. Add orzo to skillet, and stir well.
4. Scrape mixture into the prepared pan, and arrange fish on top. Sprinkle feta over fish, and cover pan with aluminum foil. Bake for 20 minutes, or until fish is opaque and cooked through and feta is melted. Serve immediately.

Note: The orzo mixture can be prepared up to 1 day in advance and refrigerated, tightly covered. Reheat it in a microwave oven before baking the fish.

Baked Parmesan and Herb-Crusted Fish

Thin fish fillets cook in so little time that there's no reason not to add this family-pleasing dish to your regular rotation. The topping can be personalized in many ways, too.

Yield: 4–6 servings | **Active time:** 10 minutes | **Start to finish:** 15 minutes

Vegetable oil spray
1¼ pounds thin white-fleshed fish fillets
2 tablespoons olive oil
Salt and freshly ground black pepper to taste
½ cup panko breadcrumbs
½ cup freshly grated Parmesan cheese
2 tablespoons chopped fresh parsley
2 teaspoons herbes de Provence

1. Preheat the oven to 425°F, line a baking sheet with aluminum foil, and grease the foil with vegetable oil spray.
2. Rinse fish, and pat dry with paper towels. Coat fish with oil, and sprinkle with salt and pepper. Arrange fish on the prepared baking sheet.
3. Combine breadcrumbs, Parmesan, parsley, and herbes de Provence in a small bowl. Sprinkle mixture on top of fish.
4. Bake fish for 5–7 minutes, or until fish flakes easily and crumbs are golden. Serve immediately.

Note: The fish can be prepared for baking up to 6 hours in advance and refrigerated, tightly covered.

Variation:
- Substitute boneless, skinless chicken breast halves, pounded between 2 sheets of plastic wrap to an even thickness of ¼ inch, for the fish. Bake chicken at 400°F for 10–12 minutes, or until chicken is cooked through and no longer pink.

Southwestern Fish Cakes

While living near the Chesapeake Bay I became enamored with traditional Old Bay seasoning used in the region's justly famed crab cakes. Fish cakes are a less expensive version, and the cilantro and green chiles are an unusual addition.

Yield: 4–6 servings | **Active time:** 15 minutes | **Start to finish:** 30 minutes

Vegetable oil spray
1 pound thin white-fleshed fish fillets
1–2 teaspoons Old Bay seasoning, or to taste
1 large egg
3 tablespoons mayonnaise
3 tablespoons plain breadcrumbs
1 large green bell pepper, seeds and ribs removed, and very finely chopped
4 scallions, white parts and 3 inches of green tops, rinsed, trimmed, and very finely chopped
2 celery ribs, rinsed, trimmed, and very finely chopped
3 tablespoons chopped canned mild green chiles, drained
3 tablespoons chopped fresh cilantro
Salt and freshly ground black pepper to taste

1. Preheat the oven to 450°F, cover a baking sheet with aluminum foil, and grease the foil with vegetable oil spray. Rinse fish and pat dry with paper towels.
2. Rub fish with Old Bay, spray with vegetable oil spray, and bake for 5–7 minutes, or until fish flakes easily. Remove fish from the oven, and break into small pieces with a fork.
3. Reduce the oven temperature to 400°F, discard foil, replace with a fresh sheet of foil, and grease the foil with vegetable oil spray.
4. Combine egg, mayonnaise, and breadcrumbs in a mixing bowl, and whisk well. Gently fold in fish, green bell pepper, scallions, celery, chiles, and cilantro. Season to taste with salt and pepper.
5. Divide mixture into 4–6 parts, and form into patties ½ inch thick. Arrange patties on the prepared baking sheet, and spray tops with vegetable oil spray. Bake for 15–20 minutes, or until browned.

Note: The fish mixture can be prepared up to 1 day in advance and refrigerated, tightly covered. Do not form the cakes or bake them until just prior to serving.

Variation:
- Substitute 3 (6-ounce) cans light tuna, drained, for the fish. The tuna requires no precooking, but add 1 teaspoon Old Bay seasoning to the egg mixture.

> While Old Bay seasoning is easy to find nationally, if you only will be using it in this dish, you can substitute Cajun or Creole seasoning, which contains many of the same ingredients.

Turkey Meatloaf "Muffins"

Just as small pieces of food for a stir-fry cook in less time than a large roast, so a meatloaf mixture baked in muffin cups is ready in far less time than it takes to bake one large loaf. Make extra of these and take them to the office for lunch; the muffins don't fall apart the way slices tend to do.

Yield: 4–6 servings | **Active time:** 15 minutes | **Start to finish:** 40 minutes

Vegetable oil spray
3 tablespoons olive oil
1 medium onion, peeled and chopped
3 garlic cloves, peeled and minced
2 carrots, peeled and grated
1 celery rib, rinsed, trimmed, and finely chopped
1¼ pounds ground turkey
2 large eggs, lightly beaten
½ cup grated mozzarella cheese
½ cup Italian breadcrumbs
¼ cup whole milk
¾ cup chili sauce or ketchup, divided
1 tablespoon Worcestershire sauce
1 teaspoon dried thyme
Salt and freshly ground black pepper to taste

1. Preheat the oven to 400°F, and spray 8–12 muffin cups with vegetable oil spray.
2. Heat oil in a medium skillet over medium-high heat. Add onion, garlic, carrots, and celery. Cook, stirring frequently, for 5 minutes, or until onion is soft.
3. While vegetables cook, combine turkey, eggs, mozzarella, breadcrumbs, milk, ¼ cup chili sauce, Worcestershire sauce, thyme, salt, and pepper in a mixing bowl. Mix well. Add sautéed vegetable mixture, and mix well again.
4. Divide mixture into the prepared muffin cups, and spread tops with remaining chili sauce. Bake for 20–25 minutes, or until an instant-read thermometer inserted into the center registers 170°F. Serve immediately.

Note: The turkey mixture can be made up to 1 day in advance and refrigerated, tightly covered. Also, the mixture can be formed into 4–6 "logs" rather than being baked in muffin cups. Bake at 375°F for 25–30 minutes.

Variations:

- Substitute ground beef, or a combination of ground beef and ground pork, for the turkey.
- Substitute plain breadcrumbs for the Italian breadcrumbs and substitute cheddar cheese for the mozzarella.
- Cook 1 (10-ounce) package frozen chopped spinach according to package directions. Place spinach in a colander, and press with the back of a spoon to extract as much liquid as possible. Combine spinach with an additional ½ cup grated mozzarella cheese, and season to taste with salt and pepper. Fill muffin tins halfway with meatloaf mixture, and top with a dollop of spinach. Enclose spinach with remaining meatloaf mixture.
- Substitute ½ pound mushrooms, wiped with a damp paper towel, trimmed, and chopped, for the carrot and celery.

Contrary to its name, chili sauce is closer to a chunky ketchup than a fiery sauce. It's a tomato-based condiment that contains onions, green peppers, vinegar, sugar, and spices. It serves as the basis for traditional cocktail sauce, too, so it's worth it to keep a bottle in the house.

Baked Chicken and Broccoli Risotto

Risotto is a traditional Italian rice dish that dates back to the Renaissance. The key ingredient is Arborio rice, which is a short, fat-grained Italian rice with a high starch content. Traditional risotto recipes require countless minutes of laborious stirring, but this recipe achieves the same results with far less work.

Yield: 4–6 servings | **Active time:** 15 minutes | **Start to finish:** 40 minutes

4 cups Chicken Stock (recipe on page 35) or purchased stock

1 (1-pound) package frozen chopped broccoli, thawed and drained, divided

3 (6-ounce) boneless, skinless chicken breast halves, cut into 1-inch cubes

Salt and freshly ground black pepper to taste

3 tablespoons unsalted butter

1 large onion, peeled and chopped

3 garlic cloves, peeled and chopped

2 cups Arborio rice

½ cup dry white wine

¾ cup freshly grated Parmesan cheese

1. Preheat the oven to 400°F, and grease a 10 x 14-inch baking pan.
2. Combine stock and ⅓ of broccoli in a food processor fitted with the steel blade or in a blender. Puree until smooth, and set aside.
3. Rinse chicken, pat dry with paper towels, and sprinkle chicken with salt and pepper. Heat butter in a large skillet over medium-high heat. Add chicken and cook, stirring frequently, for 2 minutes, or until chicken is opaque. Remove chicken from the pan with a slotted spoon, and set aside. Add onion and garlic to the pan, and cook for 3 minutes, stirring frequently, or until onion is translucent. Add rice to the pan, and cook for 2 minutes, stirring constantly.

4. Add wine to the pan, raise the heat to high, and cook for 3 minutes, stirring constantly, or until wine is almost evaporated. Add stock and chicken to pan, and bring to a boil. Scrape mixture into prepared pan, cover pan with aluminum foil, and bake for 10 minutes. Remove foil, stir in remaining broccoli, and return the pan to oven for 10–15 minutes, or until rice is soft and has absorbed liquid. Stir in Parmesan cheese, season to taste with salt and pepper, and serve immediately.

Note: The dish can be cooked up to 2 days in advance and refrigerated, tightly covered. Reheat in a 350°F oven, covered, for 20–25 minutes, or until hot.

Variations:
- Substitute asparagus for the broccoli.
- Substitute grated Swiss cheese or cheddar cheese for the Parmesan cheese.

Basic Oven-Fried Chicken

Using this easy method, chicken emerges from the oven with skin as crisp as if it was deep-fried on top of the stove, but it's less expensive because you use so little oil, and there's no mess!

Yield: 4–6 servings | **Active time:** 10 minutes | **Start to finish:** 35 minutes

1 (3½–4-pound) frying chicken, cut into serving pieces
1 cup buttermilk
2 large eggs, lightly beaten
1½ cups finely crushed corn flakes
½ cup breadcrumbs
1 cup vegetable oil, divided
3 tablespoons Cajun seasoning
Salt and freshly ground black pepper to taste

1. Preheat the oven to 400°F, and place a 10 x 14-inch baking pan in the oven as it heats. Rinse chicken and pat dry with paper towels.
2. Combine buttermilk and eggs in a shallow bowl, and whisk well. Combine crushed corn flakes, breadcrumbs, 2 tablespoons oil, Cajun seasoning, salt, and pepper in a second large bowl, and mix well.
3. Dip chicken pieces into buttermilk mixture, letting any excess drip back into the bowl. Dip pieces into crumb mixture, coating all sides. Set aside.
4. Add remaining oil to hot baking dish, and heat for 3 minutes. Add chicken pieces and turn gently with tongs to coat all sides with oil. Bake for a total of 25 minutes, turning pieces gently with tongs after 15 minutes, or until chicken is cooked through and no longer pink. Remove chicken from the pan, and pat with paper towels. Serve immediately.

Note: The chicken can be prepared for baking up to 6 hours in advance and refrigerated, tightly covered.

Variations:

- Use seasoned Italian breadcrumbs, and add ¼ cup freshly grated Parmesan cheese to the mixture.
- Use rice cereal in place of the corn flakes.
- Use fluffy panko breadcrumbs, and season them with herbes de Provence.
- Substitute smoked Spanish paprika for the Cajun seasoning, and season egg mixture to taste with salt and pepper.

It's difficult to use up a whole quart of buttermilk, and I've never been able to find it in pint containers. But there is a powdered buttermilk on the market that you can mix with water. A tin is rather expensive, but it lasts for years.

Spicy Mexican Meatloaf "Muffins"

Crushed tortilla chips and spicy jalapeño Jack cheese enliven the flavor of these tiny meatloaves. Serve them with some corn tortillas and a tossed salad.

Yield: 4–6 servings | **Active time:** 15 minutes | **Start to finish:** 35 minutes

Vegetable oil spray
2 tablespoons olive oil
1 small onion, peeled and finely chopped
4 garlic cloves, peeled and minced, divided
2 tablespoons chili powder
2 teaspoons ground cumin
1 teaspoon dried oregano
1¼ pounds ground chuck
1 large egg, lightly beaten
⅔ cup crushed tortilla chip crumbs
3 tablespoons chopped fresh cilantro
Salt and freshly ground black pepper to taste
1 cup grated jalapeño Jack cheese
¾ cup mayonnaise
2 tablespoons canned chopped mild green chiles, drained
1 tablespoon lime juice

1. Preheat the oven to 400°F, and spray 8–12 muffin cups with vegetable oil spray.
2. Heat oil in a small skillet over medium-high heat. Add onion and 3 cloves of garlic, and cook, stirring frequently, for 5 minutes, or until onion is soft. Add chili powder, cumin, and oregano, and cook for 1 minute, stirring constantly. Scrape mixture into a mixing bowl.
3. Add ground chuck, egg, tortilla chip crumbs, and cilantro to the mixing bowl. Season to taste with salt and pepper, and mix well.
4. Divide ½ of mixture into the prepared muffin cups, and divide cheese into cups on top. Fill cups with remaining meat mixture. Bake for 20–25 minutes, or until an instant-read thermometer inserted into the center registers 165°F.

5. While meatloaves bake, combine remaining 1 clove of garlic with mayonnaise, chiles, and lime juice. Stir well, and season to taste with salt and pepper. Remove meatloaves from the oven, and serve immediately, passing sauce separately.

Note: The meatloaf mixture can be made up to 1 day in advance and refrigerated, tightly covered. Also, the mixture can be formed into 4–6 "logs" rather than being baked in muffin cups. Bake at 375°F for 25–30 minutes.

Variations:
- Substitute ground turkey or ground pork for the ground chuck.
- Substitute Monterey Jack cheese for the jalapeño Jack for a milder flavor.

Ground chuck is not only reasonably priced, but it is one of the most flavorful types of ground beef. Even if something labeled "ground beef" is less expensive, select the chuck for its richness.

Quasi-Quiche with Ham and Swiss Cheese

This is not only a fast and easy version of classic quiche Lorraine, but it also serves as your master recipe for the whole quasi-quiche genre. Serve it with some crusty bread and a tossed salad.

Yield: 4–6 servings | **Active time:** 10 minutes | **Start to finish:** 30 minutes

3 tablespoons unsalted butter, divided
3 tablespoons plain breadcrumbs
1 medium onion, peeled and chopped
4 large eggs
2 cups half-and-half
2 cups grated Swiss cheese
1½ cups chopped baked ham
½ teaspoon dried thyme
Salt and freshly ground black pepper to taste

1. Preheat the oven to 425°F. Grease a 10-inch quiche pan or 10-inch-diameter deep-dish pie plate with 1 tablespoon butter and sprinkle with breadcrumbs. Set aside.

2. Heat remaining butter in a small skillet over medium heat. Add onion, and cook, stirring frequently, for 5 minutes, or until onion is soft.

3. While onion cooks, whisk eggs with half-and-half in a mixing bowl. Stir in cheese, ham, and thyme, and season to taste with salt and pepper.

4. Arrange onion in the prepared pan, and pour custard on top. Bake in the center of the oven for 20–25 minutes, or until top is brown and custard is set in the center. Remove the pan from the oven, and cut into wedges. Serve immediately.

Note: The custard can be prepared for baking up to 1 day in advance and refrigerated, tightly covered. The custard can also be baked up to 1 day in advance; serve it at room temperature or chilled.

Variations:

- Substitute 1 (10-ounce) package frozen chopped broccoli or chopped spinach, cooked according to package directions and drained in a colander, pressed with the back of a spoon to extract as much liquid as possible, for the onions. Melt the remaining 2 tablespoons butter, and add it to the custard mixture.

- Substitute leeks, white parts only, thinly sliced and rinsed well, for the onions.
- Substitute 1/4 pound mushrooms, wiped with a damp paper towel, trimmed, and sliced, for the onions.
- Substitute cheddar, Gruyère, Gouda, jalapeño Jack, Monterey Jack, or fontina, or some combination of cheeses for the Swiss cheese.
- Substitute cooked and crumbled bacon, cooked and crumbled sausage, chopped smoked or roast turkey, small cubes of cooked fish, or chopped salami for the ham.
- Substitute freshly grated Parmesan cheese for the breadcrumbs to coat the pan.
- Add 2–3 tablespoons chopped fresh herbs, such as parsley, basil, oregano, dill, or cilantro.

The reason to sprinkle the onions into the quiche pan rather than stirring them into the custard is to save time. The onions would have to be allowed to cool or they could begin to cook the eggs; this way no precious moments are wasted!

Italian Pork

Pork is my most frequent inexpensive stand-in for veal; it has the same delicate flavor and fine texture. In this dish it's layered with cheese, salami, and sage for a version of *vitello saltimbocca.* Serve it with some pasta and a tossed salad.

Yield: 4–6 servings | **Active time:** 15 minutes | **Start to finish:** 30 minutes

> 1 pound boneless pork loin
> Salt and freshly ground black pepper to taste
> 4 garlic cloves, peeled and minced
> 1 teaspoon Italian seasoning
> 2 tablespoons dried sage
> 1/4 pound thinly sliced Genoa salami
> 1/2 cup Chicken Stock (recipe on page 35) or purchased stock
> 1/2 pound whole milk mozzarella cheese, thinly sliced

1. Preheat the oven to 425°F, and line a 10 x 14-inch baking pan with aluminum foil. Rinse pork and pat dry with paper towels. Slice pork against the grain into 1/2-inch slices, and arrange slices in the pan, overlapping them slightly. Sprinkle pork with salt and pepper.
2. Combine garlic, Italian seasoning, and sage in a small cup. Sprinkle mixture on top of pork. Layer salami on top of seasonings, and drizzle stock over all. Top with cheese.
3. Bake for 15–20 minutes, or until pork is cooked through and cheese is bubbly. Serve immediately.

Note: The dish can be prepared for baking up to 6 hours in advance and refrigerated, tightly covered.

Variation:
- Substitute boneless, skinless chicken breast halves, pounded between 2 sheets of plastic wrap to an even thickness of 1/2 inch, for the pork.

Western Quasi-Quiche

If you're a fan of a Western omelet, with bits of onion, ham, and green pepper, then you'll love this custard, which also has sharp cheddar to flavor it.

Yield: 4–6 servings | **Active time:** 10 minutes | **Start to finish:** 30 minutes

3 tablespoons unsalted butter, divided
3 tablespoons plain breadcrumbs
$1/2$ medium onion, peeled and chopped
$1/2$ green bell pepper, seeds and ribs removed, and chopped
4 large eggs
2 cups half-and-half
2 cups grated sharp cheddar cheese
$1^{1}/_{4}$ cups chopped baked ham
Salt and freshly ground black pepper to taste

1. Preheat the oven to 425°F. Grease a 10-inch quiche pan or 10-inch-diameter deep-dish pie plate with 1 tablespoon butter and sprinkle with breadcrumbs. Set aside.
2. Heat remaining butter in a small skillet over medium heat. Add onion and green bell pepper, and cook, stirring frequently, for 5 minutes, or until vegetables are soft.
3. While vegetables cook, whisk eggs with half-and-half in a mixing bowl. Stir in cheese and ham, and season to taste with salt and pepper.
4. Arrange vegetables in the prepared pan, and pour custard on top. Bake in the center of the oven for 20–25 minutes, or until top is brown and custard is set in the center. Remove the pan from the oven, and cut into wedges. Serve immediately.

Note: The custard can be prepared for baking up to 1 day in advance and refrigerated, tightly covered. The custard can also be baked up to 1 day in advance; serve it at room temperature or chilled.

Variation:
- Substitute smoked cheddar cheese or Swiss cheese for the cheddar cheese.

Baked Macaroni and Cheese with Ham

Macaroni and cheese is beloved by every generation—past and present, and I'm sure future, too. The paprika and mustard add a bit of kick to this version, and it's such a yummy way to stretch leftover ham.

Yield: 4-6 servings | **Active time:** 15 minutes | **Start to finish:** 35 minutes

- $^2/_3$ pound elbow macaroni
- 3 tablespoons unsalted butter
- 3 tablespoons all-purpose flour
- 1 tablespoon paprika
- $^1/_4$ teaspoon cayenne, or to taste
- $^2/_3$ cup Chicken Stock (recipe on page 35) or purchased stock
- $1^1/_2$ cups whole milk
- 1 pound grated sharp cheddar cheese, divided
- 1 tablespoon Dijon mustard
- $^3/_4$ pound baked ham, trimmed of fat and cut into $^1/_2$-inch dice
- Salt and freshly ground black pepper to taste

1. Preheat the oven to 400°F, and grease a 10 x 14-inch baking pan. Bring a large pot of salted water to a boil. Add macaroni, and cook according to package directions until al dente. Drain, and place in the prepared pan.
2. Heat butter in saucepan over low heat. Stir in flour, paprika, and cayenne, and cook, stirring constantly, for 2 minutes. Whisk in stock, and bring to a boil over medium-high heat, whisking constantly. Reduce the heat to low, and simmer 2 minutes. Stir in milk and all but $^1/_2$ cup of grated cheese, and stir until cheese melts. Stir in mustard and ham, and season to taste with salt and pepper. Pour sauce over macaroni, and stir well.
3. Cover the pan with foil, and bake for 10 minutes. Uncover the pan, sprinkle with remaining cheese, and bake for an additional 10–15 minutes, or until bubbly. Serve immediately.

Note: The dish can be prepared up to 2 days in advance and refrigerated, tightly covered. Reheat it, covered, in a 350°F oven for 20–25 minutes, or until hot.

Variations:

- Omit the ham and substitute vegetable stock for the chicken stock for a vegetarian dish.
- Substitute roast turkey or chicken for the ham.
- Substitute jalapeño Jack for the cheddar cheese for a spicier dish.

> Macaroni is a traditional Italian pasta shape, and famed gastronome Thomas Jefferson imported one from Naples during his presidency. But macaroni and cheese is authentically American and dates from the nineteenth century.

Ham and Cheese Grits Casserole

Hominy grits are an integral part of the every Southerner's kitchen, and the addition of ham and cheese transforms them from a side dish to the star of the plate. Serve these with a fruit salad or a tossed salad, and your meal is complete.

Yield: 4–6 servings | **Active time:** 10 minutes | **Start to finish:** 25 minutes

1½ cups instant grits
2 cups boiling water
1½ cups grated sharp cheddar cheese
2 tablespoons unsalted butter, cut into small bits
1 tablespoon paprika
½ teaspoon dry mustard powder
¾ pound baked ham, trimmed of fat and cut into ½-inch dice
3 large eggs, lightly beaten
Salt and freshly ground black pepper to taste

1. Preheat the oven to 425°F, and grease a 9 x 13-inch baking pan.
2. Place grits in a large mixing bowl, and whisk in water, whisking until smooth. Whisk in cheese, butter, paprika, and mustard, and stir for 1 minute, or until cheese melts. Stir in ham and eggs, and season to taste with salt and pepper. Scrape mixture into the prepared pan.
3. Bake for 20–25 minutes, or until set at the edges and barely set in the center. Serve immediately.

Note: The casserole can be prepared for baking up to 1 day in advance and refrigerated, tightly covered. Bake, covered with foil, for 5 minutes, then discard foil and bake for an additional 20–25 minutes.

Variations:

- Substitute Swiss cheese, jalapeño Jack, or a combination of mozzarella and freshly grated Parmesan cheeses for the cheddar.
- Substitute bulk pork sausage—Italian or American—cooked for 5–7 minutes over medium-high heat, breaking up lumps with a fork, or until browned and cooked through, for the ham.
- Substitute smoked turkey for the ham.
- Add 1 cup chopped tomato to the casserole.
- Add ½ pound mushrooms, wiped with a damp paper towel, trimmed, and sliced, and then sautéed in 2 tablespoons unsalted butter and 1 tablespoon olive oil until browned.

Grits have been a part of our food history for about 400 years; they date back to around 1607 when the colonists arrived in Jamestown, Virginia. There, they were met by friendly Native Americans offering what they called *rockahominie*, a softened maize seasoned with salt and animal fat. Grits were known as "Southern oatmeal," and they were preferred over oatmeal because they could withstand the heat and humidity in the South.

Glazed Ham and Pork Meatloaf

I'm a sucker for the sweet and hot glaze served on baked ham, and when you're down to your last few cups of ham, you can replicate the taste with this meatloaf, also made with ground pork.

Yield: 4–6 servings | **Active time:** 15 minutes | **Start to finish:** 40 minutes

Vegetable oil spray
2 tablespoons unsalted butter
2 tablespoons vegetable oil
1 medium onion, peeled and chopped
½ green bell pepper, seeds and ribs removed, and chopped
1 celery rib, rinsed, trimmed, and chopped
1 garlic clove, peeled and minced
1 large egg, lightly beaten
½ cup plain breadcrumbs
¼ cup milk
¾ cup grated mozzarella cheese
2 tablespoons chopped fresh parsley
1 teaspoon dried thyme
¾ pound ground pork
2 cups finely chopped baked ham
Salt and freshly ground black pepper to taste
¼ cup apricot preserves
3 tablespoons grainy mustard
1 tablespoon grated fresh ginger

1. Preheat the oven to 400°F, cover a rimmed baking sheet with heavy-duty aluminum foil, and grease the foil with vegetable oil spray.
2. Heat butter and oil in a medium skillet over medium heat. Add onion, green bell pepper, celery, and garlic, and cook, stirring frequently, for 5–7 minutes, or until vegetables soften.
3. While vegetables cook, combine egg, breadcrumbs, milk, mozzarella, parsley, thyme, pork, and ham in a mixing bowl, and mix well. Add vegetables, season to taste with salt and pepper, and mix well again. Form meat mixture into a loaf 5 inches wide and 2 inches high on the prepared baking sheet.

4. Bake meatloaf for 15 minutes. While meatloaf bakes, combine apricot preserves, mustard, and ginger in a small bowl, and stir well. Remove meatloaf from the oven, and spread glaze on top. Bake for an additional 10 minutes, or until an instant-read thermometer registers 165°F when placed in the center. Serve immediately.

Note: The meatloaf can be baked up to 2 days in advance and refrigerated, tightly covered. It can be served cold, or it can be reheated in a 350°F oven, covered with foil, for 20–25 minutes, or until hot.

Variations:
- Substitute ground turkey for the pork, and chopped smoked turkey for the ham.
- Substitute orange marmalade or red currant jelly for the apricot preserves.

Biscuit-Topped Ham and Black-Eyed Pea Stew

Biscuits are the mainstay of the Southern diet, as are black-eyed peas. You make the cheese biscuit dough while the stew simmers, and then bake the biscuits right on top. You meal is complete in one pan.

Yield: 4–6 servings | **Active time:** 15 minutes | **Start to finish:** 35 minutes

STEW

2 tablespoons unsalted butter

1 large onion, peeled and chopped

2 garlic cloves, peeled and minced

1 carrot, peeled and thinly sliced

1 celery rib, rinsed, trimmed, and thinly sliced

2½ cups Chicken Stock (recipe on page 35) or purchased stock

2 tablespoons chopped fresh parsley

2 teaspoons dried sage

1 bay leaf

1 (15-ounce) can black-eyed peas, drained and rinsed

¾ cup frozen corn kernels, thawed

¾ pound baked ham, cut into ½-inch dice

1 tablespoon cornstarch

2 tablespoons cold water

Salt and freshly ground black pepper to taste

BISCUITS

½ cup yellow cornmeal

½ cup all-purpose flour

1½ teaspoons baking powder

½ teaspoon salt

½ teaspoon cayenne

1 cup grated Swiss cheese

½ cup whole milk

1. Preheat the oven to 425°F, and grease a 9 x 13-inch baking dish.
2. Heat butter in a large saucepan over medium-high heat. Add onion, garlic, carrot, and celery, and cook, stirring frequently, for 3 minutes, or until onion is translucent. Add stock, parsley, sage, and bay leaf, and bring to a boil over high heat, covered, stirring occasionally. Reduce the heat to low, and simmer stew, covered, for 5–7 minutes.
3. Stir in black-eyed peas, corn, and ham, and cook for an additional 5–7 minutes, or until carrots are tender. Mix cornstarch with water, and add mixture to stew. Cook for 1–2 minutes, or until slightly thickened. Remove and discard bay leaf, and season to taste with salt and pepper.
4. While stew simmers, combine cornmeal, flour, baking powder, salt, and cayenne, and whisk well. Add cheese, and toss mixture well. Add milk, and stir until dough is just combined.
5. Transfer stew to the prepared baking dish. Drop biscuit dough into 12 mounds on top of stew. Bake in the upper third of the oven for 12–15 minutes, or until biscuits are golden brown and a toothpick inserted in the center comes out clean.

Note: The stew can be prepared up to 2 days in advance and refrigerated, tightly covered. Reheat it over low heat, covered, stirring occasionally, until it simmers before baking. Do not make or bake the biscuit topping until just prior to serving.

Variation:
- Substitute cheddar cheese for the Swiss cheese, and substitute smoked turkey for the ham.

Baked Italian Sausage and Garbanzo Beans

This baked pasta casserole is similar to a *pasta fagioli*, but it's made with flavorful sausage and meaty, nutty garbanzo beans. Serve it with a tossed salad.

Yield: 4–6 servings | **Active time:** 15 minutes | **Start to finish:** 40 minutes

> ²/₃ pound penne pasta
> 1 pound bulk hot or sweet Italian sausage
> 1 large onion, peeled and chopped
> 2 garlic cloves, peeled and minced
> 1 (28-ounce) can diced tomatoes, drained
> 2 tablespoons tomato paste
> 1 (15-ounce) can garbanzo beans, drained and rinsed
> 1 teaspoon dried oregano
> ½ teaspoon dried thyme
> Salt and freshly ground black pepper to taste
> ½ cup freshly grated Parmesan cheese
> ¼ cup chopped parsley
> ¾ cup grated mozzarella cheese

1. Preheat the oven to 400°F, and grease a 10 x 14-inch baking pan. Bring a large pot of salted water to a boil. Cook pasta according to package directions until al dente. Drain, and place pasta in the prepared pan.
2. While the water heats, heat a large skillet over medium-high heat. Add sausage, breaking up lumps with a fork, and cook for 3–5 minutes, or until sausage is brown. Remove sausage from the skillet with a slotted spoon, and set aside.
3. Add onion and garlic to the skillet. Cook, stirring frequently, for 3 minutes, or until onion is translucent. Add tomatoes, tomato paste, garbanzo beans, oregano, and thyme, and simmer 5 minutes. Season to taste with salt and pepper. Stir in Parmesan and parsley, and stir mixture into pasta.

4. Cover the pan with aluminum foil, and bake for 10 minutes. Uncover the pan, sprinkle with mozzarella cheese, and bake for an additional 15 minutes, or until cheese is bubbly. Serve immediately.

Note: The dish can be prepared up to 2 days in advance and refrigerated, tightly covered. Reheat it, covered, in a 350°F oven for 20–25 minutes, or until hot.

Variations:
- Substitute ground beef or ground turkey for the sausage for a milder dish.
- Substitute kidney beans for the garbanzo beans.

This dish is extremely high in protein because in addition to the meat, when beans and pasta are joined they also create a complete protein.

Chapter 9:
Fast $1 Finales

As I promised you, the $3 per person figure pays for your entire meal, so with almost all of the dishes in the previous chapters, there's enough money left to pay for dessert! And you'll find a great range of tasty treats—each of which can be prepared along with the savory course it follows on the night you want to serve it.

You'll find a range of recipes, including fondues that are as much fun to make as they are delicious to eat. And then there are various flavors of homey puddings; you can enjoy them hot on the night you make them, and then refrigerate the rest and have it cold at a subsequent time. Or, make a double batch and know you've got a sweet treat waiting!

With the exception of apples and bananas—available and reasonably priced at all times of the year—fresh fruits should be used only when they're in season, and, therefore, the most affordable. Certain fruits—like highly perishable raspberries and succulent blackberries, are rarely affordable. But strawberries are less expensive when in season, as are blueberries and peaches.

It's also a good idea to freeze your own fruits during their brief local season. Fruits like blueberries just need rinsing, and strawberries should be hulled as well as rinsed. Freeze the fruit on a baking sheet, and then transfer it to a heavy resalable plastic bag. The quality and flavor will be superior to any frozen fruit you'd buy, and the price will be better, too.

You'll notice that the citrus desserts call for a combination of fresh fruit juice and bottled juice. Squeezing enough juice from lemons and limes for these recipes would push them beyond the fiscal restrictions of this chapter. However, there's nothing like the aroma from grated citrus zest! So I've included the zest and juice from one piece of fruit, and then filled in with less expensive bottled juice for the remainder of what is needed.

CARING FOR CHOCOLATE

While I don't adhere to the theory that you shouldn't use wine for cooking that you wouldn't drink, I am a stickler about the quality of chocolate used for chocolate desserts, and melted chocolate chips are not the answer. The supermarket shelves are now laden with good quality domestic chocolate, containing as much as 60 percent cocoa solids. The best choices for making desserts are bittersweet or semisweet chocolate.

Good quality chocolate is actually rather nutritious! It contains vitamins and minerals including calcium and magnesium. It also contains antioxidants that help to prevent cancer and heart disease. These benefits are found mostly in dark chocolate and only in high quality chocolates that use 60 percent or more cocoa solids. Cheap chocolate is mostly fat and sugar and has little nutritional value.

Almost all chocolate desserts require the chocolate to be melted. Here are the steps to follow:

Chopping the chocolate. Chopping chocolate into fine pieces makes melting easier. You can do this in a food processor fitted with a steel blade. Begin by breaking it with a heavy knife rather than breaking it with your hands. Body heat is sufficiently high to soften the chocolate so it will not chop evenly. If you don't have a food processor, place small chunks of chocolate in a heavy resealable plastic bag, cover the bag with a dish towel, and crush it by hitting it with the bottom of a heavy saucepan.

Melting the chocolate. Chocolate needs careful melting because it scorches easily. Frequently some type of liquid can be heated along with the chocolate to help shield it from the heat, but you still need to take care. While you can simply place the chocolate into a saucepan, here are some alternative ways of making a fondue:

- Melt chunks in the top of a double boiler placed over barely simmering water.

- Melt chopped chocolate in a microwave-safe bowl, and microwave on 100 percent (High) for 20 seconds. Stir, and repeat as necessary.

- Preheat the oven to 250°F. Place chopped chocolate in the oven and then turn off the heat immediately. Stir after 3 minutes, and return to the warm oven if necessary.

- Combine the chocolate with any liquid ingredients in a 2-cup slow cooker and turn it on for 15 minutes.

- Combine chocolate and cream in a heatproof bowl and place it on the warming surface of an electric coffee maker.

CARAMEL CHEMISTRY

Caramel is a very low-cost way to flavor desserts; it's simply sugar and water cooked to a high temperature. But the change from simple sugar syrup to caramel is hardly a simple one. The sugar melts and thickens into a syrup that slowly begins to change color from light yellow to deep mahogany brown.

The sugar breaks down from a single species of molecule to recombine into at least 100 different reaction products, among them sour organic acids, sweet and bitter derivatives, and brown-colored polymers. This change becomes noticeable between 320°F and 360°F because large amounts of energy are required to start the molecular changes. As the temperature of the syrup rises, there is no more moisture left to evaporate, and the color deepens. It is at about 340°F that the syrup can be called caramel.

The easiest way to judge the temperature of a sugar syrup is by using a candy or deep-frying thermometer. Place it in the middle of the pan, and not on the bottom of the pot where the temperature will be higher. But long before there were such thermometers, cooks judged the progress of a syrup by dropping drips into a cup of ice water and gauging the results. Here are the clues:

- The "soft ball" stage is between 235°F and 250°F. When you place a few drops of syrup in the water, you can pick it up between your fingers and it feels soft.

- The "hard ball" stage is the middle point before you get caramel. It's between 250°F and 275°F and a drop of the syrup forms a hard ball in the water.

Hot Banana Splits with Chocolate Caramel Sauce

The sweetness of bananas is accentuated when they're cooked, and their texture turns soft and velvety. For these sundaes, the bananas are cooked in caramel, into which chocolate is then added.

Yield: 4–6 servings | **Active time:** 15 minutes | **Start to finish:** 15 minutes

> 4 tablespoons (½ stick) unsalted butter
> 4 ripe bananas, sliced diagonally into ½-inch-thick slices
> ½ cup firmly packed dark brown sugar
> ¾ cup heavy cream
> 4 ounces bittersweet chocolate, finely chopped
> ¼ teaspoon pure vanilla extract
> 1 pint vanilla ice cream, softened

1. Melt butter in a 12-inch heavy skillet over medium-high heat. Add bananas, and sprinkle sugar over bananas. Cook bananas, turning gently with a slotted spatula, for 3 minutes. Remove bananas from the skillet with a slotted spatula, and keep warm.
2. Add cream, chocolate, and vanilla to the skillet. Cook over medium heat, stirring constantly, for 2 minutes, or until caramel dissolves.
3. To serve, place ice cream in dessert bowls and top with banana slices and sauce.

Note: The bananas can be cooked and the sauce can be completed up to 6 hours in advance. Reheat the bananas in the sauce before serving.

Variation:
- Substitute 4 peeled and sliced peaches for the bananas.

Cinnamon Apple Fondue

Think of a warm apple pie, fragrant with cinnamon. That's what this fondue is like, plus it's creamy too.

Yield: 4–6 servings | **Active time:** 5 minutes | **Start to finish:** 10 minutes

4 tablespoons (½ stick) unsalted butter
¼ cup all-purpose flour
½ cup heavy cream
1½ cups unsweetened applesauce
⅓ cup firmly packed light brown sugar
¾ teaspoon ground cinnamon

1. Melt butter in a 1-quart saucepan over medium heat. Reduce the heat to low, add flour, and cook for 2 minutes, stirring constantly.
2. Raise the heat to medium and whisk in cream, applesauce, sugar, and cinnamon. Bring to a boil, whisking until smooth. Reduce the heat to low, and simmer 1 minute.
3. To serve, transfer the fondue to a fondue pot or other pot with a heat source. Serve with hulled strawberries (halved if large), apple slices, donut holes, squares of waffle, cubes of angel food cake, cubes of pound cake, cubes of brownie, or sugar cookies.

Note: The fondue can be prepared up to 4 hours in advance and kept at room temperature. Reheat it over very low heat, stirring frequently, or in a microwave oven.

Variation:
- Substitute 2 tablespoons apple brandy or rum for 2 tablespoons of the applesauce.

While there isn't really a Pillsbury Dough Boy or an Aunt Jemima, Johnny Appleseed was a real person. Named John Chapman, he was born in Massachusetts in 1774. Unlike the artistic depictions of propagating apples by tossing seeds onto the ground, in reality he started nurseries for apple tree seedlings in the Allegheny Valley in 1800. He had pushed as far west as Indiana and Illinois to establish groves of apple trees by the time he died in 1845.

Baked Stuffed Apples

A stuffing made with cookie crumbs, nuts, and raisins elevates this homey dessert to a new level of elegance.

Yield: 4-6 servings | **Active time:** 15 minutes | **Start to finish:** 40 minutes

> 4-6 large baking apples, such as Jonathan, Northern Spy, or York Imperial
> 2 tablespoons lemon juice
> 1/2 cup chopped walnuts, toasted for 5 minutes in a 350° F oven
> 1/4 cup raisins
> 1/4 cup pure maple syrup
> 4 tablespoons unsalted butter, melted, divided
> 1/2 cup butter cookie crumbs
> 1/2-1 cup white wine

1. Preheat the oven to 375° F. Core apples, cutting a cavity about 1 inch wide but not cutting through to the bottom. Peel skin around stem end to expose 2 1/2 inches of apple flesh. Rub cut surfaces with lemon juice to prevent discoloration, and prick skin with the tip of a paring knife to prevent apples from bursting.

2. Combine nuts, raisins, maple syrup, 3 tablespoons butter, and cookie crumbs in a small bowl. Stir to blend. Gently pack stuffing into cavities of apples. Brush exposed flesh of the apples with the remaining melted butter. Arrange apples in a shallow baking dish.

3. Pour 1/4 inch of white wine into the bottom of the baking dish. Bake apples, basting them once or twice with juices in the dish for the first 10 minutes. Continue to bake until apples are just tender when pierced with a metal skewer, about 25-30 minutes total time. Do not overbake; the centers of the apples should offer some resistance. Serve warm or cold.

Note: The apples can be baked up to 2 days in advance and refrigerated, tightly covered.

Variations:
- Substitute 3 tablespoons honey for the maple syrup.
- Substitute gingersnap crumbs or graham cracker crumbs for the butter cookie crumbs.

Apple Pie Quesadillas

Flour tortillas become like crisp cookies when brushed with melted butter and sprinkled with sugar for these hot treats. And while caramel candies are a convenience food, using them means these sweet quesadillas are ready to bake within minutes.

Yield: 4–6 servings | **Active time:** 10 minutes | **Start to finish:** 30 minutes

8 (6-inch) flour tortillas
24 caramel candies, unwrapped
¼ cup whole milk
½ teaspoon ground cinnamon
2 Golden Delicious apples, peeled, cored, and thinly sliced
3 tablespoons unsalted butter, melted
⅓ cup granulated sugar

1. Preheat the oven to 400°F, and cover 2 baking sheets with aluminum foil. Soften tortillas, if necessary, by wrapping them in plastic wrap and heating them in a microwave oven on High (100 percent power) for 10–15 seconds, or until pliable.

2. Place caramel candies and milk in a small microwave safe bowl, and microwave for 45 seconds at Medium (50 percent power). Stir, and repeat as necessary until caramel is smooth. Stir in cinnamon.

3. Spread caramel mixture on tortillas to about ½ inch from the edge. Arrange apple slices over one ½ of each tortilla, and fold over the other ½. Press down with the palm of your hand.

4. Place quesadillas on the baking sheet, brush with 1 tablespoon butter, and sprinkle with 2 tablespoons sugar. Bake for 10 minutes, then turn with a spatula, brush with remaining butter, and sprinkle with remaining sugar. Bake for an additional 10 minutes or until the quesadillas are browned. Allow to sit for 3 minutes, then cut in half and serve immediately.

Note: The tortillas can be baked up to 1 day in advance and refrigerated, tightly covered. Reheat them, uncovered, in a 375°F oven for 5–7 minutes, or until hot and crispy. Do not cut them until just prior to serving.

Variation:
- Substitute peaches for the apples, and substitute ground ginger for the cinnamon.

Baked Lime Custards

Hot custards are a homey treat, and these can be made at any time of the year because they're based on readily accessible limes.

Yield: 6 servings | **Active time:** 15 minutes | **Start to finish:** 35 minutes

1 lime

3 tablespoons lime juice, or more as needed

3 large eggs, at room temperature

$\frac{1}{2}$ cup granulated sugar, divided

2 tablespoons all-purpose flour

1 cup half-and-half

$\frac{1}{4}$ teaspoon salt

$\frac{1}{4}$ cup confectioners' sugar

1. Preheat the oven to 350°F, and bring a large kettle of water up to boil over high heat. Grease 6 (6-ounce) custard cups, and place them in a baking dish. Grate zest from lime, and squeeze juice into a measuring cup; add enough bottled lime juice to measure $\frac{1}{4}$ cup. Separate eggs.

2. Whisk egg yolks and $\frac{1}{3}$ cup sugar for 2 minutes, or until thick and light in color. Whisk in lime zest and flour, and then whisk in lime juice and half-and-half. Set aside.

3. Place egg whites in a grease-free mixing bowl and beat at medium speed with an electric mixer until frothy. Add salt, raise the speed to high, and beat until soft peaks form. Add remaining sugar, 1 tablespoon at a time, and continue to beat until stiff peaks form.

4. Fold yolk mixture into whites, and divide batter into the prepared cups. Place the pan in the oven, and add boiling water to reach halfway up the sides of the custard cups.

5. Bake for 20–25 minutes, or until puddings are puffed and lightly browned. Dust tops of custards with confectioners' sugar, and serve immediately.

Note: The custards can be baked up to 4 hours in advance and served at room temperature. Do not dust with confectioners' sugar until just prior to serving.

Variation:
- Substitute lemon zest and lemon juice for the lime zest and lime juice.

Lemon Pudding

Either hot or cold, this pudding seems like the essence of spring. You can fold berries into it, or top it with berries, too.

Yield: 6 servings | **Active time:** 15 minutes | **Start to finish:** 15 minutes

1 lemon
⅓ cup lemon juice, or more as needed
¾ cup granulated sugar
¼ cup cornstarch
2 cups whole milk
½ cup half-and-half
3 large egg yolks, lightly beaten
Pinch of salt
2 tablespoons unsalted butter, cut into bits
1 pint vanilla or strawberry ice cream

1. Grate zest from lemon, and squeeze juice into a measuring cup; add enough bottled lemon juice to measure ½ cup.
2. Whisk sugar and cornstarch in a medium saucepan. Add milk and half-and-half, and whisk until smooth. Beat in egg yolks, lemon zest, lemon juice, and salt. Cook over medium heat, whisking constantly, until mixture comes to a boil and thickens. Reduce the heat to low, and simmer 1 minute.
3. Remove the pan from the stove, and whisk in butter. Serve immediately, topped with ice cream.

Note: The pudding can be prepared up to 2 days in advance and refrigerated, with a sheet of plastic wrap pushed directly into the surface to prevent a skin from forming. Serve cold; do not reheat.

Variation:
- Substitute 1 lime and lime juice for the lemon and lemon juice.

Caramelized Pineapple

Pineapples are frequently on sale, and that's when you should make this fast and easy dessert. To choose the ripest pineapple, smell them and see which one has the strongest fragrance.

Yield: 6–8 servings | **Active time:** 10 minutes | **Start to finish:** 20 minutes

> 1 small (2–2½ pound) ripe pineapple
> 3 tablespoons unsalted butter
> ⅓ cup firmly packed dark brown sugar
> ½ cup orange juice
> 2 tablespoons dark rum
> 2 cups vanilla ice cream

1. Cut green top and base from pineapple so it sits firmly on the cutting board. Cut off rind using a serrated knife, turning pineapple over as necessary. Cut pineapple in half lengthwise, and discard woody core. Cut each half into 3–4 lengthwise slices, and cut each slice in half horizontally.

2. While preparing pineapple, heat butter, brown sugar, orange juice, and rum in a large skillet over medium heat, stirring just until the sugar is moistened. Add pineapple wedges in one layer, bring to a boil, cover the skillet, and cook for 5 minutes without stirring.

3. Uncover the skillet, raise the heat to medium-high, turn wedges gently with a slotted spatula, and cook, uncovered, for 5–7 minutes, or until syrup is thick. Turn wedges gently to coat with caramel, and transfer to individual serving plates. Place ⅓ cup ice cream next to pineapple wedges, and spoon caramel over ice cream. Serve immediately.

Note: The pineapple can be prepared up to 4 hours in advance and kept in the skillet. Reheat over low heat until bubbly, then serve.

Variation:
- Substitute peeled fresh peaches for the pineapple, allowing 1 peach per person.

Peach Skillet Cake

Summer's ripe peaches should be enjoyed as often as possible, and one reason why this cake is such a treat is that it's only briefly under the broiler, so cooking it doesn't heat up the oven.

Yield: 6–8 servings | **Active time:** 10 minutes | **Start to finish:** 30 minutes

3 tablespoons unsalted butter
3 ripe peaches, peeled, seeded, and cut into 8 wedges each
¼ cup granulated sugar, divided
1 cup cottage cheese
¾ cup sour cream
1 teaspoon pure vanilla extract
¾ cup all-purpose flour
3 large eggs
1 tablespoon confectioners' sugar
Sweetened whipped cream for serving (optional)

1. Preheat the oven broiler. Melt butter in a 12-inch ovenproof skillet. Arrange peach wedges in one layer in the skillet and sprinkle them with ½ of granulated sugar. Cook over medium heat for 5 minutes, turn wedges over with a slotted spatula, and cook for 3 minutes.
2. While peaches cook, combine cottage cheese, sour cream, vanilla, flour, eggs, and remaining granulated sugar in a food processor fitted with the steel blade or in a blender. Puree until smooth.
3. Pour batter over peaches in the skillet. Cover and cook over low heat on top of the stove for 6 minutes. Uncover the skillet, and broil 8 inches from the broiler element for 6–8 minutes, or until browned. Invert cake onto a serving plate. Sprinkle with the confectioners' sugar, cut into wedges, and serve immediately, passing whipped cream separately, if using.

Note: The batter and peaches can be prepared up to 6 hours in advance. Do not cook the cake until just prior to serving.

Variation:
- Substitute apples for the peaches, slicing them thinly.

> Rather than blanching peaches in boiling water to peel them, it's easier and faster to use a vegetable peeler.

Blueberry Clafouti

Clafouti is basically a dessert that combines fruit and a batter. Any fruit that holds its shape while baking can be used.

Yield: 6–8 servings | **Active time:** 10 minutes | **Start to finish:** 30 minutes

1 cup granulated sugar, divided
6 tablespoons all-purpose flour
6 large eggs
2 cups whole milk
2 teaspoons pure vanilla extract
½ teaspoon salt
2 cups fresh blueberries, rinsed
2 tablespoons unsalted butter, cut into bits
Vanilla ice cream (optional)

1. Preheat the oven to 400°F, and grease a 9 x 13-inch baking pan.
2. Reserve 3 tablespoons sugar; combine remaining sugar, flour, eggs, milk, vanilla extract, and salt in a food processor fitted with the steel blade or in a blender. Puree until smooth.
3. Arrange blueberries in the prepared baking pan, and pour custard over them. Bake for 20–25 minutes, or until top is puffed and springy to the touch.
4. Remove the pan from the oven, and increase the oven temperature to broil. Sprinkle with remaining 3 tablespoons sugar, dot with butter, and broil clafouti under the broiler about 4 inches from the heat for 1–1½ minutes, or until it is browned. Serve immediately with ice cream, if using.

Note: The batter can be prepared up to 1 day in advance and refrigerated, tightly covered. Do not bake or broil cake until just prior to serving.

Variation:
- Substitute halved cherries, chopped peaches, sliced pears, or chopped fresh apricots for the blueberries.

Although it's more expensive, always buy real vanilla extract. The imitation stuff is only slightly less expensive and gives food such a chemical taste. You use so little vanilla in any given dish that it's probably not more than a penny difference.

Strawberry Shortcake

What would summer be without strawberry shortcake? This an authentic recipe, and the rich and buttery shortcake itself has the texture of a biscuit. You'll never buy those premade sponges in the produce department again!

Yield: 6 servings | **Active time:** 15 minutes | **Start to finish:** 35 minutes

> 3 cups all-purpose flour
> $^3/_4$ cup granulated sugar, divided
> 1 tablespoon cream of tartar
> $2^1/_4$ teaspoons baking soda
> $^1/_4$ teaspoon salt
> $^1/_2$ pound (2 sticks) unsalted butter, divided
> 2 cups heavy cream, divided
> 1 quart fresh strawberries
> $^1/_3$ cup confectioners' sugar

1. Preheat the oven to 375°F, and grease 2 baking sheets. Combine flour, $^1/_3$ cup sugar, cream of tartar, baking soda, and salt in a medium mixing bowl. Melt 3 tablespoons butter, and set aside. Cut remaining butter into $^1/_4$-inch cubes.
2. Cut butter into flour mixture using a pastry blender, two knives, or your fingertips until mixture resembles coarse meal. Add 1 cup cream, and blend until just blended.
3. Scrape dough onto a floured surface, and knead lightly. Roll dough $^3/_4$ inch thick. Cut out 6 (4-inch) rounds and place them on the baking sheet. Brush rounds with melted butter. Cut out 6 ($2^1/_2$-inch) rounds and place them on top of larger rounds. Brush tops with butter.
4. Bake for 15–17 minutes, or until shortcakes are golden brown. Cool for at least 5 minutes on a wire rack.
5. While shortcakes bake, rinse strawberries, discard green caps, and slice. Toss strawberries with remaining sugar. Set aside. Just prior to serving, whip remaining cream with confectioners' sugar until stiff peaks form.
6. To serve, mound strawberries on larger round, and top with whipped cream and smaller round. Serve immediately.

Note: The shortcakes can be prepared up to 2 days in advance and kept at room temperature, tightly covered.

Variations:
- Substitute blueberries, sliced peaches, or fruit salad for the strawberries.
- Add 2 teaspoons orange zest to the shortcake dough.

Cream of tartar comes from the acid deposited inside wine barrels. It's used in conjunction with baking soda to produce the same chemical reaction as that caused by baking powder.

Classic Chocolate Fondue

As an unabashed chocoholic, to me this gooey, rich fondue is the ultimate dessert! And there are so many inexpensive items you can use as dippers to enjoy every bite.

Yield: 6–8 servings | **Active time:** 15 minutes | **Start to finish:** 15 minutes

½ cup heavy cream

10 ounces bittersweet chocolate, chopped

2–3 tablespoons liquor or liqueur (your favorite: rum, bourbon, tequila, Cognac, brandy, triple sec, Grand Marnier, Chambord, kirsch, amaretto, Frangelico, crème de cacao, crème de banana, Irish cream liqueur, Kahlúa)

1. Combine cream and chocolate in a heavy 1-quart saucepan. Stir over very low heat to melt chocolate. When mixture is smooth and the chocolate is melted, stir in liquor.
2. Transfer fondue to a fondue pot or other pot with a heat source, and serve with hulled strawberries (halved if large), banana chunks, apple slices, donut holes, waffle squares, butter cookies, angel food cake cubes, cake cubes, brownie cubes, biscotti, or sugar cookies.

Note: The fondue can be prepared up to 4 hours in advance and kept at room temperature. Reheat it over very low heat, stirring frequently, or in a microwave oven.

Variation:

- If you're serving the fondue to children or adults who cannot tolerate alcohol, you can substitute ¼ to ½ teaspoon pure extract plus 2 tablespoons water for the liquor or liqueur.

One of the additional health benefits of chocolate is that it has been found to contain catechins—some of the same antioxidants found in green tea. The catechins attack free radicals, which damage cells and are thought to lead to cancer and heart disease. So eating chocolate may help to prevent heart disease and cancer!

Chocolate Honey Almond Fondue

This fondue has the wonderful flavor of a Toblerone candy bar, with crunchy almonds and sweet honey as accents in the creamy chocolate base.

Yield: 6 servings | **Active time:** 15 minutes | **Start to finish:** 15 minutes

½ cup heavy cream

¼ cup honey

8 ounces bittersweet chocolate, chopped

1 ounce unsweetened chocolate, chopped

½ cup sliced almonds, toasted in a 350°F oven for 5–7 minutes, or until lightly browned, chopped

3 tablespoons almond liqueur, such as Amaretto, or light rum

½ teaspoon pure almond extract

1. Combine heavy cream, honey, bittersweet chocolate, and unsweetened chocolate in a 1-quart heavy saucepan. Stir over very low heat until chocolate melts. Stir in almonds, liqueur, and almond extract.

2. To serve, transfer fondue to a fondue pot or other pot with a heat source. Serve with hulled strawberries (halved if large), banana chunks, apple slices, donut holes, squares of waffle, butter cookies, cubes of angel food cake, cubes of pound cake, almond biscotti, or sugar cookies.

Note: The fondue can be prepared up to 4 hours in advance and kept at room temperature. Reheat it over very low heat, stirring frequently, or in a microwave oven.

Variation:

- Substitute hazelnuts for the almonds, and substitute hazelnut liqueur, such as Frangelico, for the almond liqueur.

Candy Bar Quesadillas

There's no reason why cream cheese can't become the *queso* for these quesadillas, and there are myriad ways to personalize them with your favorite candy bar. They're so fast and easy to make that you can decide even after dinner is finished that you want a dessert!

Yield: 4–6 servings | **Active time:** 5 minutes | **Start to finish:** 15 minutes

> 8 (6-inch) flour tortillas
> 1 (8-ounce) package cream cheese, softened
> 4 (1½–2-ounce) plain or flavored chocolate, broken into small pieces
> 4 tablespoons unsalted butter, melted
> ¼ cup granulated sugar

1. Preheat the oven to 450°F, and cover a baking sheet with aluminum foil. Soften tortillas, if necessary, by wrapping them in plastic wrap and heating them in a microwave oven on High (100 percent power) for 10–15 seconds, or until pliable.
2. Lay tortillas out on a counter, and divide cream cheese amongst them. Spread cream cheese over ½ of each circle, and top with equal amounts of candy bar slices. Press quesadillas together gently into half circles, and place them on the baking sheet. Brush the tops with the melted butter, and sprinkle with ½ of sugar.
3. Bake for 5 minutes. Turn quesadillas with a spatula, brush the second side with butter, and sprinkle with remaining sugar. Bake an additional 3–4 minutes, or until the quesadillas are browned. Remove from the oven, and serve immediately.

Note: The quesadillas can be baked up to 1 day in advance and refrigerated, tightly covered. Reheat them, uncovered, in a 375°F oven for 5–7 minutes, or until hot and crispy. Do not cut them until just prior to serving.

Variation:
- Substitute a candy bar with additional ingredients, like a Snickers, Almond Joy, or Three Musketeers, for the chocolate bars.

Hot Chocolate Mini-Tortes

Warm chocolate tortes have become all the rage in the past few years, and they are really so easy to make that you can wow guests. The center remains runny, so it's like a sauce for the portion of the tortes that are set.

Yield: 4 servings | **Active time:** 15 minutes | **Start to finish:** 35 minutes

¼ pound (1 stick) unsalted butter, plus additional for greasing cups
2 tablespoons granulated sugar
¼ pound bittersweet chocolate, chopped
2 large eggs
2 large egg yolks
⅓ cup confectioners' sugar
¾ teaspoon pure vanilla extract
4 tablespoons all-purpose flour
2 tablespoons unsweetened cocoa powder
Sweetened whipped cream (optional)

1. Preheat the oven to 400°F. Grease 4 (6-ounce) custard cups with butter, and sprinkle with granulated sugar. Place cups on a baking sheet pan and set aside.

2. Combine remaining butter and chopped semisweet chocolate in a small saucepan, and melt over low heat, stirring frequently. Remove the pan from the heat and cool.

3. Beat eggs, egg yolks, confectioners' sugar, and vanilla extract with a hand-held electric mixer set on high speed for 5 minutes, or until mixture is thick and pale yellow. Beat in chocolate mixture on medium speed. Sift flour and cocoa powder over chocolate mixture, and beat on low speed just until blended. Spoon batter into the prepared custard cups.

4. Bake for 12–14 minutes, or until cakes rise slightly and feel firm at the edges and softer in the center when pressed gently. Cool in custard cups for 5 minutes. Invert with pot holders onto dessert plates, and serve with sweetened whipped cream, if using.

Note: The cups can be prepared for baking up to 2 hours in advance, and kept at room temperature.

Variation:
- Place a white chocolate truffle in the center of each cup before baking.

Chocolate Pudding

One bite of this and I promise you'll be transported back to childhood, and once you've seen that it takes but minutes to make, you'll never spend money on a mix again.

Yield: 4–6 servings | **Active time:** 10 minutes | **Start to finish:** 10 minutes

> 1 cup granulated sugar
> 4 tablespoons cornstarch
> ½ pound bittersweet chocolate, chopped
> Pinch of salt
> 2⅔ cups whole milk
> 2 large egg yolks, lightly beaten
> 2 tablespoons unsalted butter
> ½ teaspoon pure vanilla extract
> 1½–2 cups vanilla ice cream

1. Combine sugar, cornstarch, chocolate, and salt in a heavy saucepan. Add milk and egg yolks, and whisk well.
2. Place the saucepan over medium heat, and bring to a boil, whisking constantly. Simmer 1 minute, whisking constantly. Remove the pan from the heat, and whisk in butter and vanilla. Serve immediately, topped with ice cream.

Note: The pudding can be prepared up to 2 days in advance and refrigerated, with a sheet of plastic wrap pressed directly into the surface to prevent a skin from forming. Serve it chilled; do not reheat it.

Variations:
- Add 1 tablespoon instant coffee powder for mocha pudding.
- Substitute 2 tablespoons of your favorite liquor or liqueur for 2 tablespoons milk to flavor the pudding.

> Cornstarch prevents eggs from scrambling when they're cooked and come to a boil. That's why this pudding can simmer while a custard cannot.

Chocolate Sauce

Everyone should know how to make chocolate sauce; it's so much better than any you can buy and it's so easy you can always have it around. This is very intensely flavored from the combination of chocolate and cocoa.

Yield: 3 cups | **Active time:** 15 minutes | **Start to finish:** 15 minutes

    10 ounces good-quality bittersweet chocolate
    1 cup heavy cream
    1/4 cup cocoa powder
    1/2 teaspoon pure vanilla extract
    Pinch of salt

1. Chop chocolate into pieces no larger than a lima bean, and set aside.
2. Pour cream into a 2-quart saucepan, and place over medium heat. Whisk in cocoa powder, vanilla, and salt. Bring to a boil, whisking frequently, until mixture is smooth.
3. When cream begins to boil, remove pan from the heat. Add chocolate, cover pan, and allow to sit for 5 minutes; whisk well until sauce is smooth. If lumps remain, place sauce over low heat and continue to whisk until smooth.
4. Scrape mixture into a container, and refrigerate for up to 1 week or freeze for up to 3 months. To serve, microwave sauce on Medium (50 percent power) for 30-second intervals or until liquid and warm, stirring well between microwave times.

Variations:
- Add 2 tablespoons instant coffee powder along with the cocoa for mocha sauce.
- Add 2 tablespoons of your favorite liquor or liqueur to flavor the sauce more complexly.
- Add 1/2 cup chopped toasted nuts of any type.

Because chocolate can absorb aromas and flavors from other foods, it should always be wrapped tightly after being opened. Store chocolate in a cool, dry place, but do not refrigerate or freeze it. If stored at a high temperature, the fat will rise to the surface and become a whitish powder called a bloom. It will disappear, however, as soon as the chocolate is melted.

Caramel Rum Fondue

This is one of my favorite fondues because I adore the rich and buttery taste of caramel sauce. It seems to complement just about every fruit.

Yield: 4–6 servings | **Active time:** 15 minutes | **Start to finish:** 30 minutes

> 2 cups granulated sugar
> ½ cup water
> ¼ pound (1 stick) unsalted butter, softened and cut into small pieces
> 2 cups heavy cream
> ¼ cup rum
> 1 teaspoon pure vanilla extract

1. Combine sugar and water in a 1-quart saucepan. Bring to a simmer over medium heat, swirling occasionally. Cover the pan, raise the heat to medium-high, and cook until the liquid gives off thick, large bubbles. Remove the cover and cook until the syrup reaches a golden brown.
2. Remove the pan from the heat, and stir in the butter with a long-handled wooden spoon. Add cream, stirring constantly, and then add rum and vanilla. Return the pan to a low flame, and stir constantly until the lumps have melted and the syrup is smooth.
3. To serve, transfer fondue to a fondue pot or other pot with a heat source. Serve with banana chunks, apple slices, dried apricots, donut holes, squares of waffle, cubes of angel food cake, cubes of pound cake, cubes of brownie, coconut macaroons, or sugar cookies.

Note: The fondue can be prepared up to 4 hours in advance and kept at room temperature. Reheat it over very low heat, stirring frequently, or in a microwave oven.

Variation:
- Substitute a fruit- or nut-flavored liqueur for the rum.

Caramel Sauce

Caramel is simply sugar and water cooked to a high temperature. Once that's done, just add some butter and cream you've got caramel sauce.

Yield: 3 cups | **Active time:** 15 minutes | **Start to finish:** 15 minutes

    3 cups granulated sugar
    1 cup water
    6 tablespoons (¾ stick) unsalted butter, cut into small pieces
    2 cups heavy cream
    2 teaspoons pure vanilla extract

1. Combine sugar and water in a 2-quart saucepan, and bring to a boil over medium-high heat. Swirl the pan by the handle but do not stir. Raise the heat to high, and allow syrup to cook until it reaches a walnut brown color, swirling the pot by the handle frequently.

2. Remove the pan from the heat, and stir in butter and cream with a long-handled spoon; the mixture will bubble furiously at first. Return the pan to low heat and stir until lumps melt and sauce is smooth. Stir in vanilla, and transfer to a jar. Serve hot, room temperature, or cold.

Note: The sauce can be refrigerated for up to 1 week, tightly covered.

Variation:
  • Reduce the vanilla to ½ teaspoon and add 2 tablespoons of brandy, rum, or a liqueur.

The easiest way to clean a pan in which you've caramelized sugar or made caramel sauce is to fill the pan with water and place it back on the stove. Stir as the water comes to a boil and the pan will be virtually clean.

Mock Tiramisù

The name tiramisù means "pick me up" in Italian, probably based on the strong espresso into which the ladyfingers are dipped. What makes this "mock" is that the creamy part is a combination of cream cheese, butter, and cream rather than expensive mascarpone.

Yield: 6–8 servings | **Active time:** 20 minutes | **Start to finish:** 20 minutes

> 3 tablespoons instant espresso powder
> ⅓ cup boiling water
> ¾ cup cold water
> 1 (8-ounce) package cream cheese, softened
> 3 tablespoons unsalted butter, softened
> ½ cup heavy cream
> ¼ cup sweet Marsala wine or sweet sherry
> ⅔ cup granulated sugar
> 2 (3-ounce) packages soft ladyfingers
> 2 tablespoons unsweetened cocoa powder

1. Place espresso powder in a mixing bowl, and add boiling water. Stir well to dissolve granules, and then add cold water and set aside.
2. Combine cream cheese, butter, cream, Marsala, and sugar in a mixing bowl. Beat at medium speed with an electric mixer for 5 minutes, or until light and fluffy.
3. Spread ¼ of cheese mixture into the bottom of a 2-quart serving dish. Separate halves of ladyfingers, and dip cut sides into espresso. Create two layers of cheese and dipped ladyfingers. Sprinkle with cocoa, and serve immediately.

Note: The dish can be prepared up to 1 day in advance and refrigerated, tightly covered. Do not dust with cocoa until just prior to serving.

Variation:
- Add 2–3 tablespoons Tia Maria or other coffee liqueur to the coffee mixture.

Butterscotch Pudding

Butterscotch is merely caramel made with brown sugar instead of granulated sugar, and this easy pudding can be made with ingredients you probably have around the house.

Yield: 6 servings | **Active time:** 10 minutes | **Start to finish:** 15 minutes

⅔ cup firmly packed light brown sugar

3 tablespoons cornstarch

2 cups half-and-half

3 tablespoons unsalted butter, cut into bits

1 teaspoon pure vanilla extract

Pinch of salt

1 pint ice cream (your favorite flavor)

1. Combine sugar, cornstarch, and half-and-half in a heavy saucepan, and whisk well. Bring to a boil over medium heat, whisking frequently. Boil for 2 minutes, whisking constantly.

2. Remove the pan from the stove, and whisk in butter, vanilla, and salt. Serve immediately, topped with ice cream.

Note: The pudding can be prepared up to 2 days in advance and refrigerated, with a sheet of plastic wrap pushed directly into the surface to prevent a skin from forming. Serve cold; do not reheat.

Variation:

- Substitute 2 tablespoons rum or Scotch for 2 tablespoons of the half-and-half.

Appendix A:
Metric Conversion Tables

The scientifically precise calculations needed for baking are not necessary when cooking conventionally. The tables in this appendix are designed for general cooking. If making conversions for baking, grab your calculator and compute the exact figure.

CONVERTING OUNCES TO GRAMS

The numbers in the following table are approximate. To reach the exact quantity of grams, multiply the number of ounces by 28.35.

Ounces	Grams
1 ounce	30 grams
2 ounces	60 grams
3 ounces	85 grams
4 ounces	115 grams
5 ounces	140 grams
6 ounces	180 grams
7 ounces	200 grams
8 ounces	225 grams
9 ounces	250 grams
10 ounces	285 grams
11 ounces	300 grams
12 ounces	340 grams
13 ounces	370 grams
14 ounces	400 grams
15 ounces	425 grams
16 ounces	450 grams

CONVERTING QUARTS TO LITERS

The numbers in the following table are approximate. To reach the exact amount of liters, multiply the number of quarts by 0.95.

Quarts	Liter
1 cup (¼ quart)	¼ liter
1 pint (½ quart)	½ liter
1 quart	1 liter
2 quarts	2 liters
2½ quarts	2½ liters
3 quarts	2¾ liters
4 quarts	3¾ liters
5 quarts	4¾ liters
6 quarts	5½ liters
7 quarts	6½ liters
8 quarts	7½ liters

CONVERTING POUNDS TO GRAMS AND KILOGRAMS

The numbers in the following table are approximate. To reach the exact quantity of grams, multiply the number of pounds by 453.6.

Pounds	Grams; Kilograms
1 pound	450 grams
1½ pounds	675 grams
2 pounds	900 grams
2½ pounds	1,125 grams; 1¼ kilograms
3 pounds	1,350 grams
3½ pounds	1,500 grams; 1½ kilograms
4 pounds	1,800 grams
4½ pounds	2 kilograms
5 pounds	2¼ kilograms
5½ pounds	2½ kilograms
6 pounds	2¾ kilograms
6½ pounds	3 kilograms
7 pounds	3¼ kilograms
7½ pounds	3½ kilograms
8 pounds	3¾ kilograms

CONVERTING FAHRENHEIT TO CELSIUS

The numbers in the following table are approximate. To reach the exact temperature, subtract 32 from the Fahrenheit reading, multiply the number by 5, and then divide by 9.

Degrees Fahrenheit	Degrees Celsius
170°F	77°C
180°F	82°C
190°F	88°C
200°F	95°C
225°F	110°C
250°F	120°C
300°F	150°C
325°F	165°C
350°F	180°C
375°F	190°C
400°F	205°C
425°F	220°C
450°F	230°C
475°F	245°C
500°F	260°C

CONVERTING INCHES TO CENTIMETERS

The numbers in the following table are approximate. To reach the exact number of centimeters, multiply the number of inches by 2.54.

Inches	Centimeters
½ inch	1.5 centimeters
1 inch	2.5 centimeters
2 inches	5 centimeters
3 inches	8 centimeters
4 inches	10 centimeters
5 inches	13 centimeters
6 inches	15 centimeters
7 inches	18 centimeters
8 inches	20 centimeters
9 inches	23 centimeters
10 inches	25 centimeters
11 inches	28 centimeters
12 inches	30 centimeters

Appendix B:
Table of Weights and Measures of Common Ingredients

Food	Quantity	Yield
Apples	1 pound	2½–3 cups sliced
Avocado	1 pound	1 cup mashed
Bananas	1 medium	1 cup sliced
Bell peppers	1 pound	3–4 cups sliced
Blueberries	1 pound	3⅓ cups
Butter	¼ pound (1 stick)	8 tablespoons
Cabbage	1 pound	4 cups packed shredded
Carrots	1 pound	3 cups diced or sliced
Chocolate, morsels	12 ounces	2 cups
Chocolate, bulk	1 ounce	3 tablespoons grated
Cocoa powder	1 ounce	¼ cup
Coconut, flaked	7 ounces	2½ cups
Cream	½ pint (1 cup)	2 cups whipped
Cream cheese	8 ounces	1 cup
Flour	1 pound	4 cups
Lemons	1 medium	3 tablespoons juice
Lemons	1 medium	2 teaspoons zest
Milk	1 quart	4 cups
Molasses	12 ounces	1½ cups
Mushrooms	1 pound	5 cups sliced
Onions	1 medium	½ cup chopped
Peaches	1 pound	2 cups sliced
Peanuts	5 ounces	1 cup
Pecans	6 ounces	1½ cups
Pineapple	1 medium	3 cups diced
Potatoes	1 pound	3 cups sliced
Raisins	1 pound	3 cups
Rice	1 pound	2 to 2½ cups raw
Spinach	1 pound	¾ cup cooked
Squash, summer	1 pound	3½ cups sliced
Strawberries	1 pint	1½ cups sliced

Food	Quantity	Yield
Sugar, brown	1 pound	2$\frac{1}{4}$ cups, packed
Sugar, confectioners'	1 pound	4 cups
Sugar, granulated	1 pound	2$\frac{1}{4}$ cups
Tomatoes	1 pound	1$\frac{1}{2}$ cups pulp
Walnuts	4 ounces	1 cup

TABLE OF LIQUID MEASUREMENTS

Dash	=	less than $\frac{1}{8}$ teaspoon
3 teaspoons	=	1 tablespoon
2 tablespoons	=	1 ounce
8 tablespoons	=	$\frac{1}{2}$ cup
2 cups	=	1 pint
1 quart	=	2 pints
1 gallon	=	4 quarts

Index